SOUTHERN BASTARDS

**Volume 1**
HERE WAS A MAN

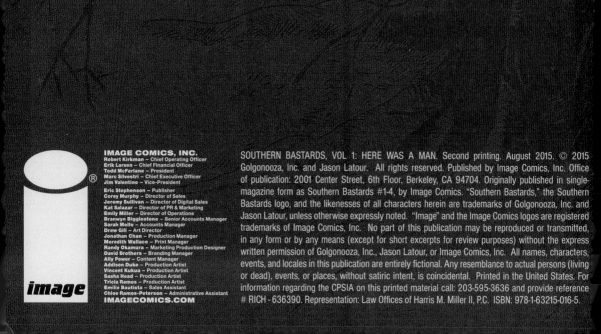

**IMAGE COMICS, INC.**
Robert Kirkman – Chief Operating Officer
Erik Larsen – Chief Financial Officer
Todd McFarlane – President
Marc Silvestri – Chief Executive Officer
Jim Valentino – Vice-President

Eric Stephenson – Publisher
Corey Murphy – Director of Sales
Jeremy Sullivan – Director of Digital Sales
Kat Salazar – Director of PR & Marketing
Emily Miller – Director of Operations
Branwyn Bigglestone – Senior Accounts Manager
Sarah Mello – Accounts Manager
Drew Gill – Art Director
Jonathan Chan – Production Manager
Meredith Wallace – Print Manager
Randy Okamura – Marketing Production Designer
David Brothers – Branding Manager
Ally Power – Content Manager
Addison Duke – Production Artist
Vincent Kukua – Production Artist
Sasha Head – Production Artist
Tricia Ramos – Production Artist
Emilio Bautista – Sales Assistant
Chloe Ramos-Peterson – Administrative Assistant
IMAGECOMICS.COM

# SOUTHERN BASTARDS

## "HERE WAS A MAN"

created by
JASON AARON & JASON LATOUR

**JASON AARON** writer
**JASON LATOUR** art & color

JARED K. FLETCHER letters
RICO RENZI color assist issues 1 & 2
SEBASTIAN GIRNER editor

Special thanks to...
Paul Azaceta
David B. Cooper
Capt. Rob Gibson USMC

I love the south.

The south also scares the living shit out of me.

I was born in Alabama. In a dry county, in a town called Jasper, birthplace of the guy who played "Goober" on the Andy Griffith Show and the 400 pound fighter they call "Butterbean." My grandfather was a Baptist preacher and a coal miner. My great grandfather died of rabies. My great great grandfather once stabbed a man to death in an argument over some sheep. I was raised on "Hee-Haw," the Crimson Tide, pork rinds and Jesus. I've memorized songs by all three generations of Hanks. I still get choked up whenever I hear Bear Bryant's voice. I've stood in William Faulkner's house.

I love being from the south.

But I don't live there anymore. And I don't plan on ever moving back.

The south is more peaceful than any other place I've ever been. But more primal too. More timeless. But more haunted. More spiritual. More hateful. More beautiful. More scarred.

And that's what this series is about. About a place you can love and hate and miss and fear all at the same time. I've always considered myself a Southern writer, and I think you can see that in a lot of the stuff I've done over the years. In the characters of SCALPED. In the way I wrote WOLVERINE for Marvel. Hell, even in my THOR GOD OF THUNDER.

But with this series, I finally get to go full country. So expect lots of BBQ. And football. And rednecks and senseless violence. And maybe even a laugh or two. Thanks for dropping by. Hope you'll stick around for a spell. We've got lots of bastards we'd like to introduce you to.

--Jason Aaron


I was born and raised in a Carolina's border town called Charlotte. A place that was about as far "North" as I ever really knew growing up. See back then places like New York were for superheroes. If we had any of those I was never given any cause to look up and see them.

When I got older I finally worked up the courage to travel some. For a while I moved deeper into the South's syrupy bloodstream--first to Atlanta and then to Florida, where I spent equal time avoiding the weirdness and the sunshine. I criss crossed the country until eventually I found myself walking around Brooklyn in the snow--Listening to country music--Getting angry. Angry for letting The South beat me. For letting them run me off. For letting them steal my home from me.

So I wrote LOOSE ENDS. I got a great job writing and drawing all those superheroes I used to dream about being. I moved back home and stared The South in her face. It ain't always easy, but I'm probably happier than I've ever been. Today I can and often do laugh about all the drama and stress this place has caused me. A lot of it's absurdity is even endearing.

And yet, somehow...deep down...I'm still angry as hell.

So this book is for them. The assholes you might think Southerners are. The rednecks we're afraid we might really be. This book is designed to bury them sons of bitches. To spit on their graves. Because I fucking hate those bastards with every part of me.

Because I love The South with all I've got.

--Jason Latour

Chapter 1

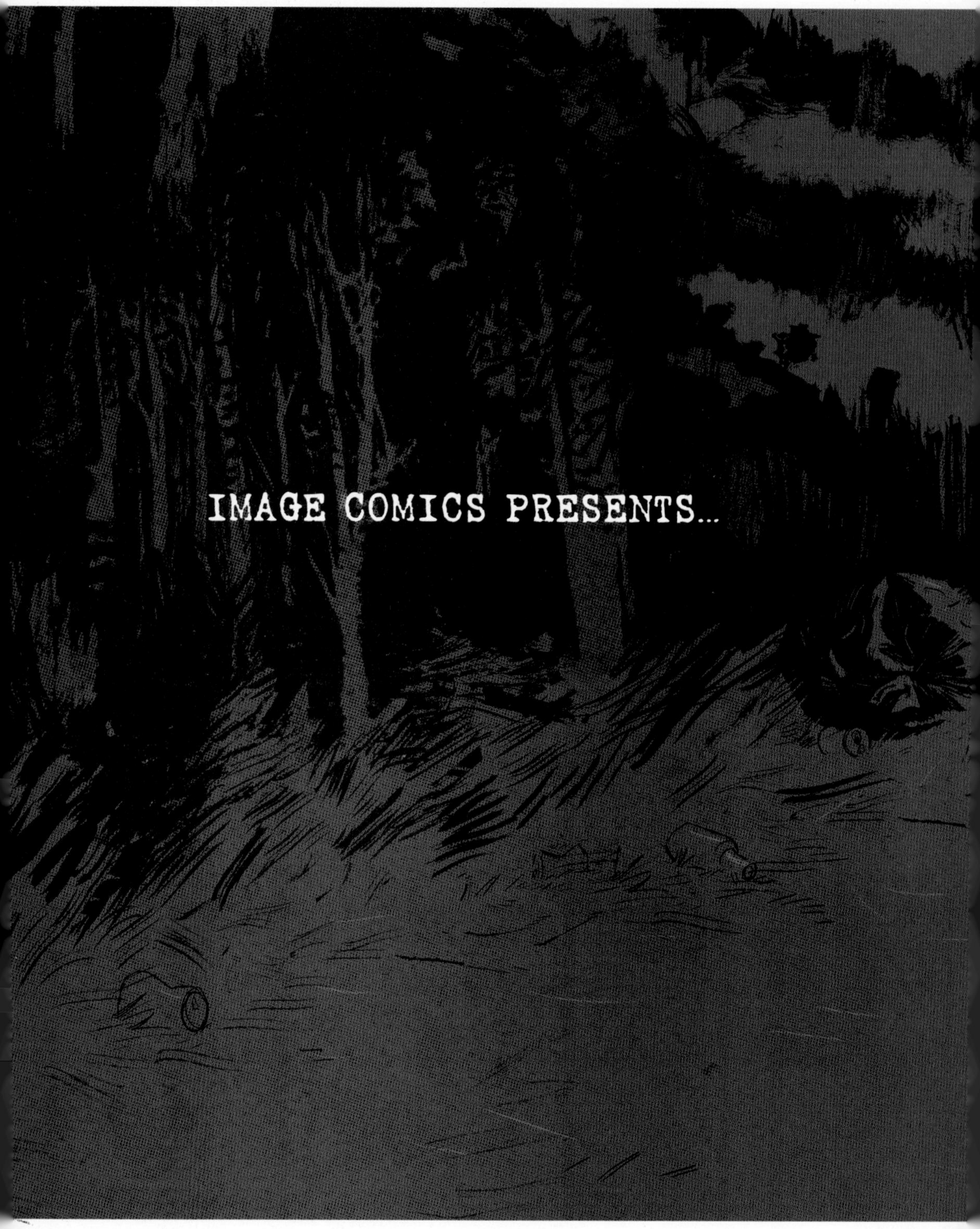
IMAGE COMICS PRESENTS...

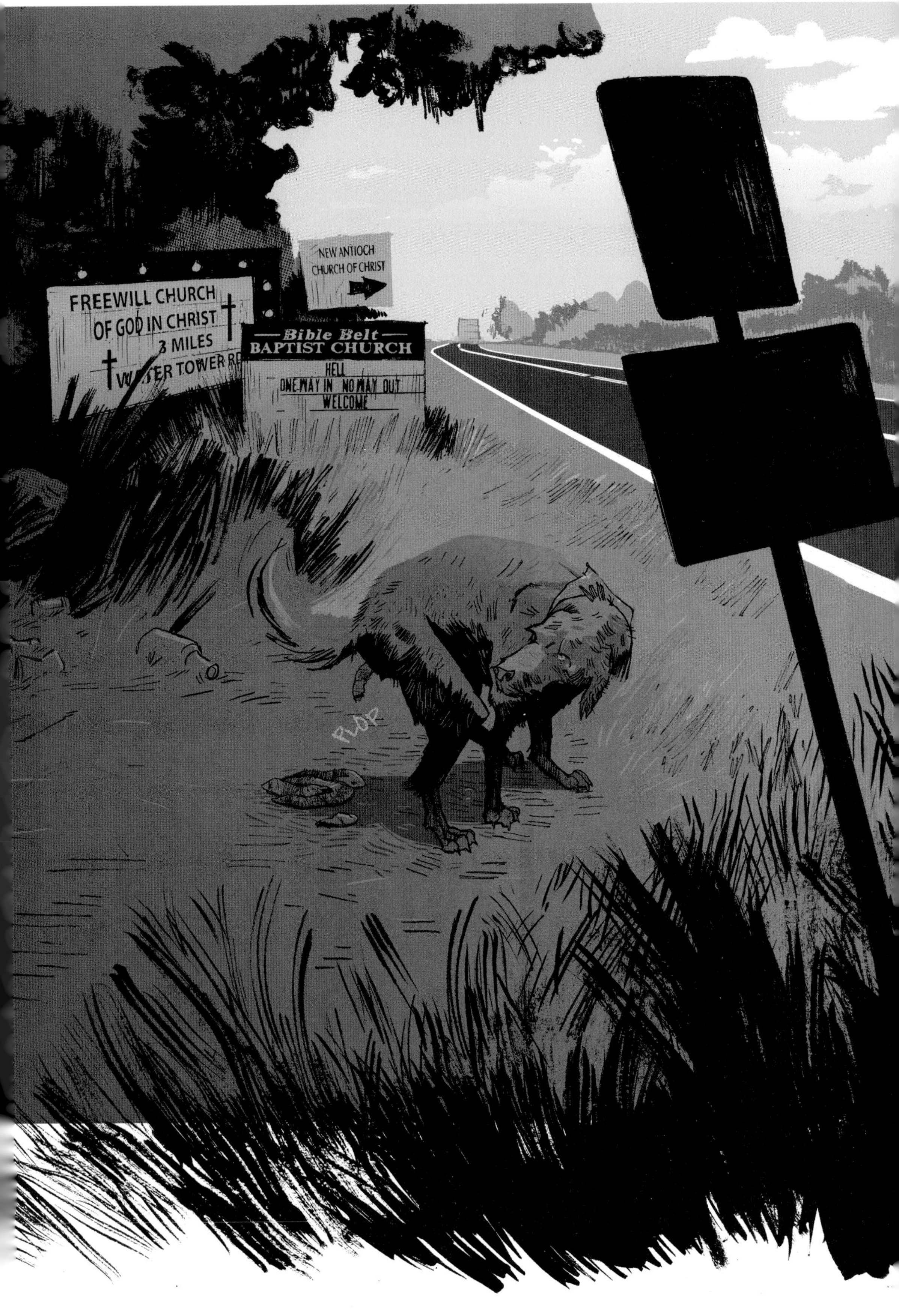
FREEWILL CHURCH
OF GOD IN CHRIST
3 MILES
WATER TOWER RD
NEW ANTIOCH
CHURCH OF CHRIST
Bible Belt
BAPTIST CHURCH
HELL
ONE WAY IN NO WAY OUT
WELCOME
PLOP

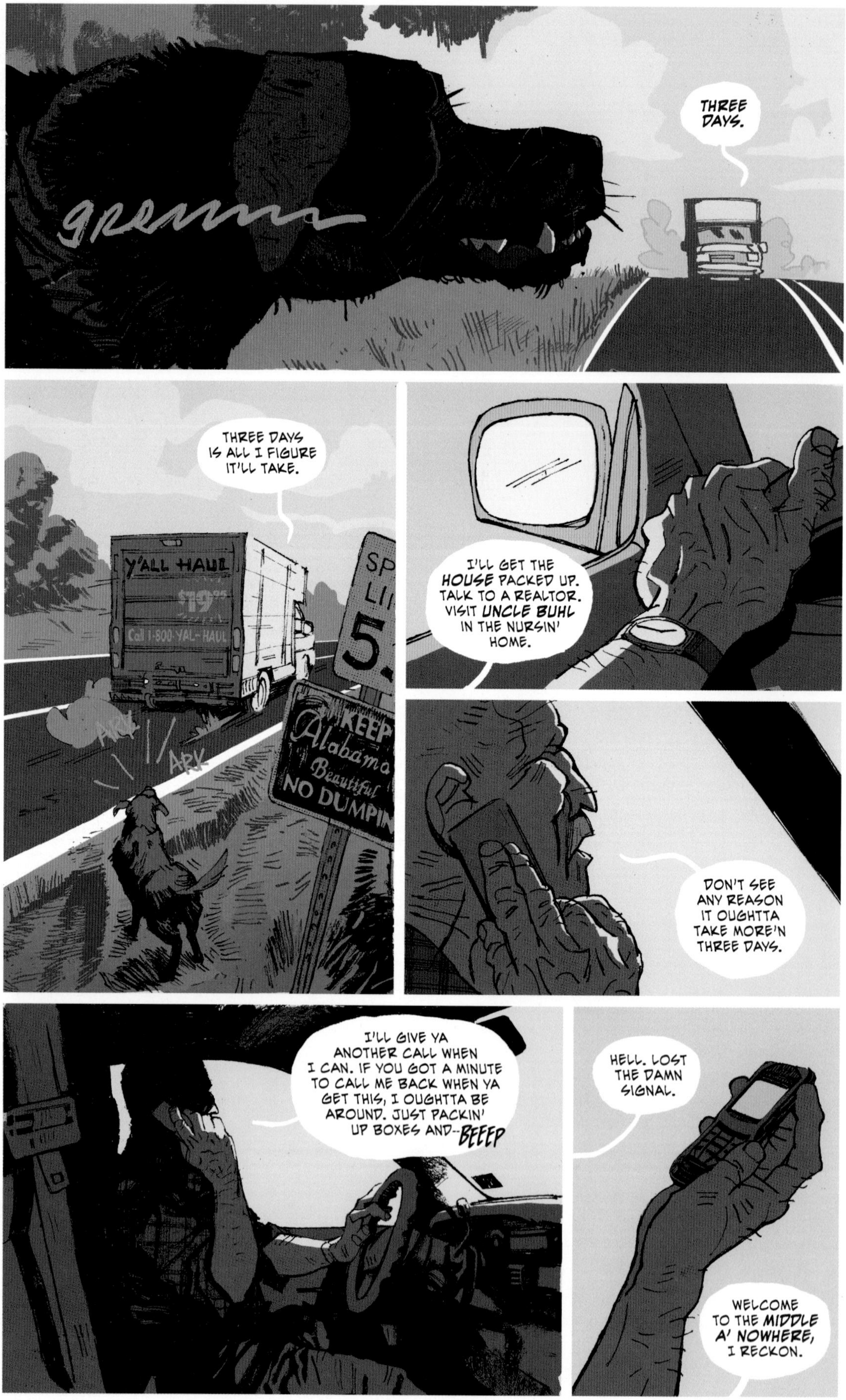
grrrrrr
THREE DAYS.
THREE DAYS IS ALL I FIGURE IT'LL TAKE.
Y'ALL HAUL
Call 1-800-YAL-HAUL
KEEP Alabama Beautiful NO DUMPIN
ARK
ARK
I'LL GET THE HOUSE PACKED UP. TALK TO A REALTOR. VISIT UNCLE BUHL IN THE NURSIN' HOME.
DON'T SEE ANY REASON IT OUGHTTA TAKE MORE'N THREE DAYS.
I'LL GIVE YA ANOTHER CALL WHEN I CAN. IF YOU GOT A MINUTE TO CALL ME BACK WHEN YA GET THIS, I OUGHTTA BE AROUND. JUST PACKIN' UP BOXES AND--BEEEP
HELL. LOST THE DAMN SIGNAL.
WELCOME TO THE MIDDLE A' NOWHERE, I RECKON.

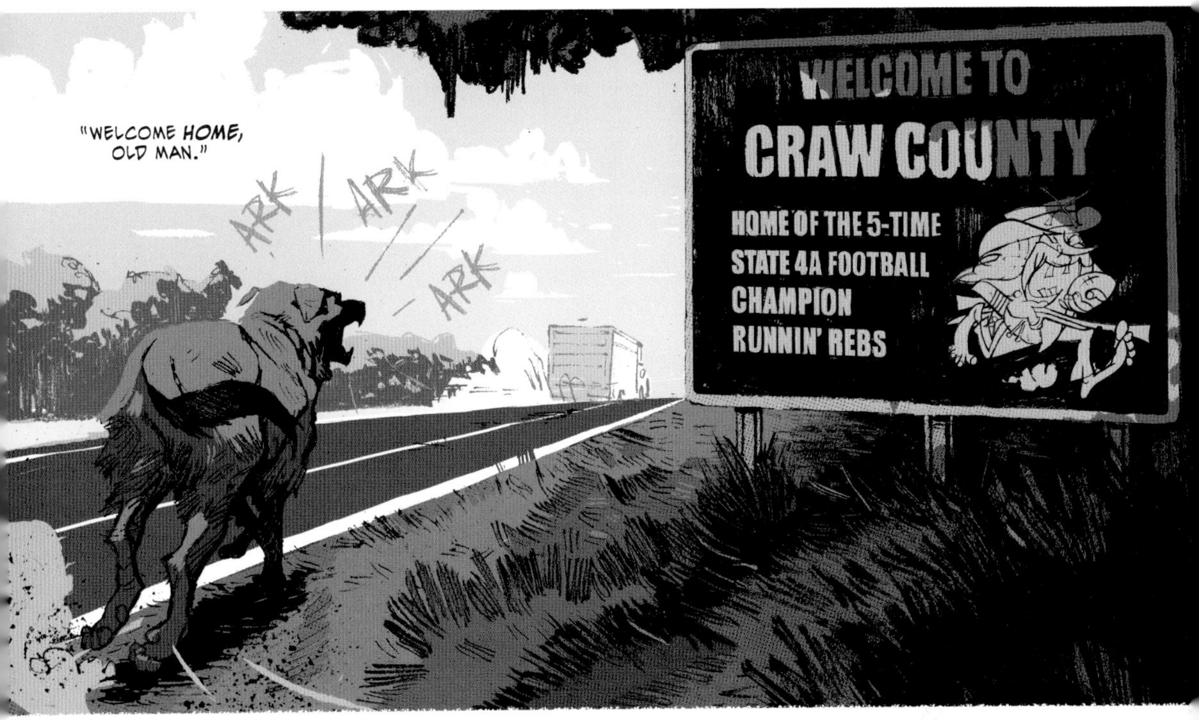
"WELCOME HOME, OLD MAN."
ARK
ARK
ARK
WELCOME TO
CRAW COUNTY
HOME OF THE 5-TIME
STATE 4A FOOTBALL
CHAMPION
RUNNIN' REBS

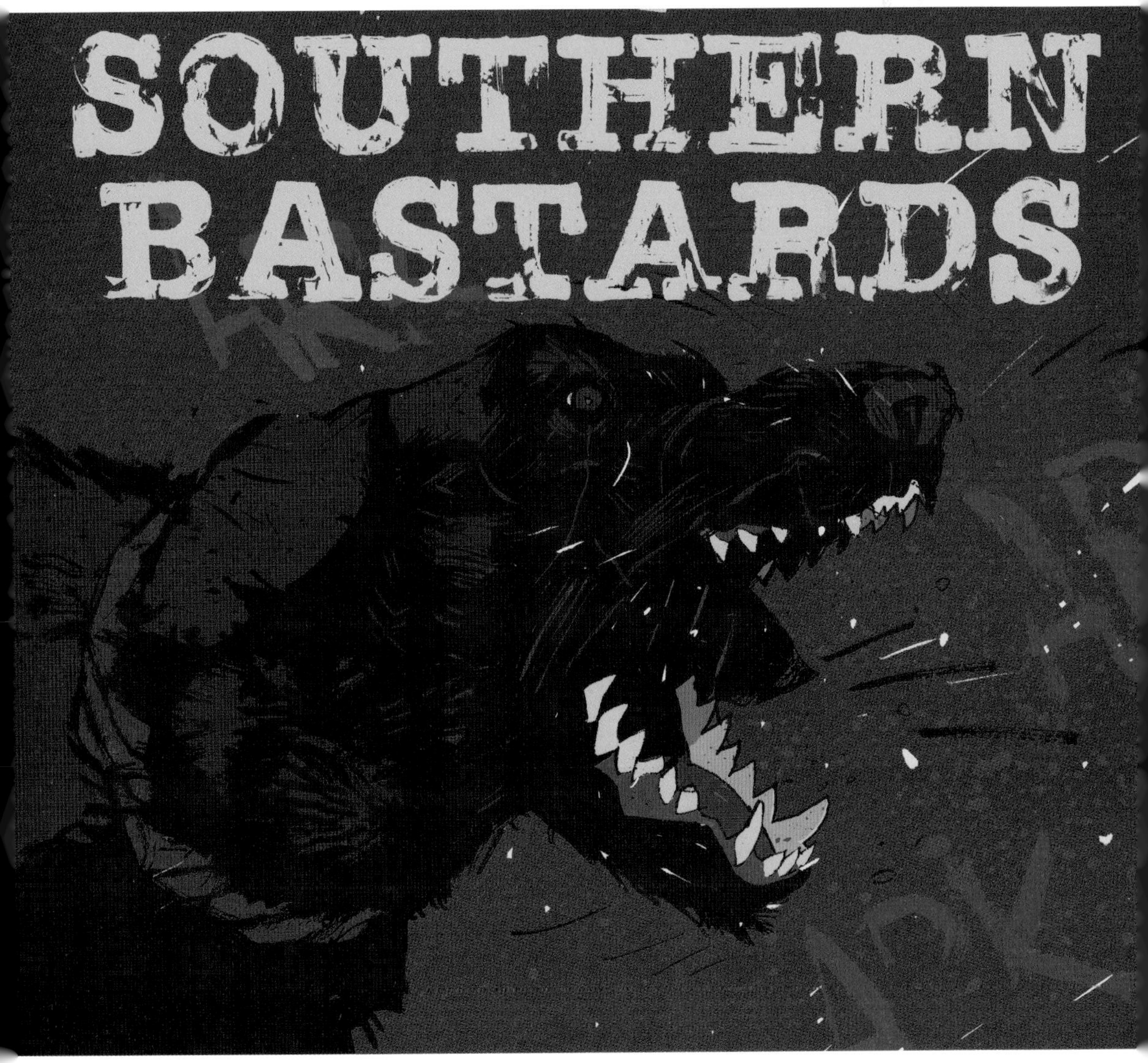
SOUTHERN
BASTARDS

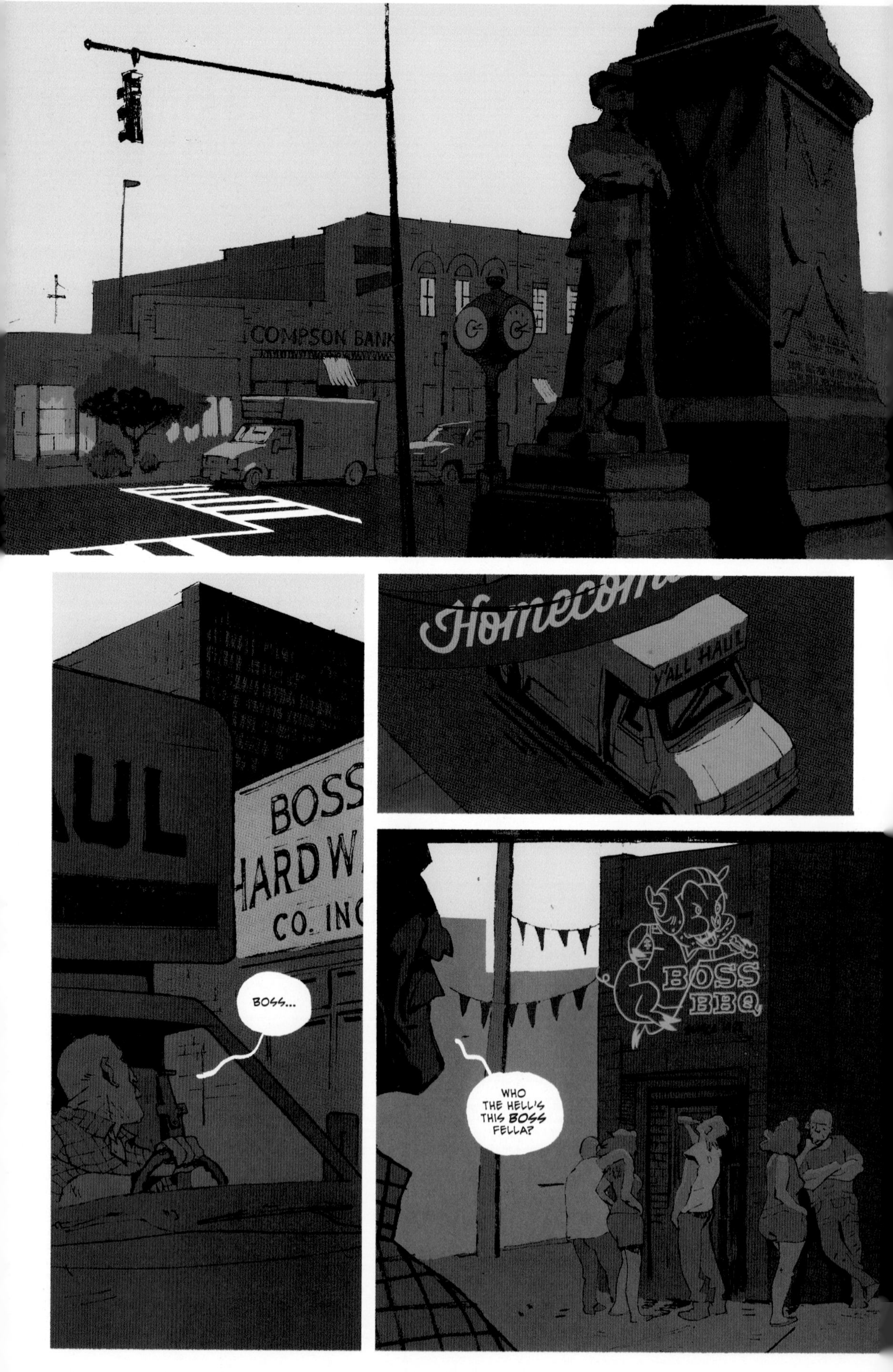
COMPSON BANK
Y'ALL HAUL
BOSS...
BOSS BBQ
WHO THE HELL'S THIS BOSS FELLA?

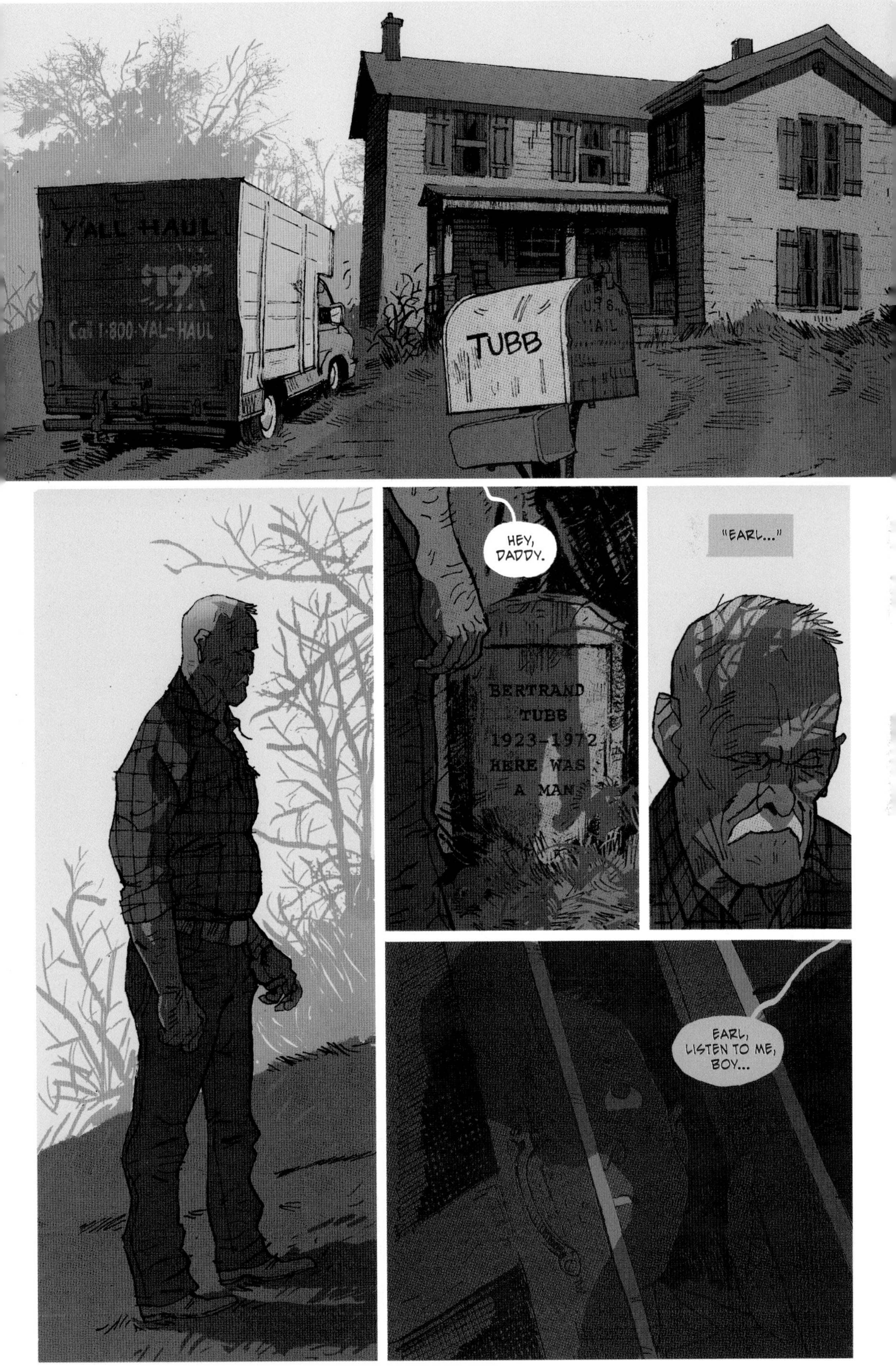
Y'ALL HAUL
Call 1-800-YAL-HAUL
TUBB
HEY, DADDY.
BERTRAND TUBB 1923-1972 HERE WAS A MAN
"EARL..."
EARL, LISTEN TO ME, BOY...

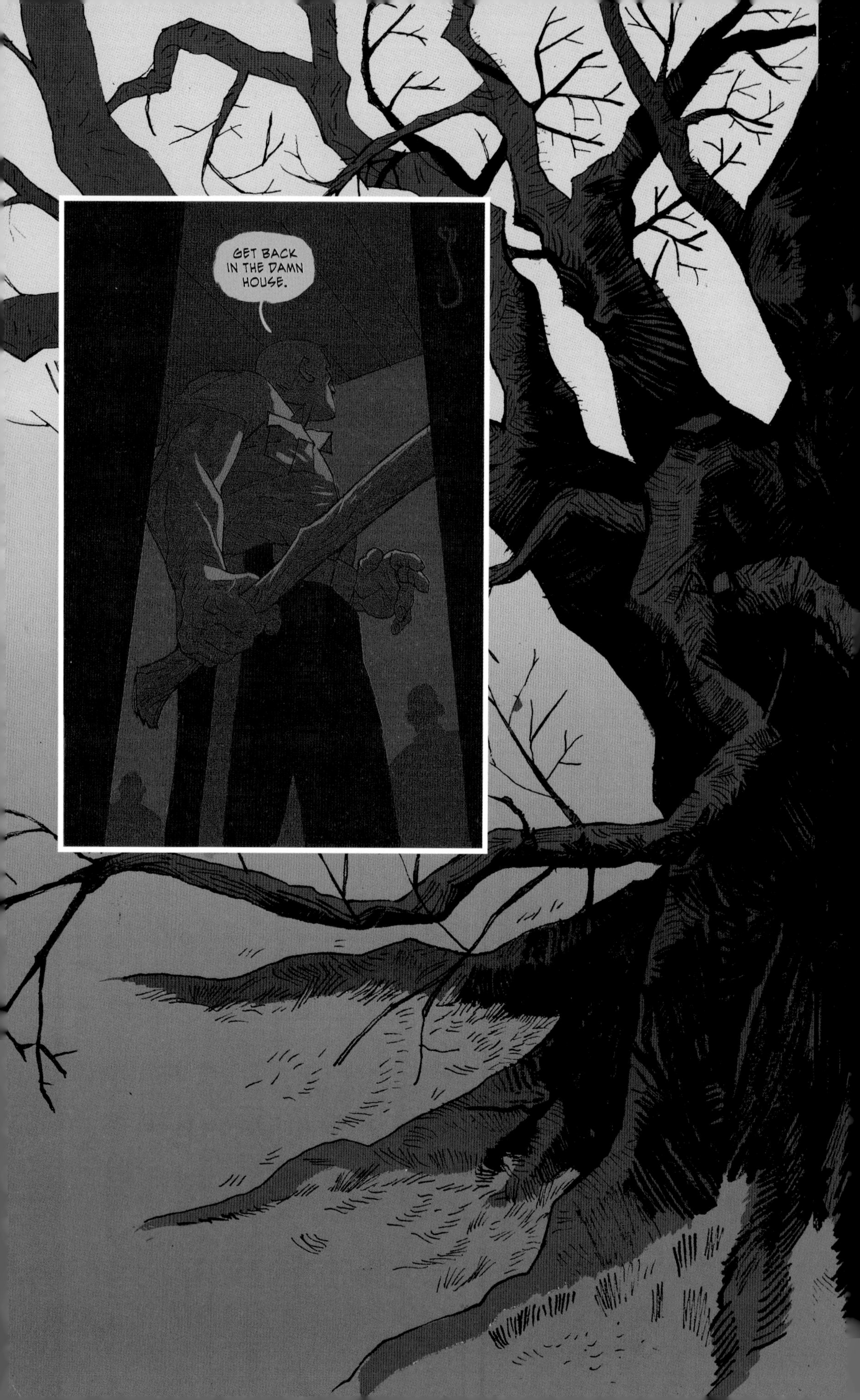
GET BACK IN THE DAMN HOUSE.

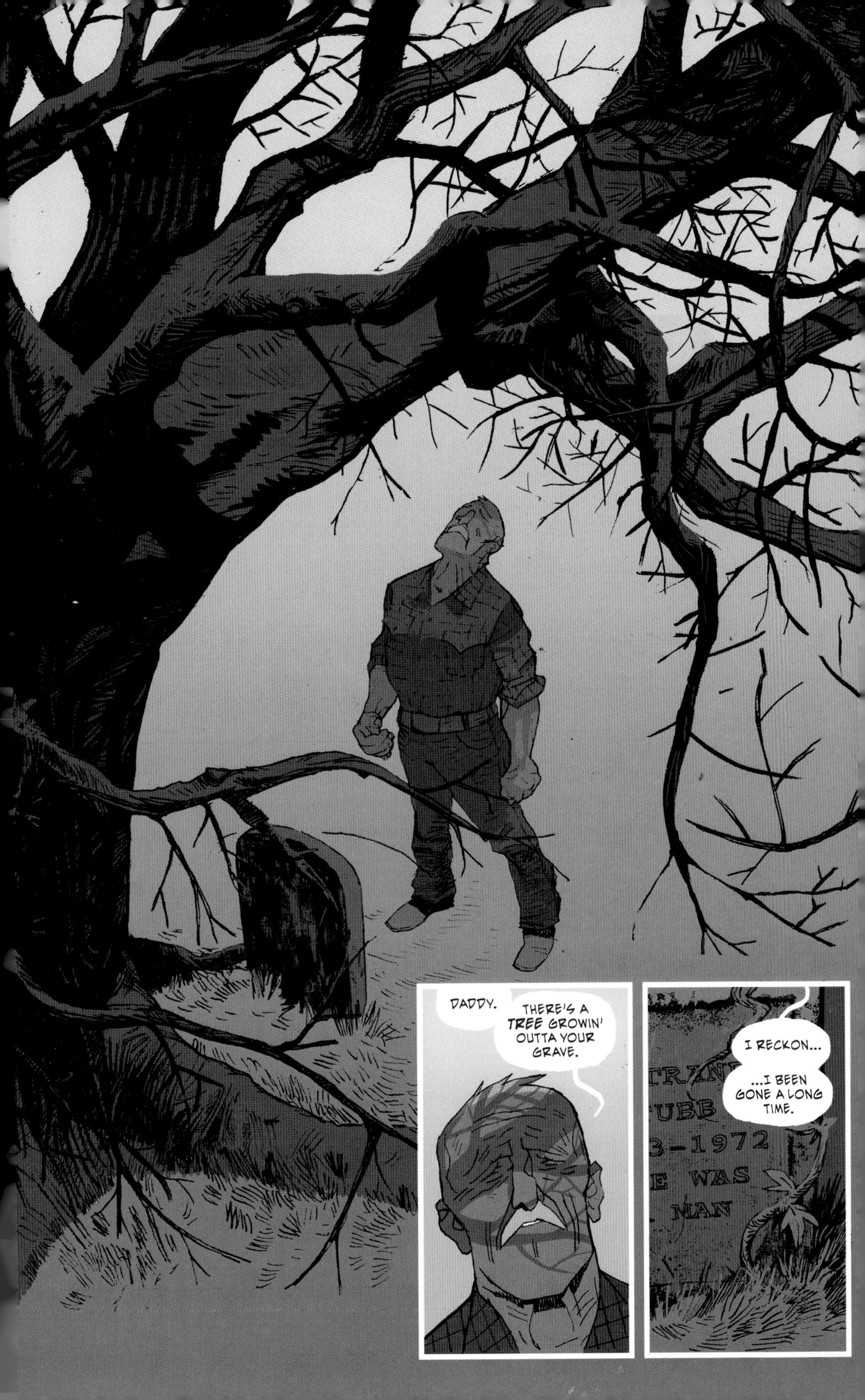
DADDY.
THERE'S A *TREE* GROWIN' OUTTA YOUR GRAVE.
I RECKON...
...I BEEN GONE A LONG TIME.

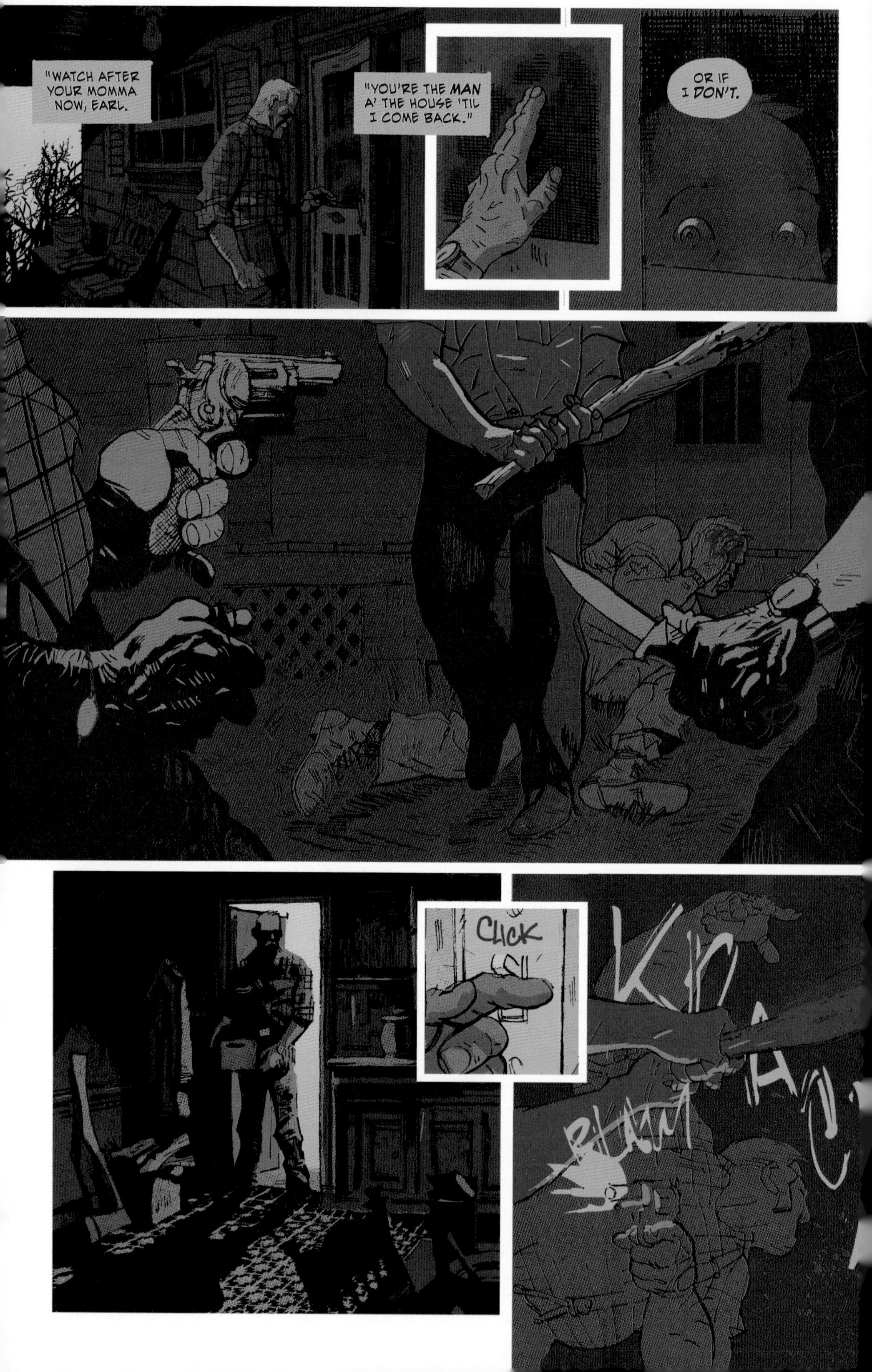
"WATCH AFTER YOUR MOMMA NOW, EARL.
"YOU'RE THE MAN A' THE HOUSE 'TIL I COME BACK."
OR IF I DON'T.
CLICK

SHERIFF SHOT

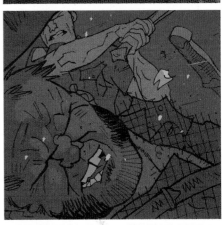

H BACK TO WALL TUBB
OK LAW IN OWN HANDS

his one-man battle agains
ssful syndicate of crooks
riff Bertrand Tubb of Craw
Alabama, was said to have
en the law into his own hands
a number of occasions. And
of the law-abiding citizens
he community said he was
justified in doing so.

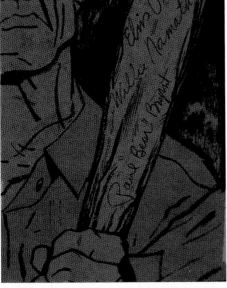

THE STICK THAT
SAVED CRAW COUNTY
OW ONE ALABAMA SHERIFF T

ATTACKED AT HOM
SHERIFF TUBB VOW
NOT TO QUIT

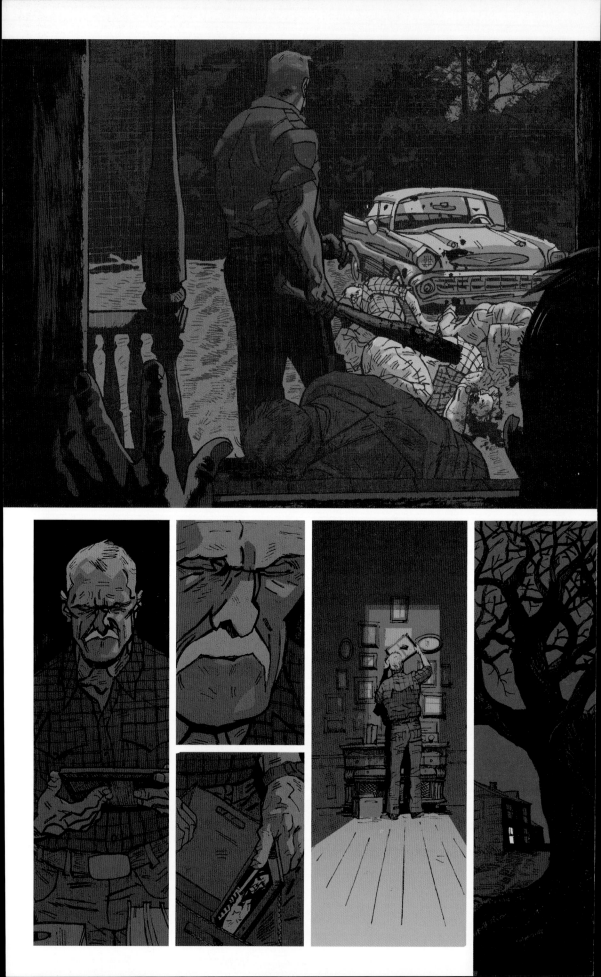

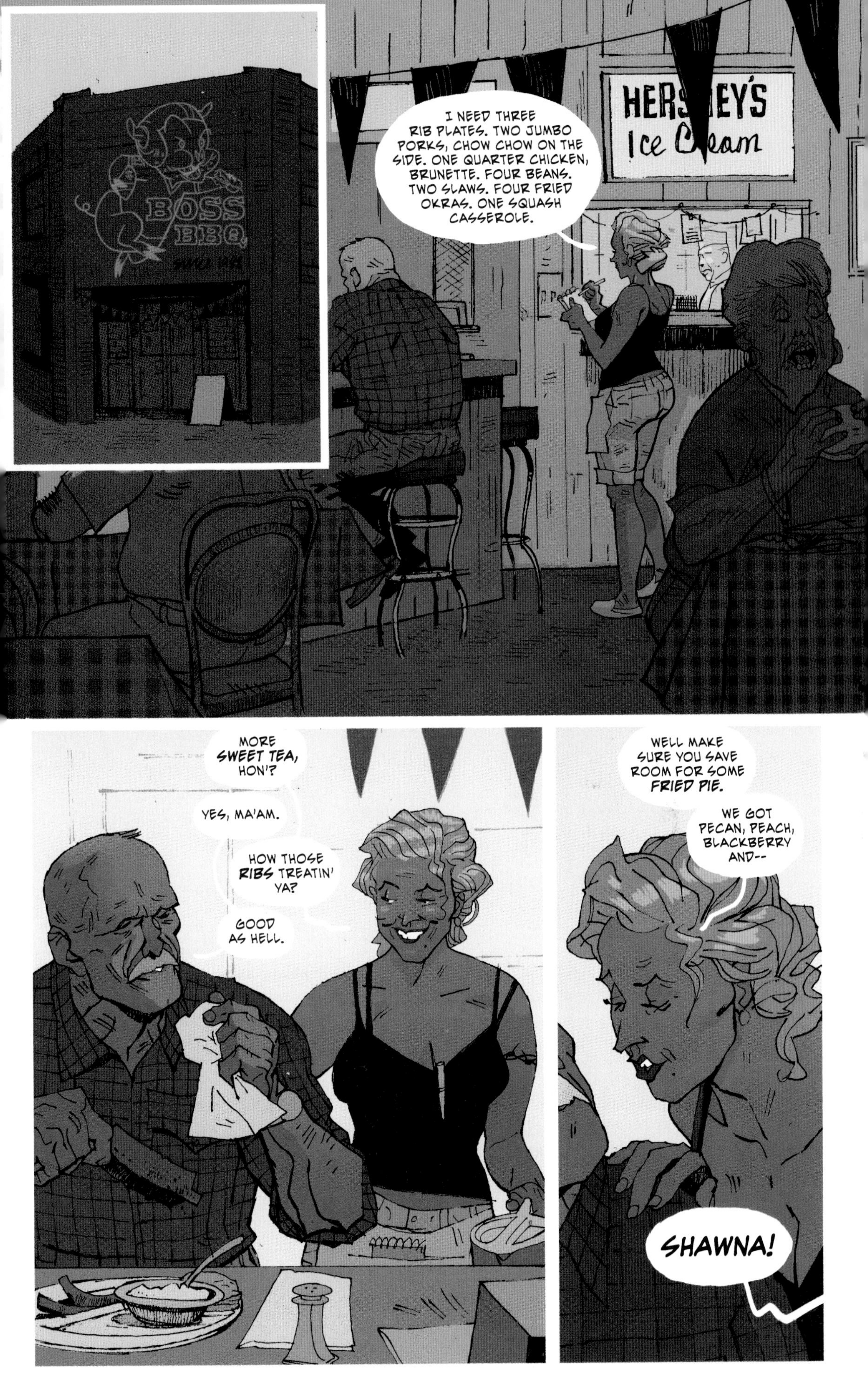
BOSS
BBQ
I NEED THREE RIB PLATES. TWO JUMBO PORKS, CHOW CHOW ON THE SIDE. ONE QUARTER CHICKEN, BRUNETTE. FOUR BEANS. TWO SLAWS. FOUR FRIED OKRAS. ONE SQUASH CASSEROLE.
MORE **SWEET TEA,** HON'?
YES, MA'AM.
HOW THOSE **RIBS** TREATIN' YA?
GOOD AS HELL.
WELL MAKE SURE YOU SAVE ROOM FOR SOME **FRIED PIE.**
WE GOT PECAN, PEACH, BLACKBERRY AND--
SHAWNA!

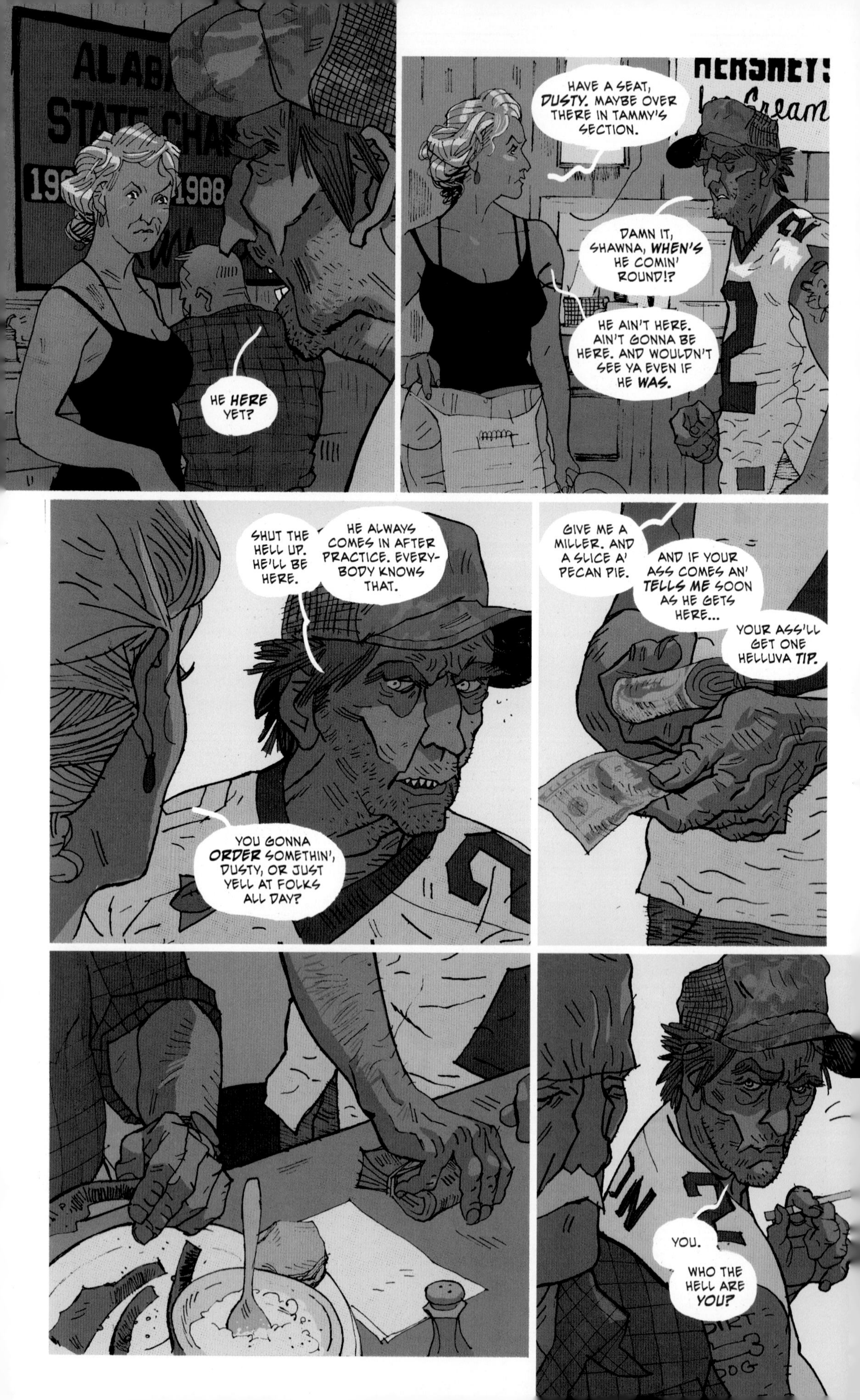
ALABA
STATE CHA
19 1988
HE HERE YET?
HAVE A SEAT, DUSTY. MAYBE OVER THERE IN TAMMY'S SECTION.
HERSHEY'S
Ice Cream
DAMN IT, SHAWNA, WHEN'S HE COMIN' ROUND!?
HE AIN'T HERE. AIN'T GONNA BE HERE. AND WOULDN'T SEE YA EVEN IF HE WAS.
SHUT THE HELL UP. HE'LL BE HERE.
HE ALWAYS COMES IN AFTER PRACTICE. EVERYBODY KNOWS THAT.
YOU GONNA ORDER SOMETHIN', DUSTY, OR JUST YELL AT FOLKS ALL DAY?
GIVE ME A MILLER. AND A SLICE A' PECAN PIE.
AND IF YOUR ASS COMES AN' TELLS ME SOON AS HE GETS HERE...
YOUR ASS'LL GET ONE HELLUVA TIP.
YOU.
WHO THE HELL ARE YOU?

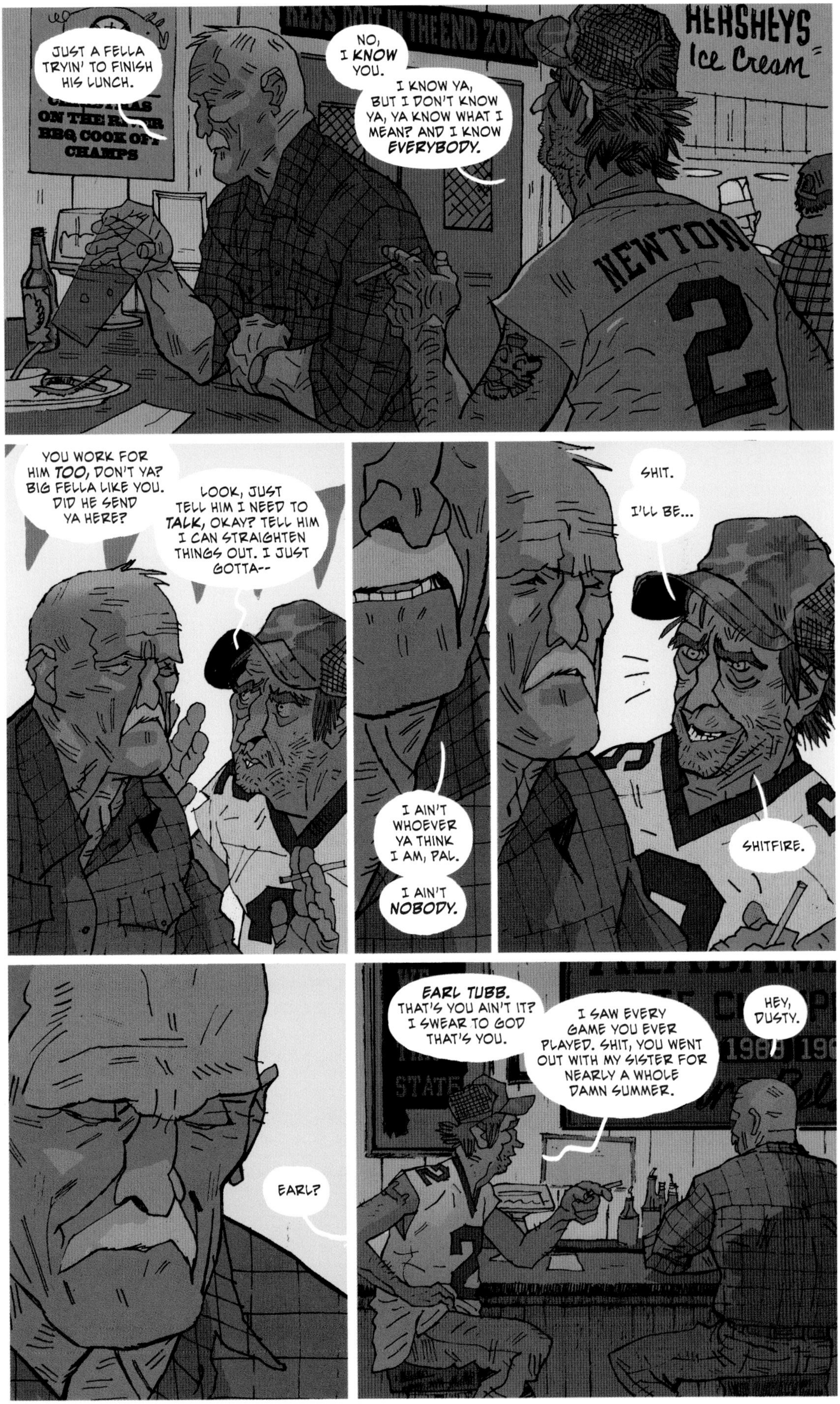

JUST A FELLA TRYIN' TO FINISH HIS LUNCH.
NO, I **KNOW** YOU.
I KNOW YA, BUT I DON'T KNOW YA, YA KNOW WHAT I MEAN? AND I KNOW *EVERYBODY.*
HERSHEYS Ice Cream
NEWTON 2
YOU WORK FOR HIM *TOO,* DON'T YA? BIG FELLA LIKE YOU. DID HE SEND YA HERE?
LOOK, JUST TELL HIM I NEED TO *TALK,* OKAY? TELL HIM I CAN STRAIGHTEN THINGS OUT. I JUST GOTTA--
I AIN'T WHOEVER YA THINK I AM, PAL.
I AIN'T *NOBODY.*
SHIT.
I'LL BE...
SHITFIRE.
EARL?
***EARL TUBB.*** THAT'S YOU AIN'T IT? I SWEAR TO GOD THAT'S YOU.
I SAW EVERY GAME YOU EVER PLAYED. SHIT, YOU WENT OUT WITH MY SISTER FOR NEARLY A WHOLE DAMN SUMMER.
HEY, DUSTY.

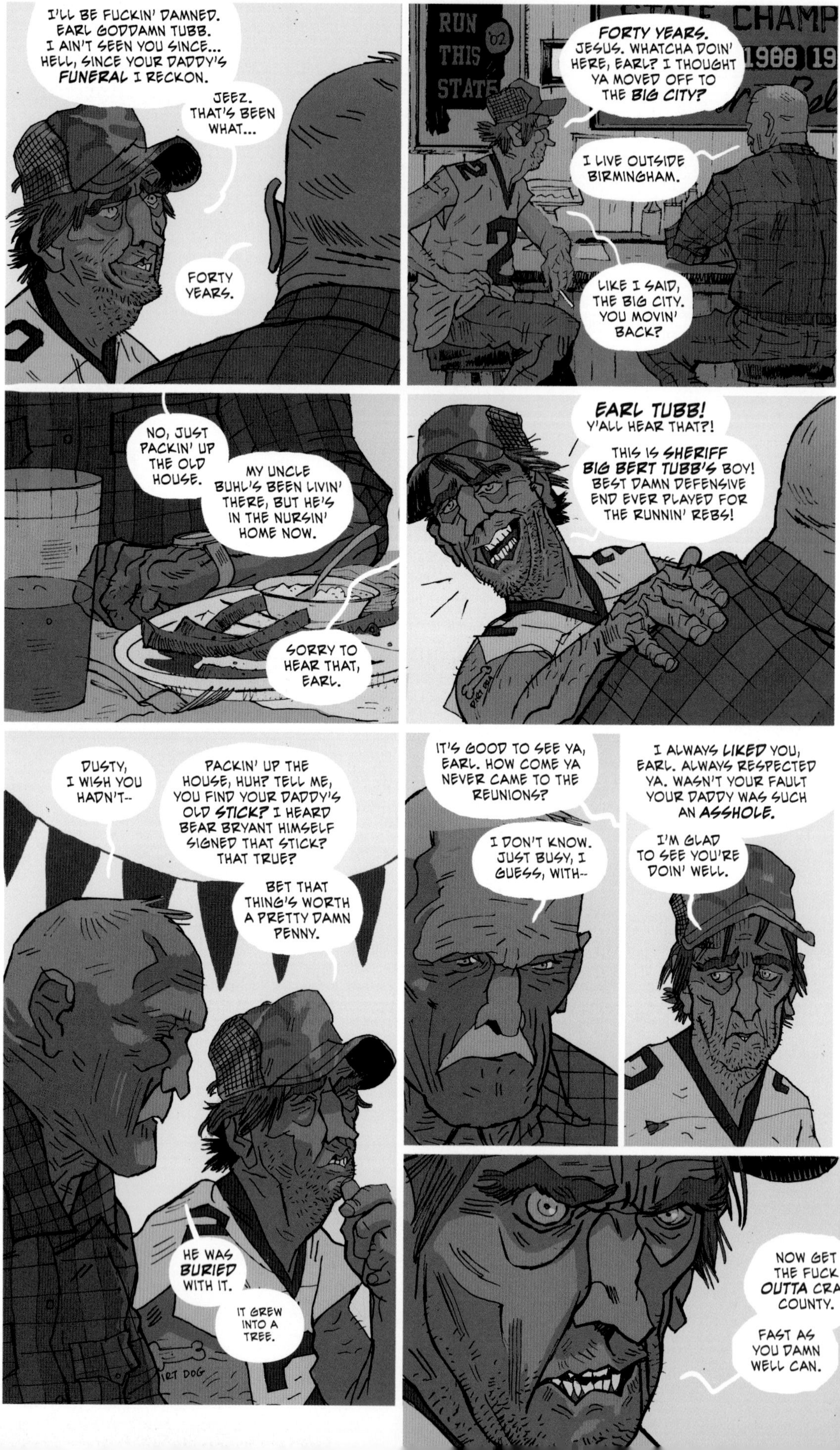
I'LL BE FUCKIN' DAMNED. EARL GODDAMN TUBB. I AIN'T SEEN YOU SINCE... HELL, SINCE YOUR DADDY'S FUNERAL I RECKON.
JEEZ. THAT'S BEEN WHAT...
FORTY YEARS.
RUN THIS STATE
'02
STATE CHAMP
1988
FORTY YEARS. JESUS. WHATCHA DOIN' HERE, EARL? I THOUGHT YA MOVED OFF TO THE BIG CITY?
I LIVE OUTSIDE BIRMINGHAM.
LIKE I SAID, THE BIG CITY. YOU MOVIN' BACK?
NO, JUST PACKIN' UP THE OLD HOUSE.
MY UNCLE BUHL'S BEEN LIVIN' THERE, BUT HE'S IN THE NURSIN' HOME NOW.
SORRY TO HEAR THAT, EARL.
EARL TUBB! Y'ALL HEAR THAT?!
THIS IS SHERIFF BIG BERT TUBB'S BOY! BEST DAMN DEFENSIVE END EVER PLAYED FOR THE RUNNIN' REBS!
DUSTY, I WISH YOU HADN'T--
PACKIN' UP THE HOUSE, HUH? TELL ME, YOU FIND YOUR DADDY'S OLD STICK? I HEARD BEAR BRYANT HIMSELF SIGNED THAT STICK? THAT TRUE?
BET THAT THING'S WORTH A PRETTY DAMN PENNY.
HE WAS BURIED WITH IT.
IT GREW INTO A TREE.
IT'S GOOD TO SEE YA, EARL. HOW COME YA NEVER CAME TO THE REUNIONS?
I DON'T KNOW. JUST BUSY, I GUESS, WITH--
I ALWAYS LIKED YOU, EARL. ALWAYS RESPECTED YA. WASN'T YOUR FAULT YOUR DADDY WAS SUCH AN ASSHOLE.
I'M GLAD TO SEE YOU'RE DOIN' WELL.
NOW GET THE FUCK OUTTA CRAW COUNTY.
FAST AS YOU DAMN WELL CAN.

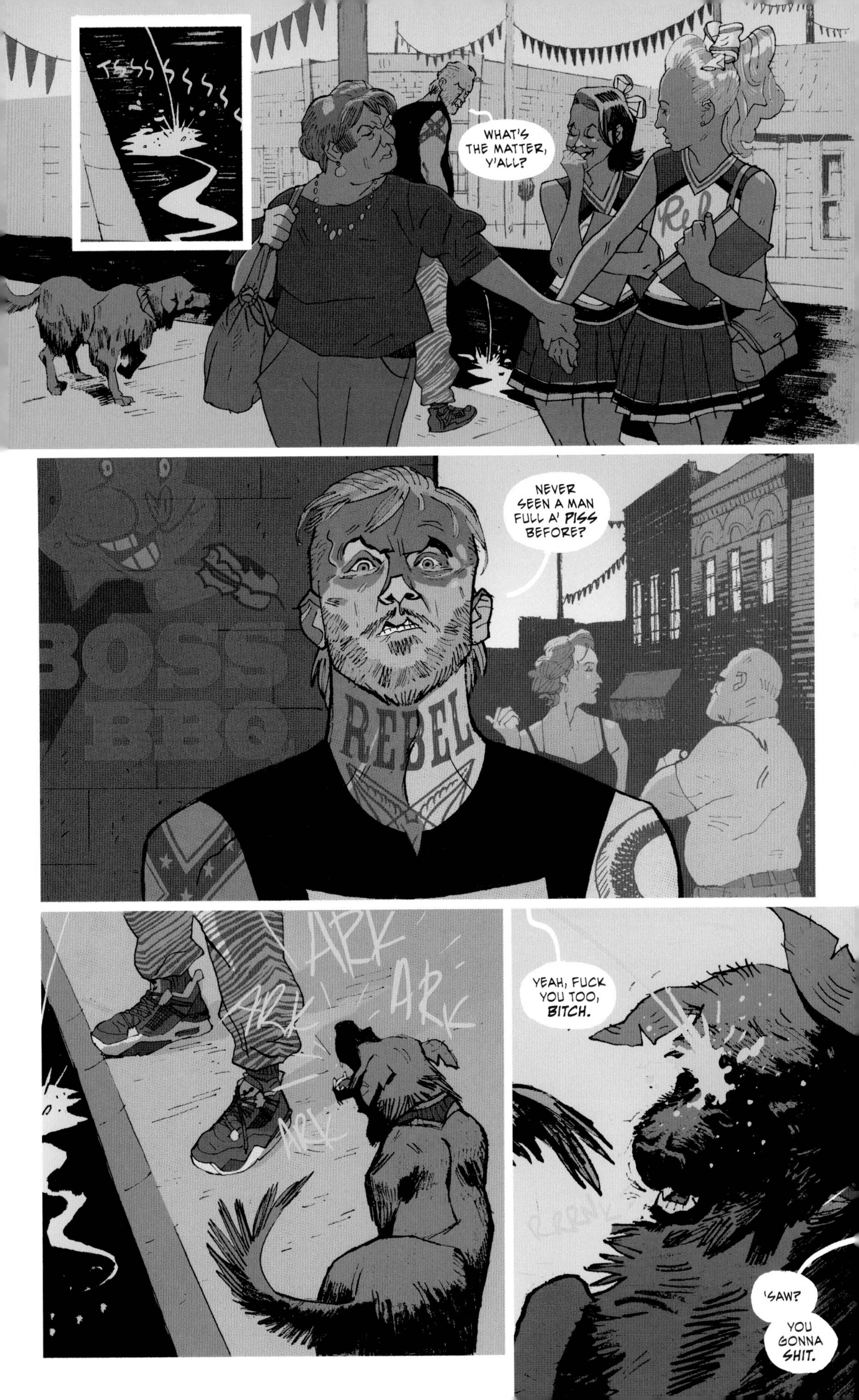
TSSSSSSSSS
WHAT'S THE MATTER, Y'ALL?
NEVER SEEN A MAN FULL A' PISS BEFORE?
BOSS BBQ
REBEL
ARK
ARK
ARK
ARK
YEAH, FUCK YOU TOO, BITCH.
'SAW?
YOU GONNA SHIT.

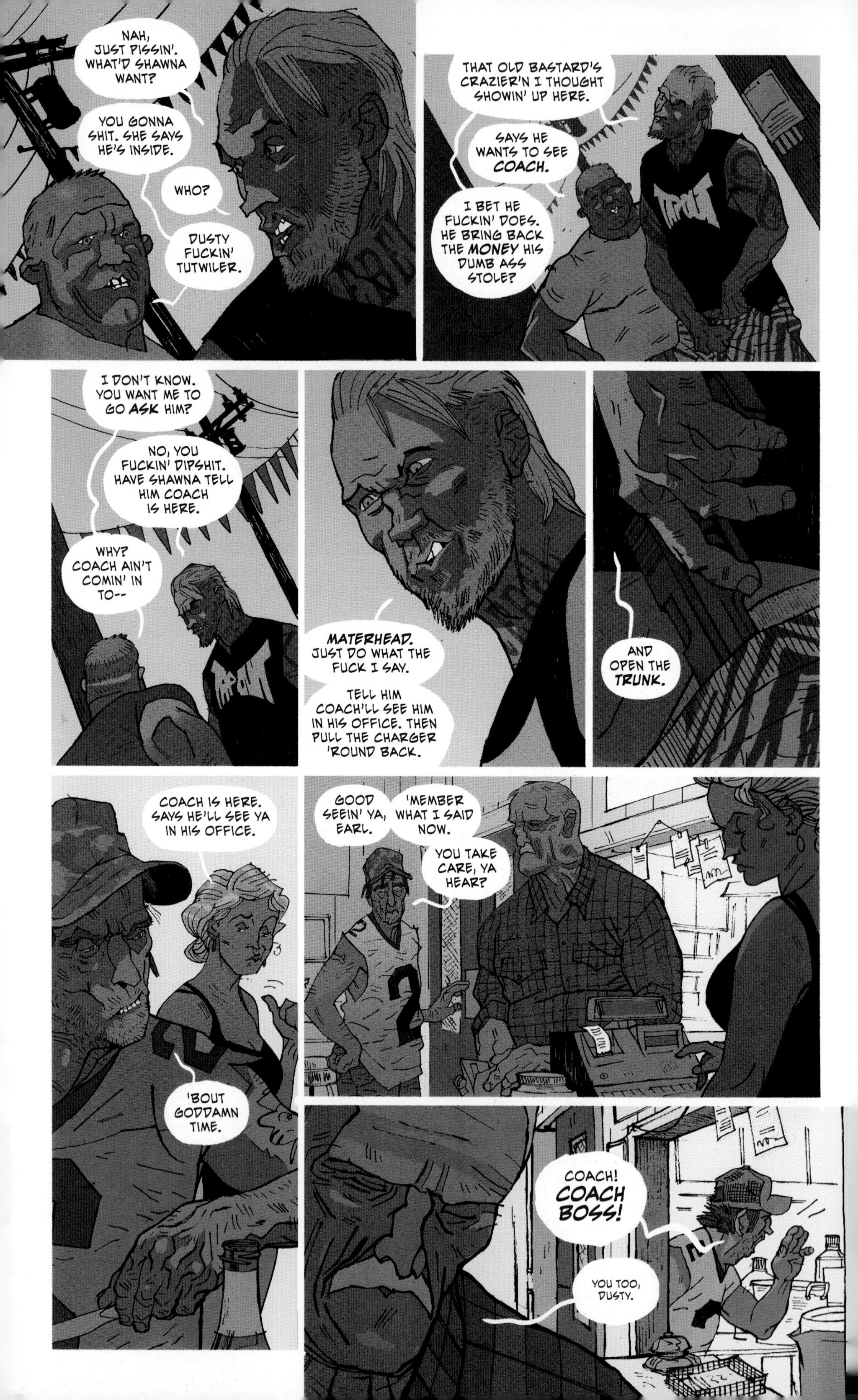
NAH, JUST PISSIN'. WHAT'D SHAWNA WANT?
YOU GONNA SHIT. SHE SAYS HE'S INSIDE.
WHO?
DUSTY FUCKIN' TUTWILER.
THAT OLD BASTARD'S CRAZIER'N I THOUGHT SHOWIN' UP HERE.
SAYS HE WANTS TO SEE COACH.
I BET HE FUCKIN' DOES. HE BRING BACK THE MONEY HIS DUMB ASS STOLE?
I DON'T KNOW. YOU WANT ME TO GO ASK HIM?
NO, YOU FUCKIN' DIPSHIT. HAVE SHAWNA TELL HIM COACH IS HERE.
WHY? COACH AIN'T COMIN' IN TO--
MATERHEAD. JUST DO WHAT THE FUCK I SAY.
TELL HIM COACH'LL SEE HIM IN HIS OFFICE. THEN PULL THE CHARGER 'ROUND BACK.
AND OPEN THE TRUNK.
COACH IS HERE. SAYS HE'LL SEE YA IN HIS OFFICE.
'BOUT GODDAMN TIME.
GOOD SEEIN' YA, EARL.
'MEMBER WHAT I SAID NOW.
YOU TAKE CARE, YA HEAR?
COACH! COACH BOSS!
YOU TOO, DUSTY.

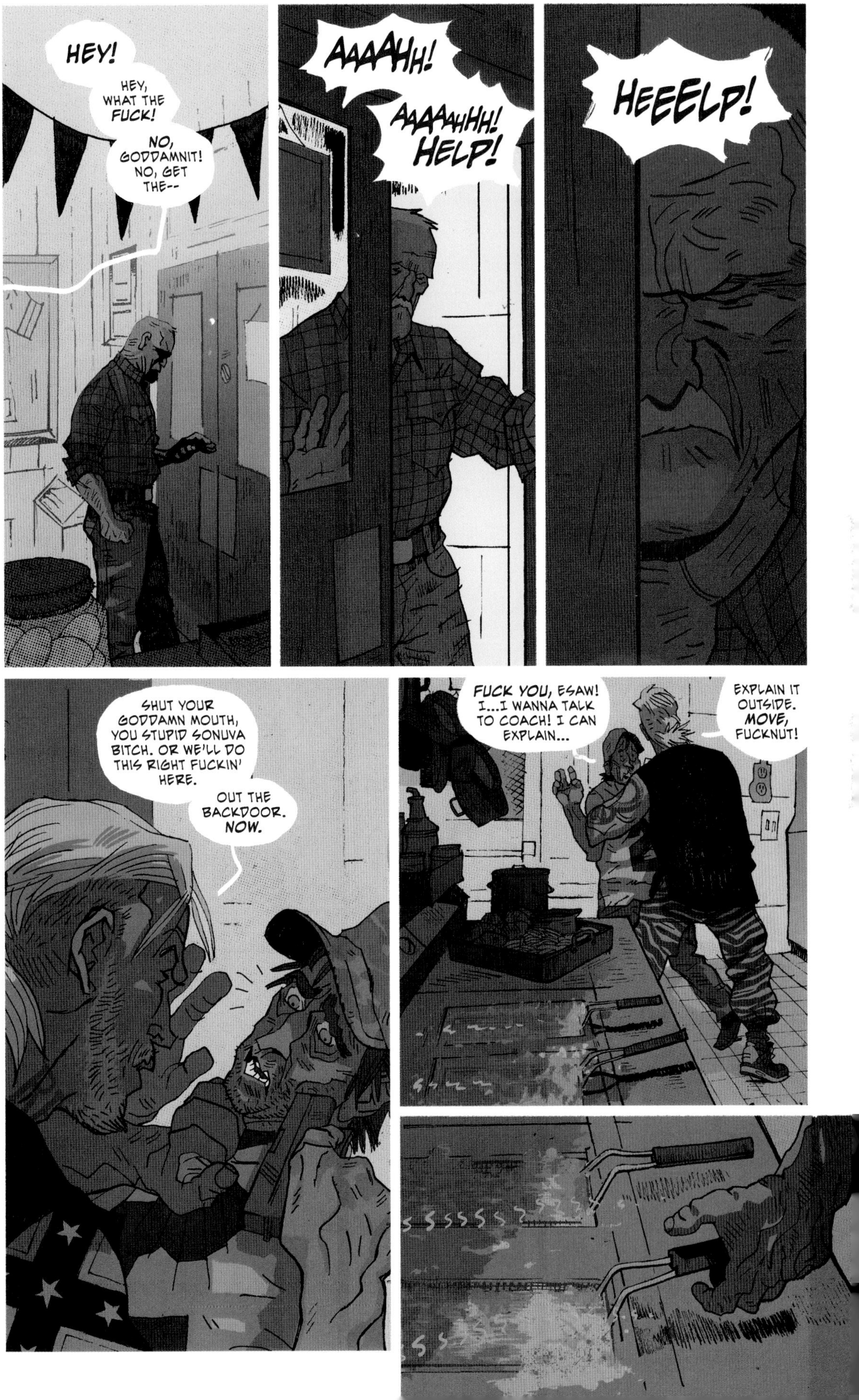

HEY!
HEY, WHAT THE FUCK!
NO, GODDAMNIT! NO, GET THE--
AAAAHH!
AAAAAHHH! HELP!
HEEELP!
SHUT YOUR GODDAMN MOUTH, YOU STUPID SONUVA BITCH. OR WE'LL DO THIS RIGHT FUCKIN' HERE.
OUT THE BACKDOOR. NOW.
FUCK YOU, ESAW! I...I WANNA TALK TO COACH! I CAN EXPLAIN...
EXPLAIN IT OUTSIDE. MOVE, FUCKNUT!

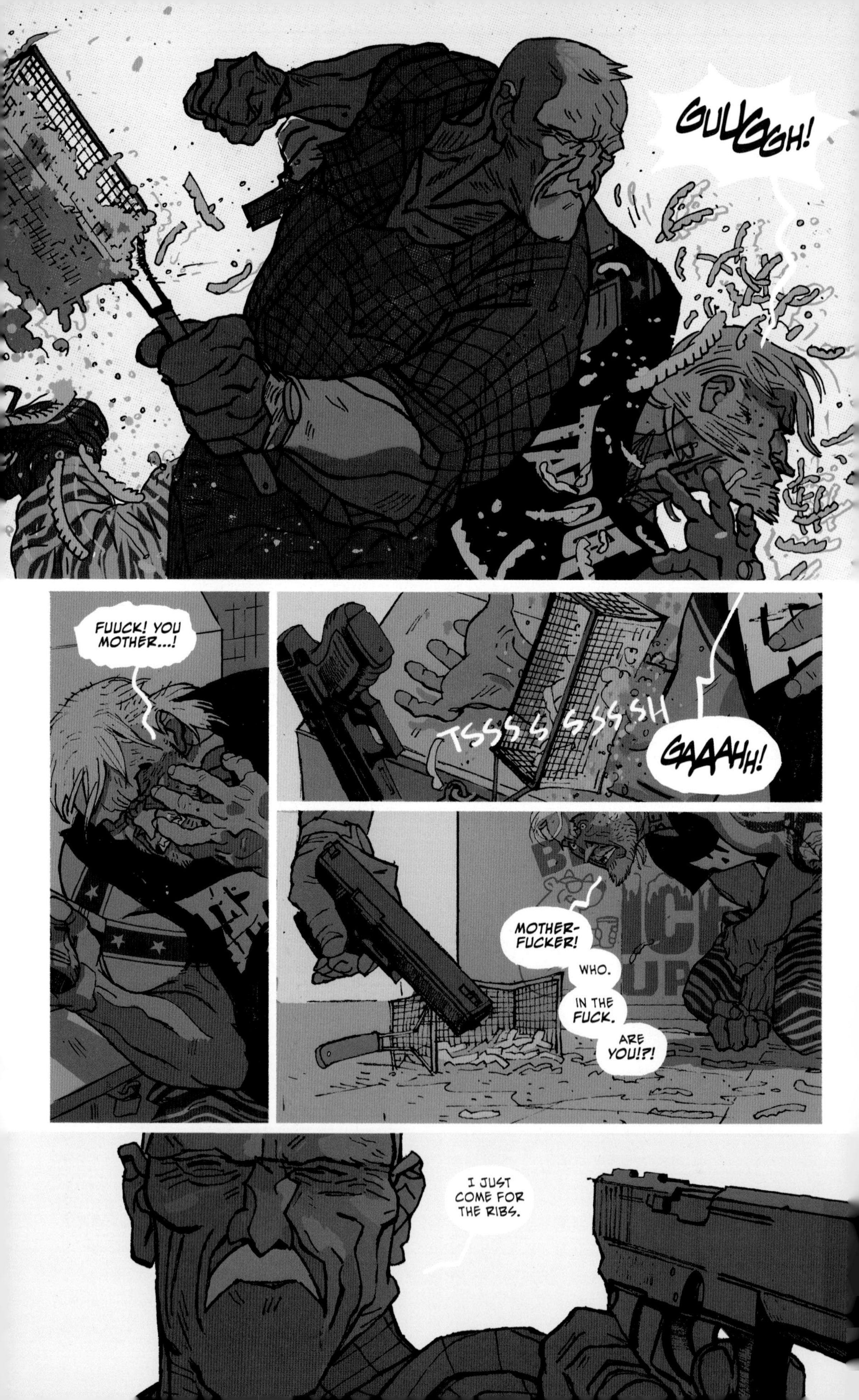
GULUGGH!
FUUCK! YOU MOTHER...!
TSSSSSSSSSH
GAAAHH!
MOTHER-FUCKER!
WHO.
IN THE FUCK.
ARE YOU!?!
I JUST COME FOR THE RIBS.

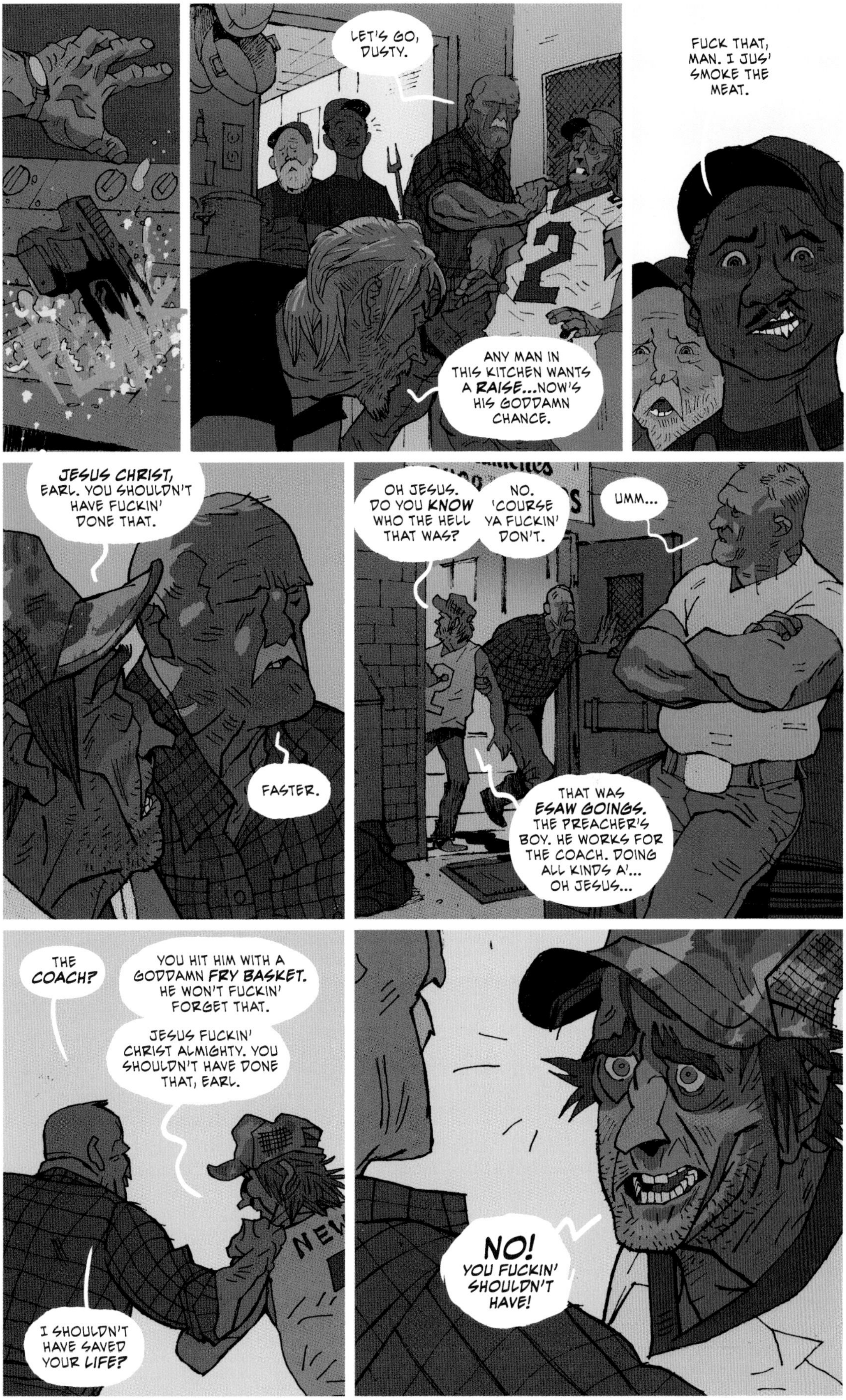
LET'S GO, DUSTY.
ANY MAN IN THIS KITCHEN WANTS A **RAISE...**NOW'S HIS GODDAMN CHANCE.
FUCK THAT, MAN. I JUS' SMOKE THE MEAT.
***JESUS CHRIST,*** EARL. YOU SHOULDN'T HAVE FUCKIN' DONE THAT.
FASTER.
OH JESUS. DO YOU **KNOW** WHO THE HELL THAT WAS?
NO. 'COURSE YA FUCKIN' DON'T.
UMM...
THAT WAS ***ESAW GOINGS.*** THE PREACHER'S BOY. HE WORKS FOR THE COACH. DOING ALL KINDS A'... OH JESUS...
THE ***COACH?***
YOU HIT HIM WITH A GODDAMN **FRY BASKET.** HE WON'T FUCKIN' FORGET THAT.
JESUS FUCKIN' CHRIST ALMIGHTY. YOU SHOULDN'T HAVE DONE THAT, EARL.
I SHOULDN'T HAVE SAVED YOUR ***LIFE?***
**NO!** YOU FUCKIN' SHOULDN'T HAVE!

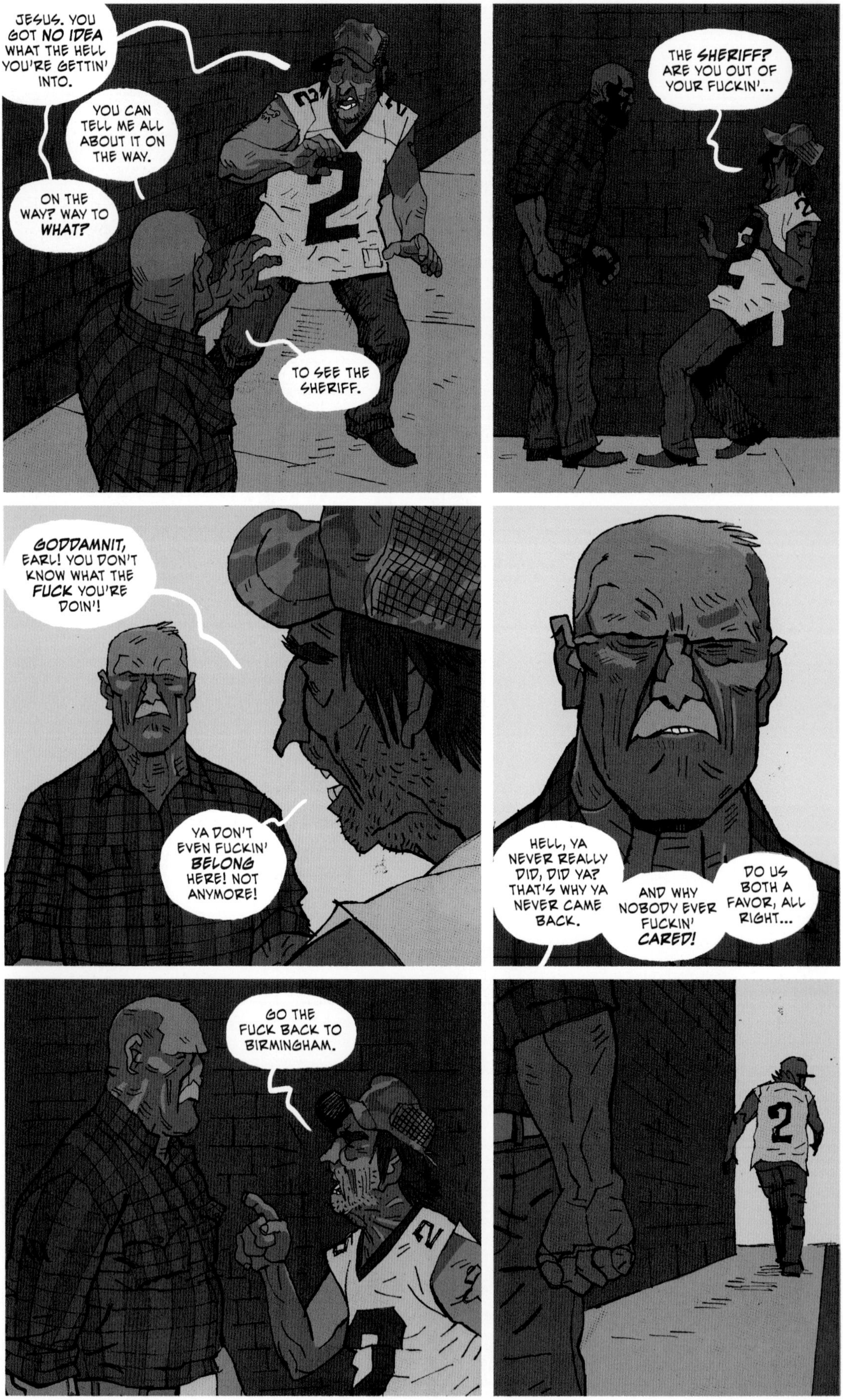
JESUS. YOU GOT NO IDEA WHAT THE HELL YOU'RE GETTIN' INTO.
YOU CAN TELL ME ALL ABOUT IT ON THE WAY.
ON THE WAY? WAY TO WHAT?
TO SEE THE SHERIFF.
THE SHERIFF? ARE YOU OUT OF YOUR FUCKIN'...
GODDAMNIT, EARL! YOU DON'T KNOW WHAT THE FUCK YOU'RE DOIN'!
YA DON'T EVEN FUCKIN' BELONG HERE! NOT ANYMORE!
HELL, YA NEVER REALLY DID, DID YA? THAT'S WHY YA NEVER CAME BACK.
AND WHY NOBODY EVER FUCKIN' CARED!
DO US BOTH A FAVOR, ALL RIGHT...
GO THE FUCK BACK TO BIRMINGHAM.

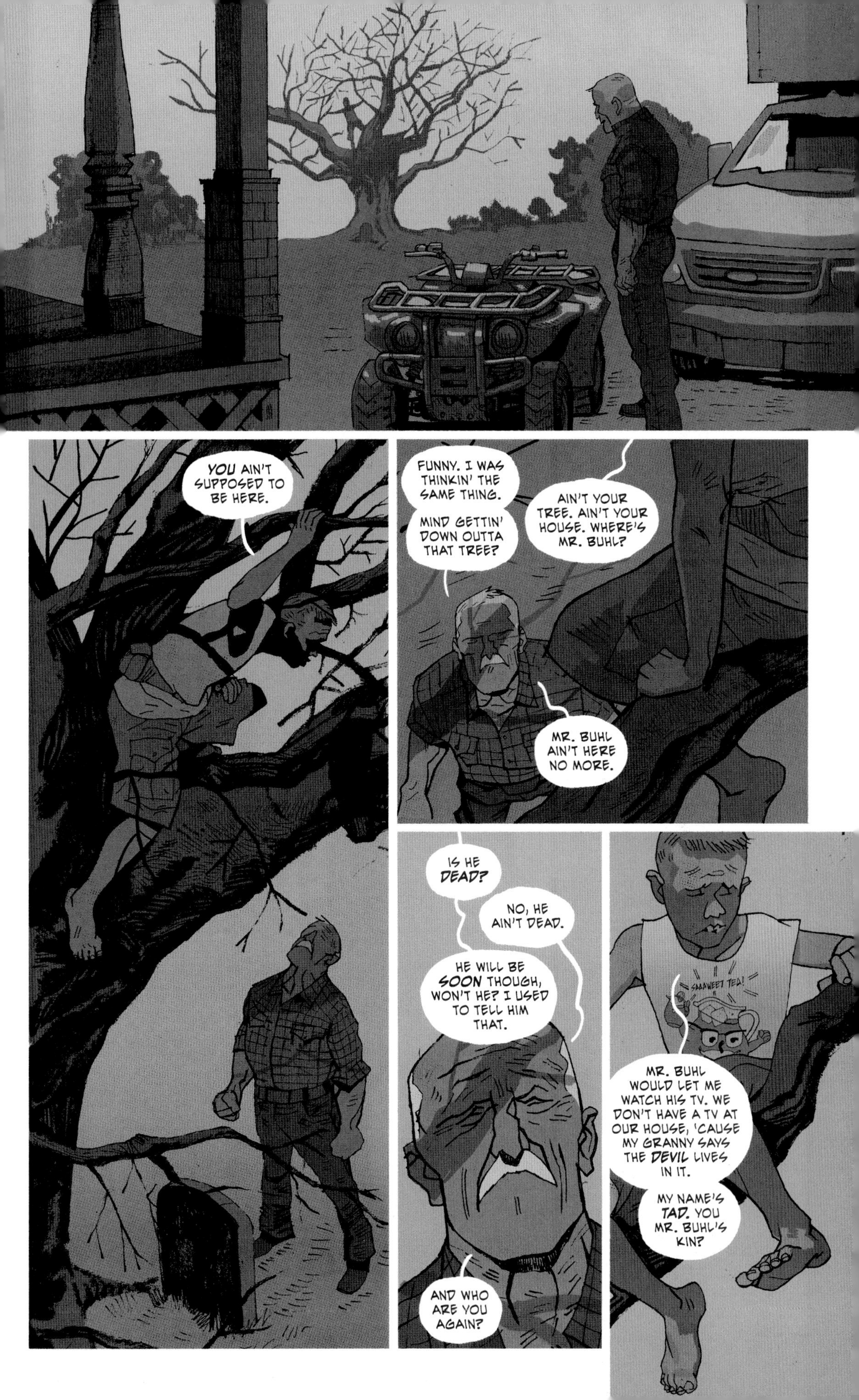
YOU AIN'T SUPPOSED TO BE HERE.
FUNNY. I WAS THINKIN' THE SAME THING.
MIND GETTIN' DOWN OUTTA THAT TREE?
AIN'T YOUR TREE. AIN'T YOUR HOUSE. WHERE'S MR. BUHL?
MR. BUHL AIN'T HERE NO MORE.
IS HE DEAD?
NO, HE AIN'T DEAD.
HE WILL BE SOON THOUGH, WON'T HE? I USED TO TELL HIM THAT.
AND WHO ARE YOU AGAIN?
SAAAWEET TEA!
MR. BUHL WOULD LET ME WATCH HIS TV. WE DON'T HAVE A TV AT OUR HOUSE, 'CAUSE MY GRANNY SAYS THE DEVIL LIVES IN IT.
MY NAME'S TAD. YOU MR. BUHL'S KIN?

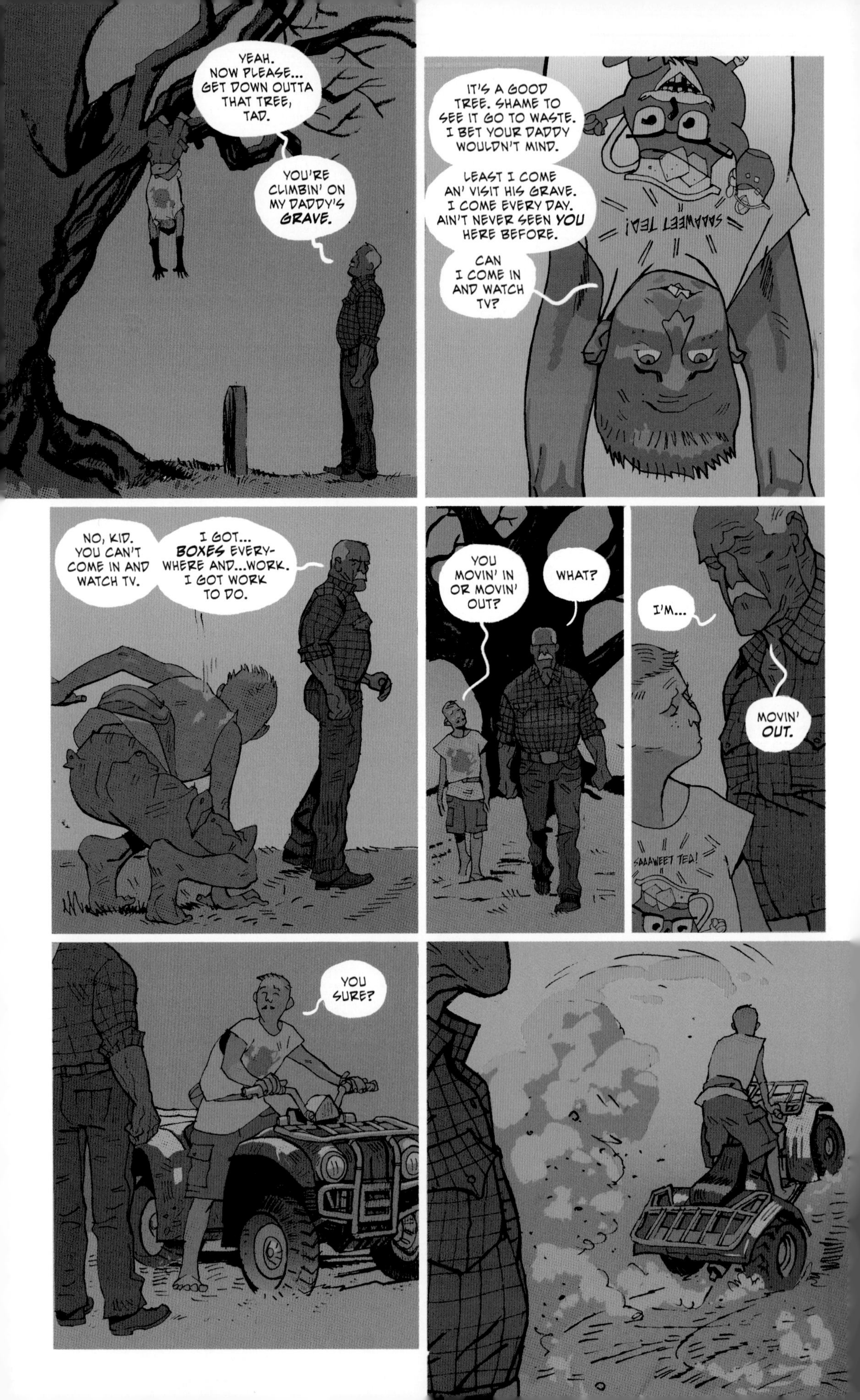
YEAH. NOW PLEASE... GET DOWN OUTTA THAT TREE, TAD.
YOU'RE CLIMBIN' ON MY DADDY'S GRAVE.
IT'S A GOOD TREE. SHAME TO SEE IT GO TO WASTE. I BET YOUR DADDY WOULDN'T MIND.
LEAST I COME AN' VISIT HIS GRAVE. I COME EVERY DAY. AIN'T NEVER SEEN YOU HERE BEFORE.
CAN I COME IN AND WATCH TV?
SAAAWEET TEA!
NO, KID. YOU CAN'T COME IN AND WATCH TV.
I GOT... BOXES EVERYWHERE AND...WORK. I GOT WORK TO DO.
YOU MOVIN' IN OR MOVIN' OUT?
WHAT?
I'M...
MOVIN' OUT.
SAAAWEET TEA!
YOU SURE?

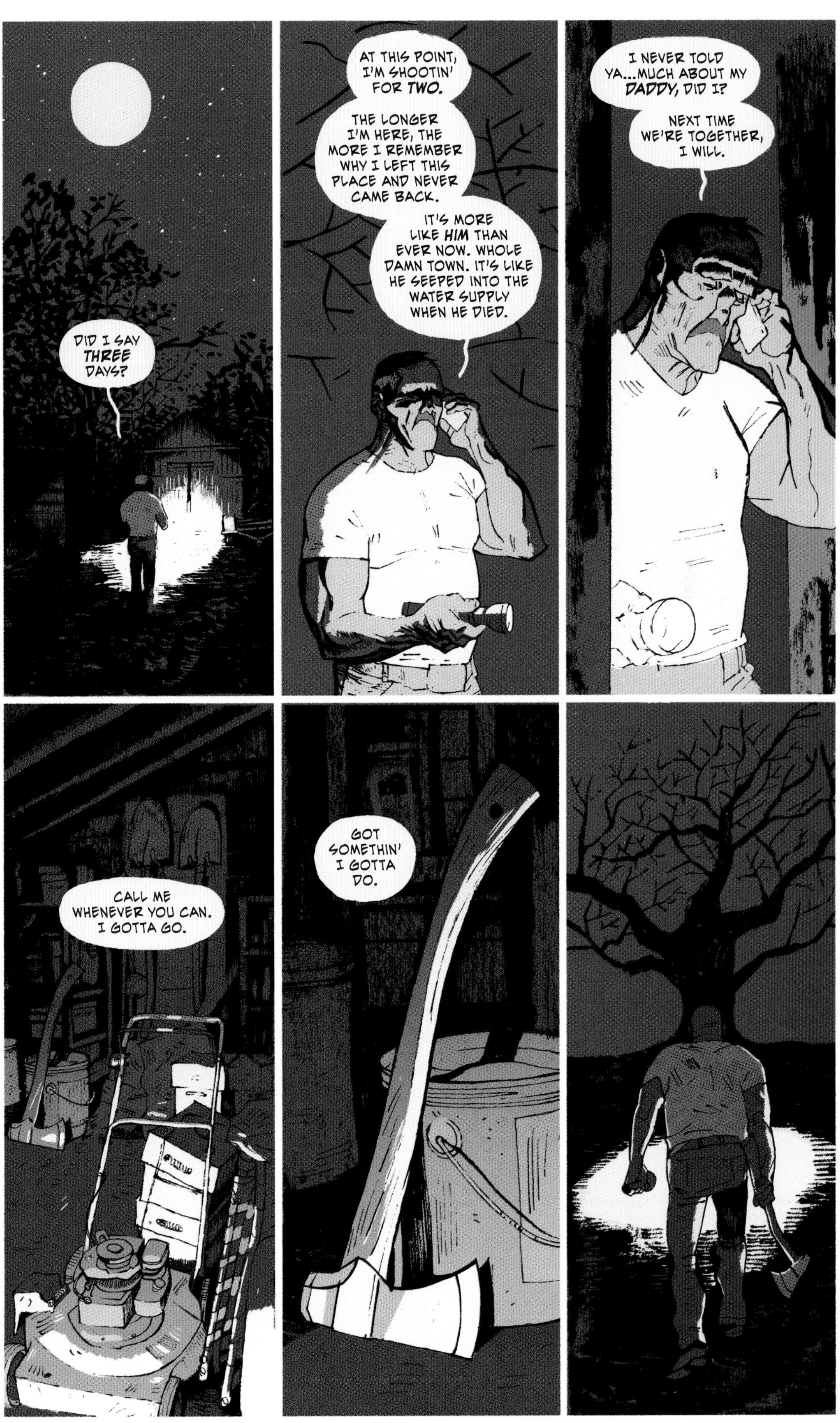
DID I SAY THREE DAYS?
AT THIS POINT, I'M SHOOTIN' FOR TWO.
THE LONGER I'M HERE, THE MORE I REMEMBER WHY I LEFT THIS PLACE AND NEVER CAME BACK.
IT'S MORE LIKE HIM THAN EVER NOW. WHOLE DAMN TOWN. IT'S LIKE HE SEEPED INTO THE WATER SUPPLY WHEN HE DIED.
I NEVER TOLD YA...MUCH ABOUT MY DADDY, DID I?
NEXT TIME WE'RE TOGETHER, I WILL.
CALL ME WHENEVER YOU CAN. I GOTTA GO.
GOT SOMETHIN' I GOTTA DO.

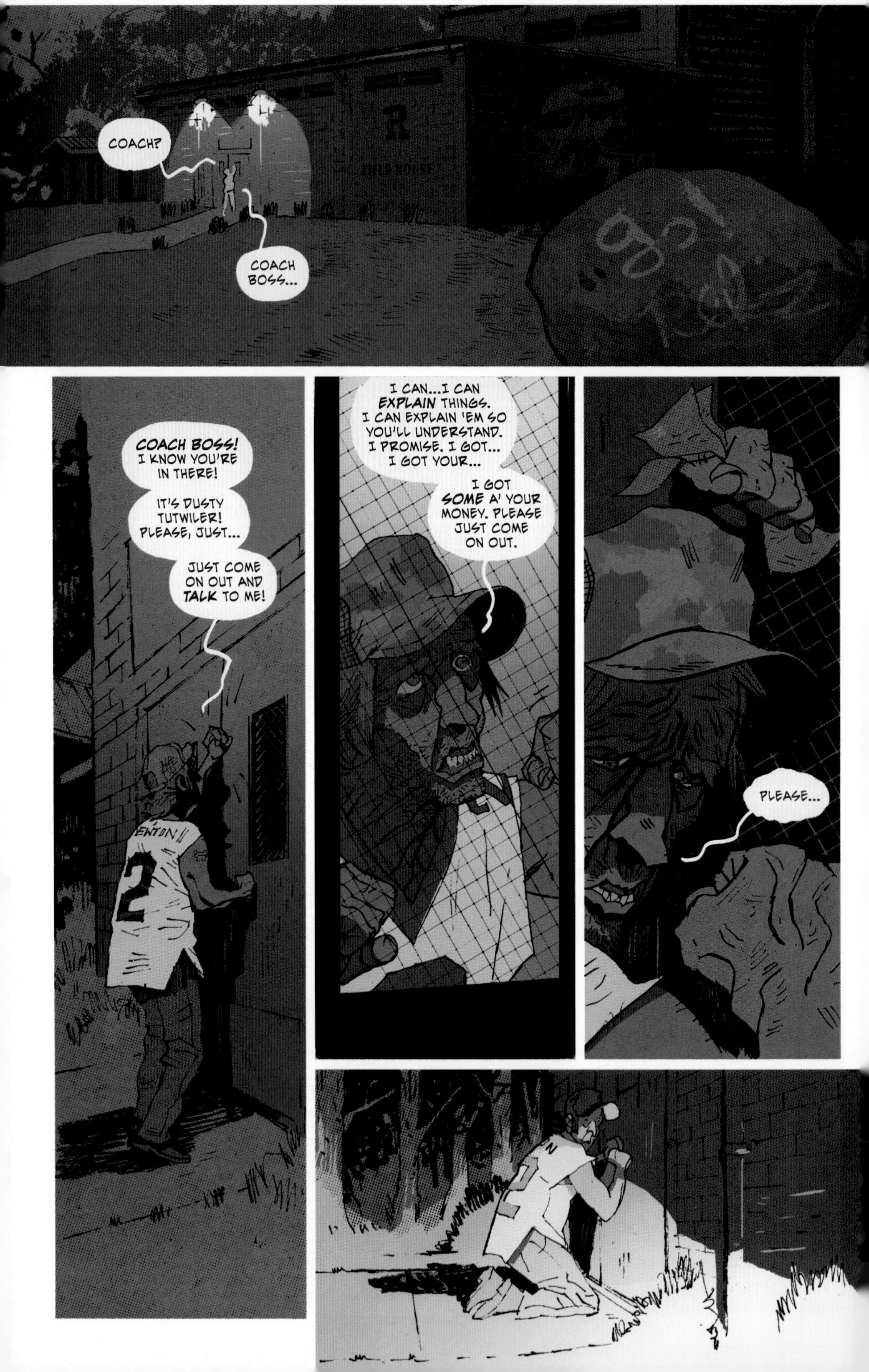
COACH?
COACH BOSS...
FIELD HOUSE
COACH BOSS! I KNOW YOU'RE IN THERE!
IT'S DUSTY TUTWILER! PLEASE, JUST...
JUST COME ON OUT AND TALK TO ME!
I CAN...I CAN EXPLAIN THINGS. I CAN EXPLAIN 'EM SO YOU'LL UNDERSTAND. I PROMISE. I GOT... I GOT YOUR...
I GOT SOME A' YOUR MONEY. PLEASE JUST COME ON OUT.
PLEASE...

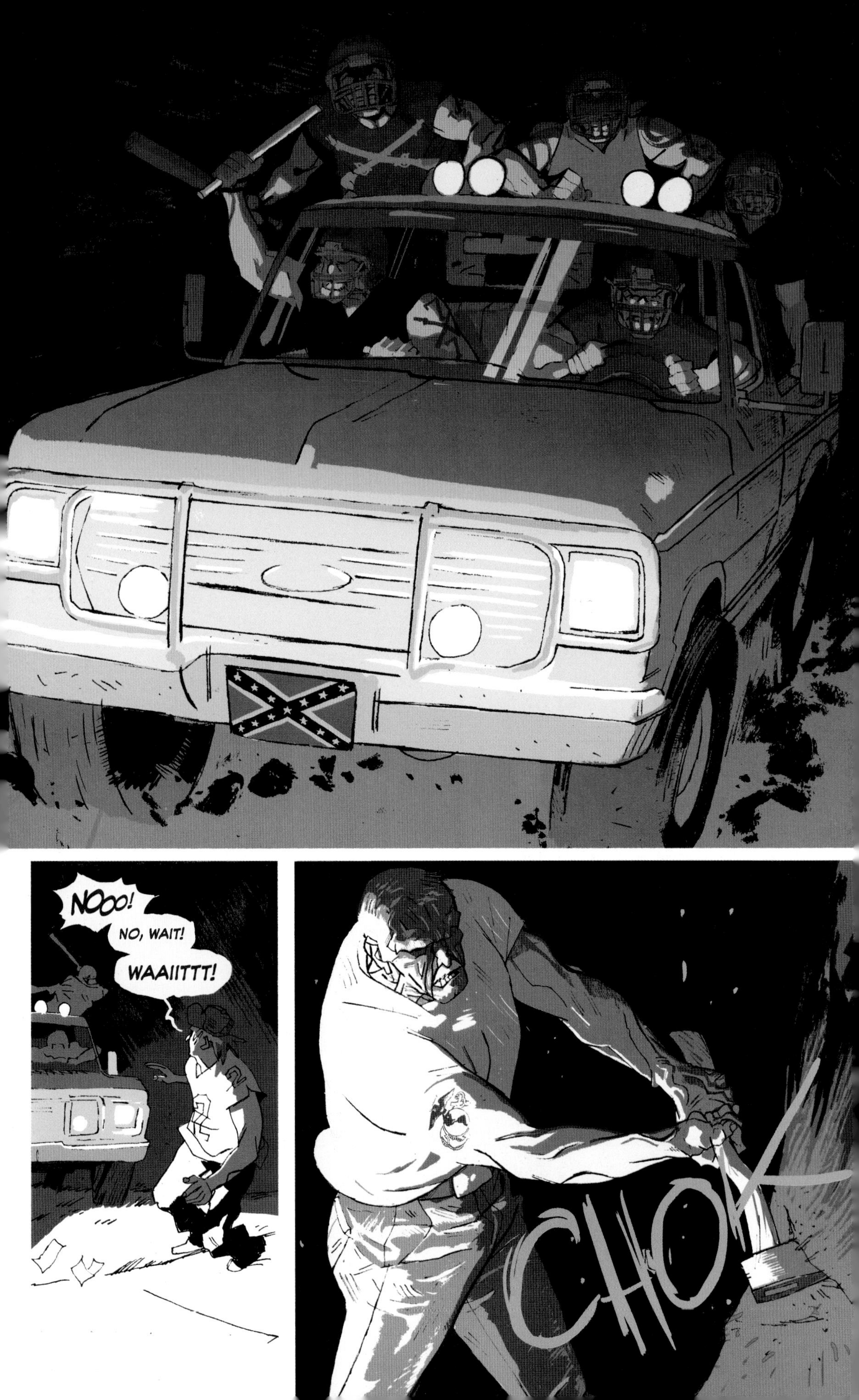
NOOO!
NO, WAIT!
WAAIITTT!
CHOK

UGGH

AH, FUCK...

WAIT...
WAIT,
I GOT...

TAKE IT.

TAKE IT,
JUS'...

HNGH
HNGH
HNGH

HNGH

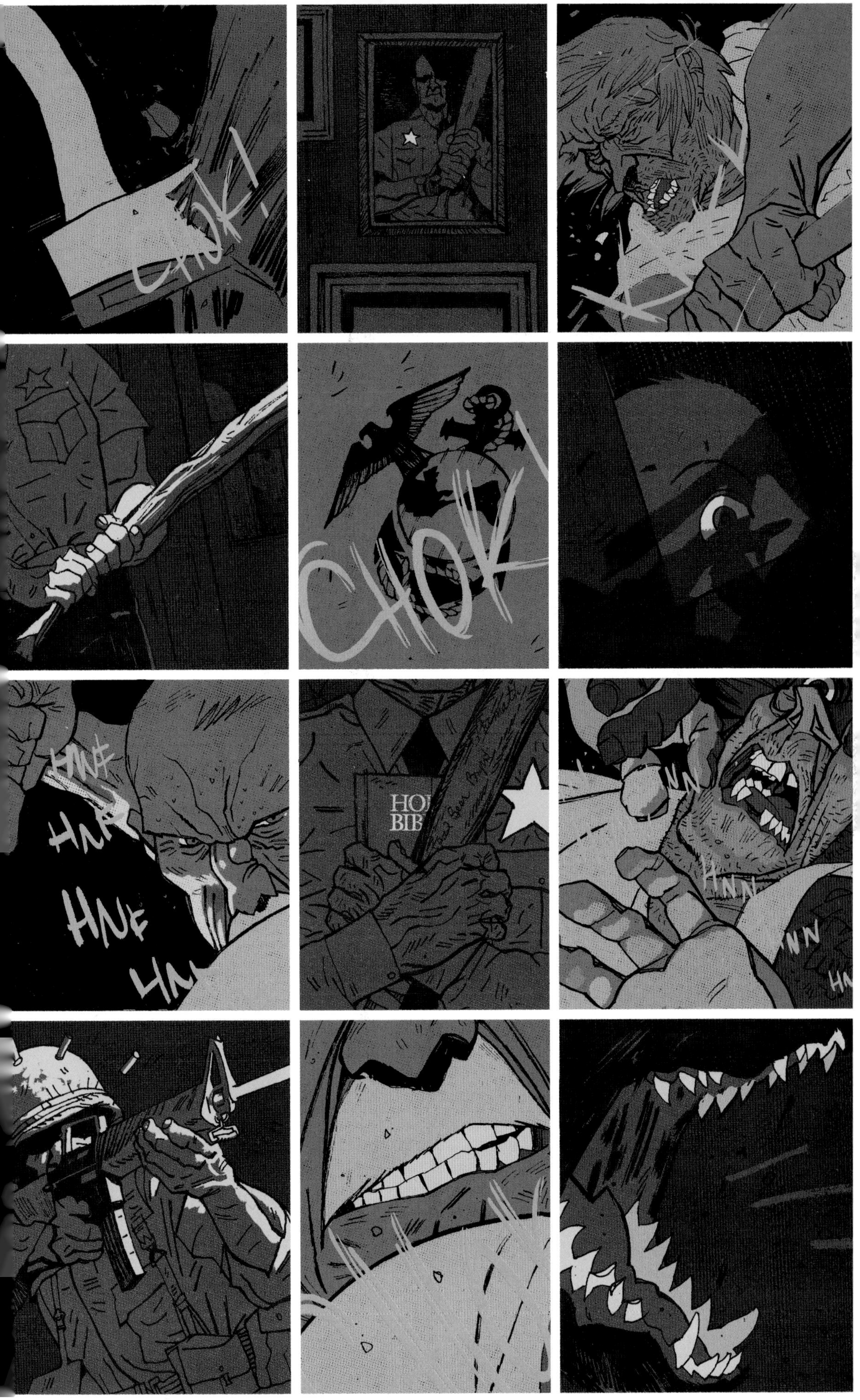
CHOK!
CHOK!
HNF
HNF
HNF
HOL
BIB
HNN

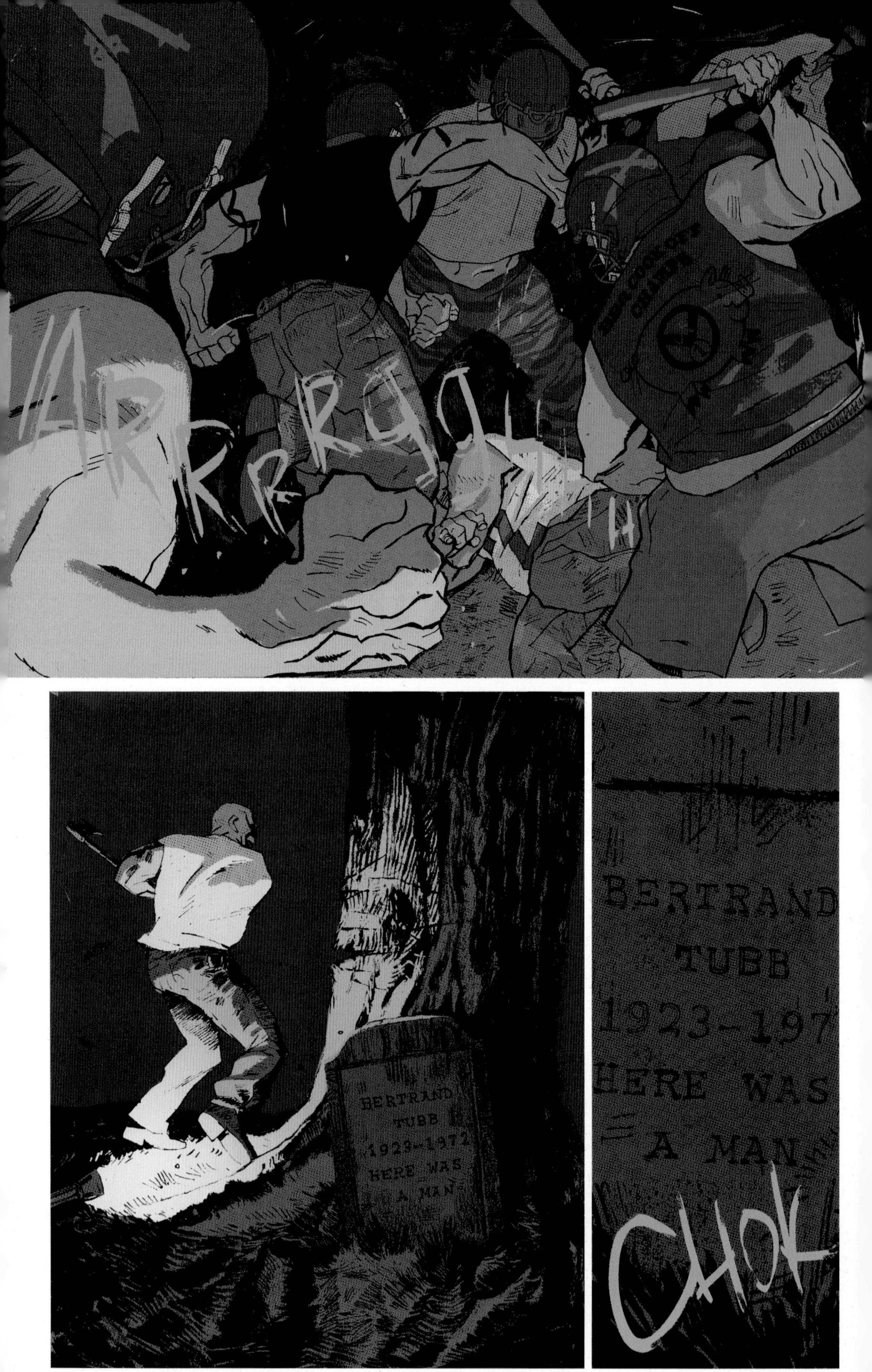
ARRRGGHH
BERTRAND
TUBB
1923-1972
HERE WAS
A MAN
BERTRAND
TUBB
1923-197
HERE WAS
A MAN
CHOK

Chapter 2

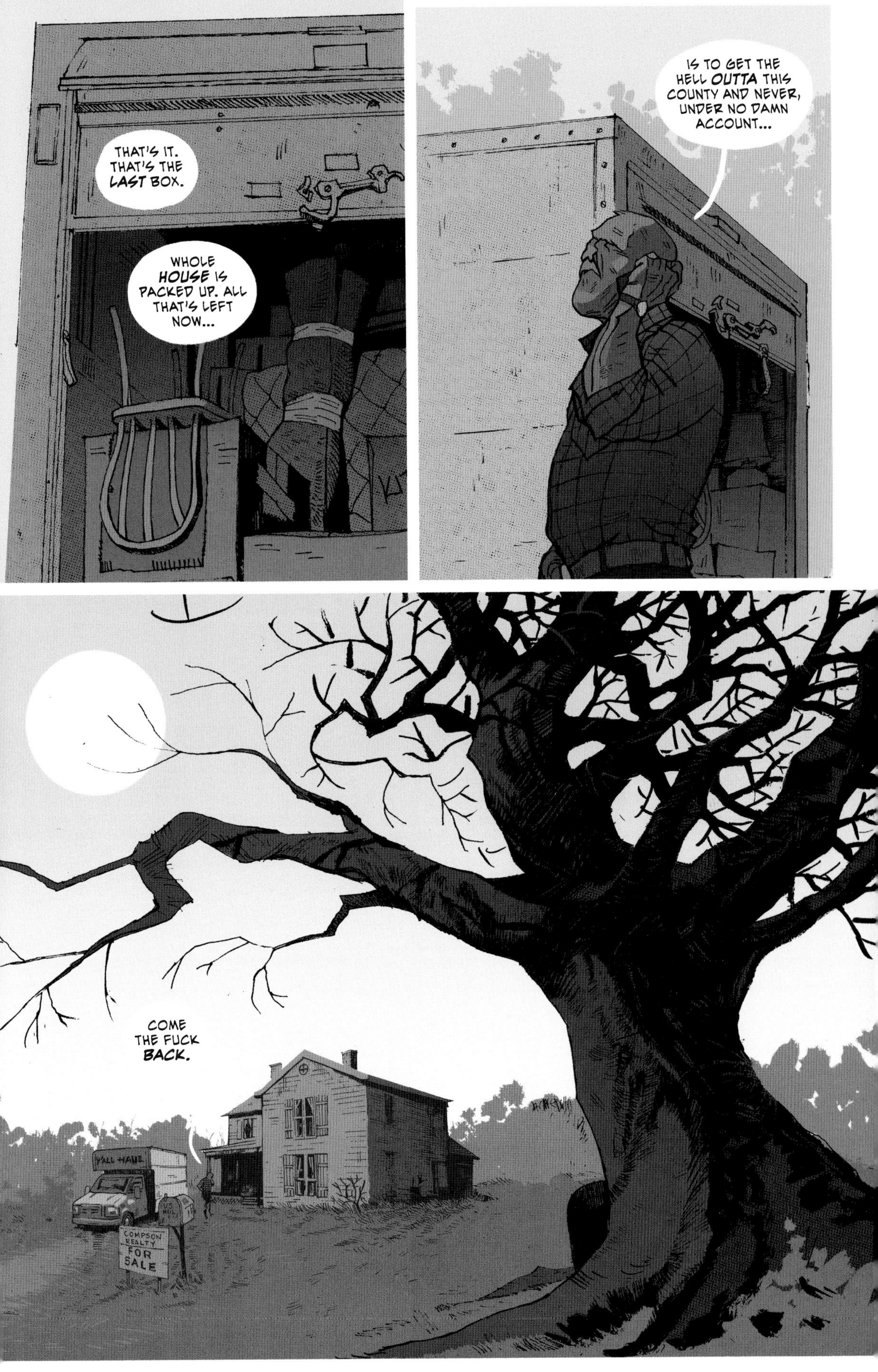
THAT'S IT. THAT'S THE *LAST* BOX.
WHOLE *HOUSE* IS PACKED UP. ALL THAT'S LEFT NOW...
IS TO GET THE HELL *OUTTA* THIS COUNTY AND NEVER, UNDER NO DAMN ACCOUNT...
COME THE FUCK *BACK*.
Y'ALL HAUL
US MAIL
COMPSON REALTY
FOR SALE

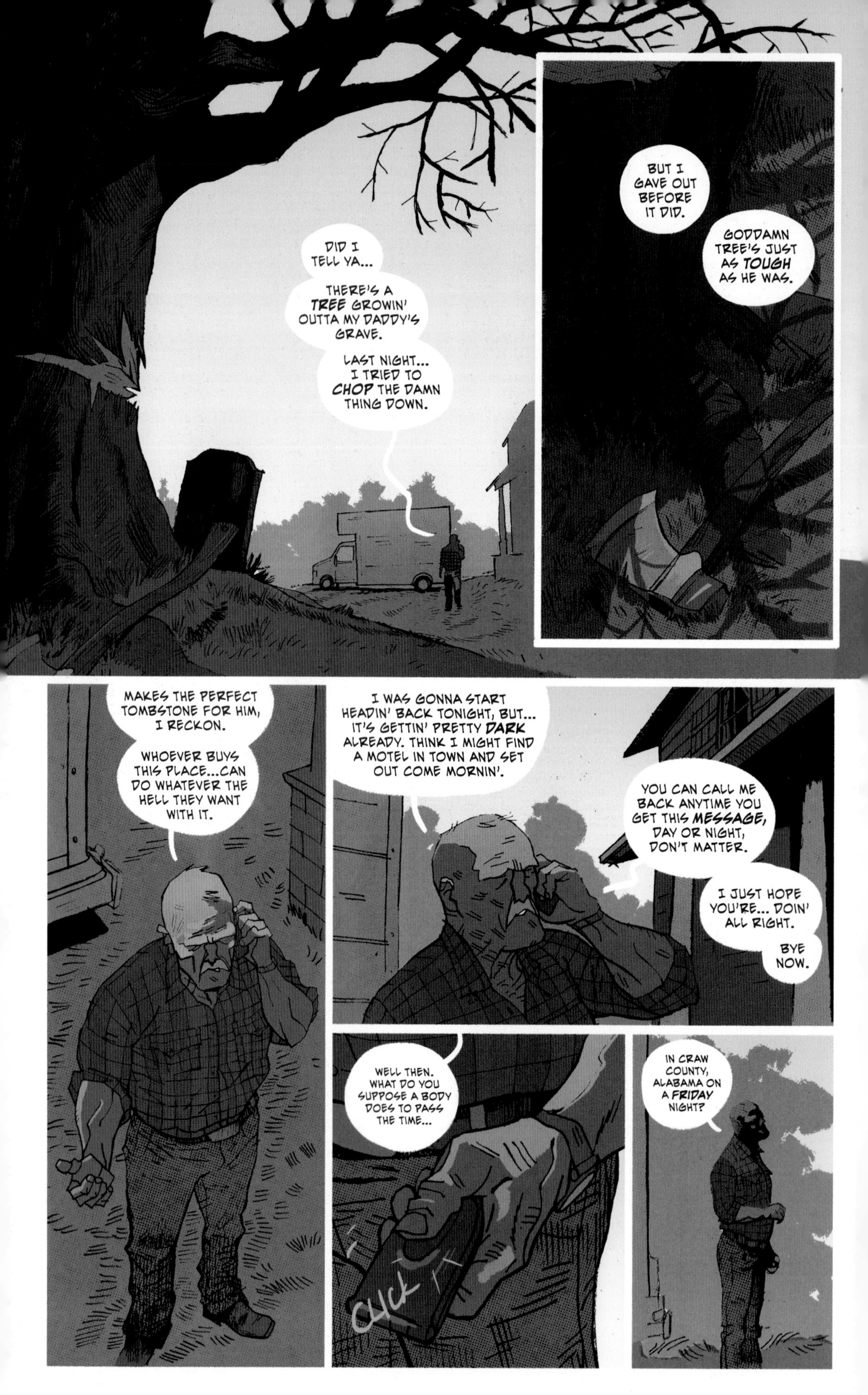
DID I TELL YA...
THERE'S A TREE GROWIN' OUTTA MY DADDY'S GRAVE.
LAST NIGHT... I TRIED TO CHOP THE DAMN THING DOWN.
BUT I GAVE OUT BEFORE IT DID.
GODDAMN TREE'S JUST AS TOUGH AS HE WAS.
MAKES THE PERFECT TOMBSTONE FOR HIM, I RECKON.
WHOEVER BUYS THIS PLACE...CAN DO WHATEVER THE HELL THEY WANT WITH IT.
I WAS GONNA START HEADIN' BACK TONIGHT, BUT... IT'S GETTIN' PRETTY DARK ALREADY. THINK I MIGHT FIND A MOTEL IN TOWN AND SET OUT COME MORNIN'.
YOU CAN CALL ME BACK ANYTIME YOU GET THIS MESSAGE, DAY OR NIGHT, DON'T MATTER.
I JUST HOPE YOU'RE... DOIN' ALL RIGHT.
BYE NOW.
WELL THEN. WHAT DO YOU SUPPOSE A BODY DOES TO PASS THE TIME...
CLICK
IN CRAW COUNTY, ALABAMA ON A FRIDAY NIGHT?

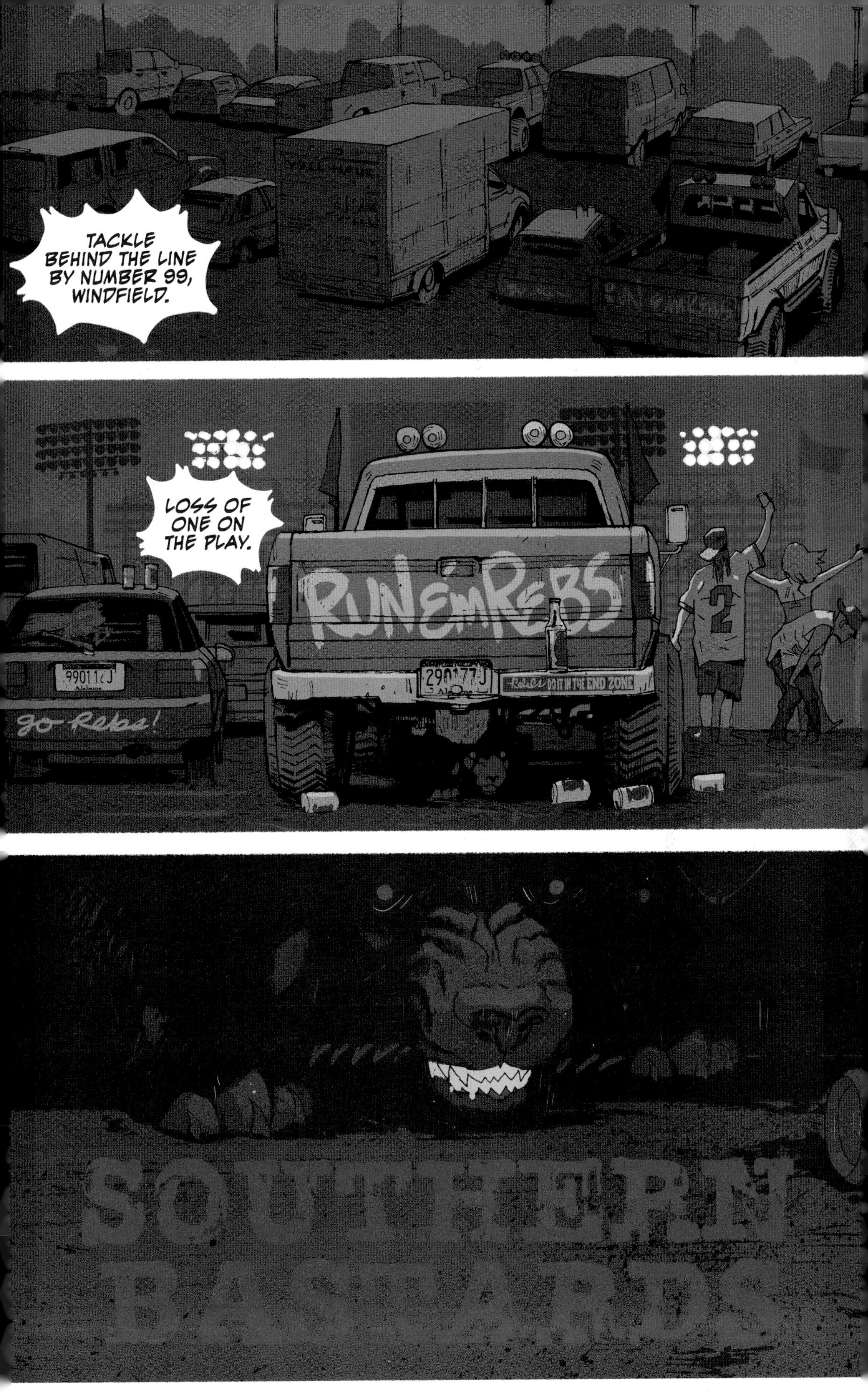

TACKLE BEHIND THE LINE BY NUMBER 99, WINDFIELD.
LOSS OF ONE ON THE PLAY.
RUN'EM REBS
go Rebs!
Rebs DO IT IN THE END ZONE
SOUTHERN BASTARDS

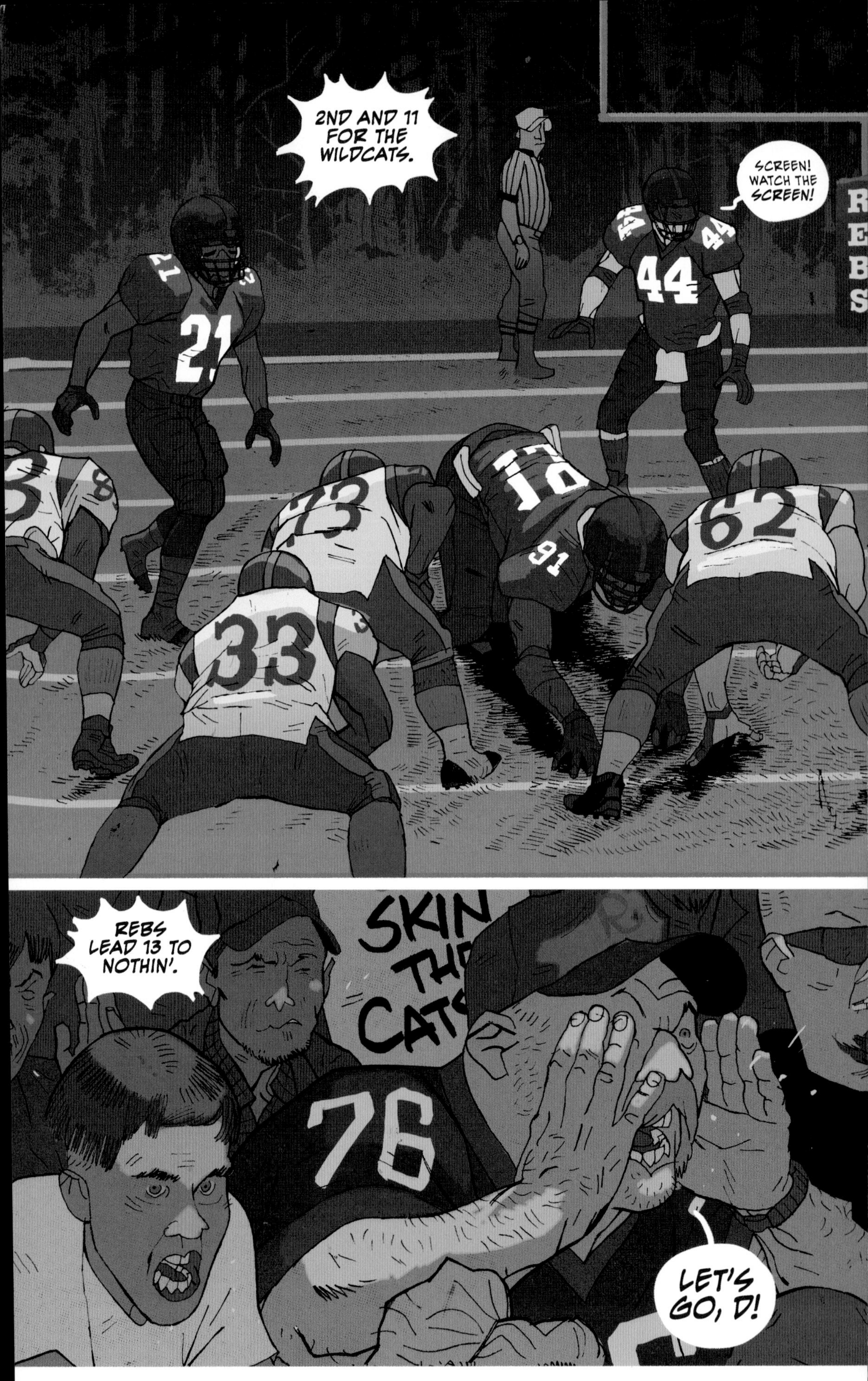
2ND AND 11 FOR THE WILDCATS.
SCREEN! WATCH THE SCREEN!
REBS
REBS LEAD 13 TO NOTHIN'.
SKIN
LET'S GO, D!

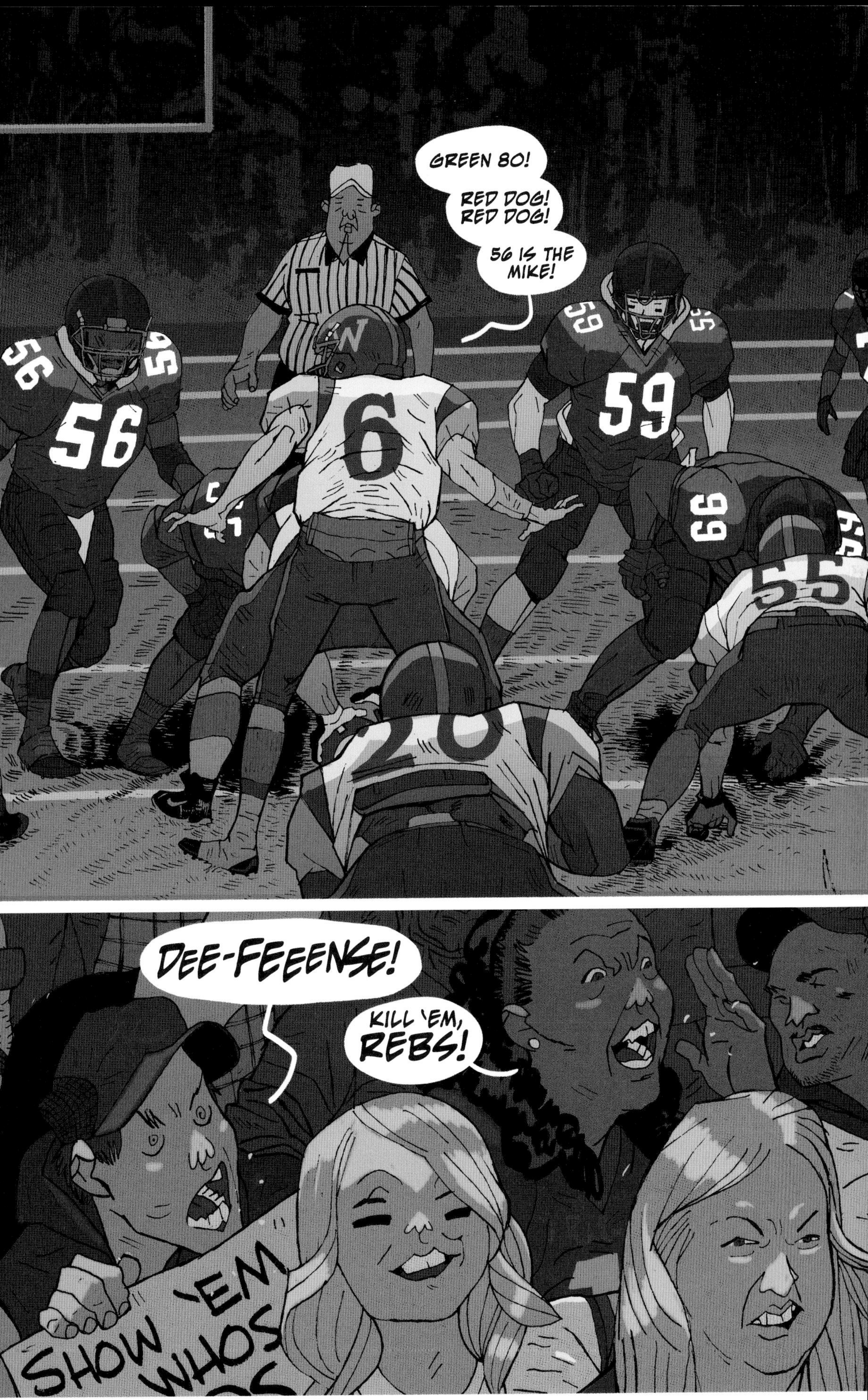
GREEN 80!
RED DOG! RED DOG!
56 IS THE MIKE!
DEE-FEEENSE!
KILL 'EM, REBS!
SHOW 'EM WHOS

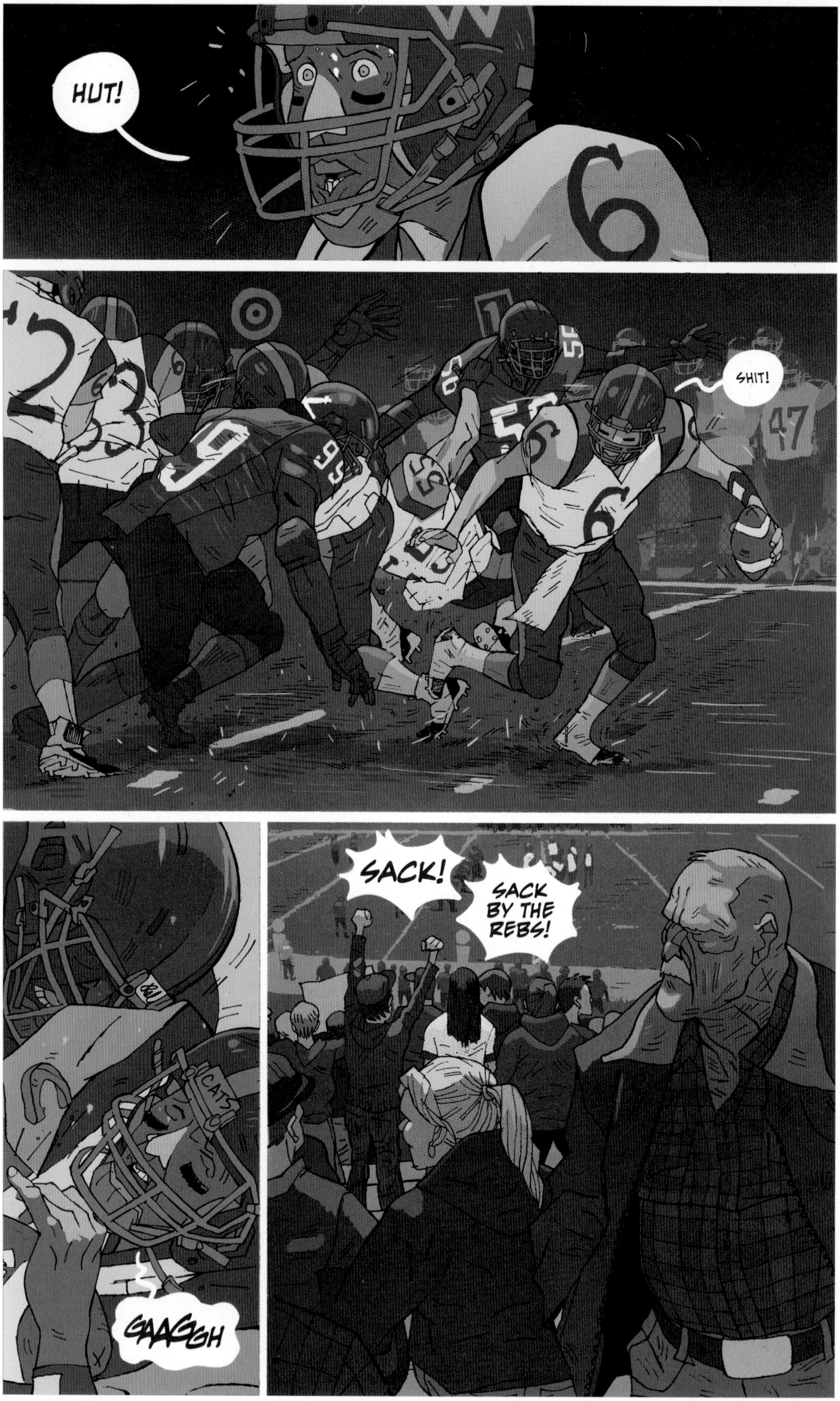
HUT!
SHIT!
GAAGGH
SACK!
SACK BY THE REBS!

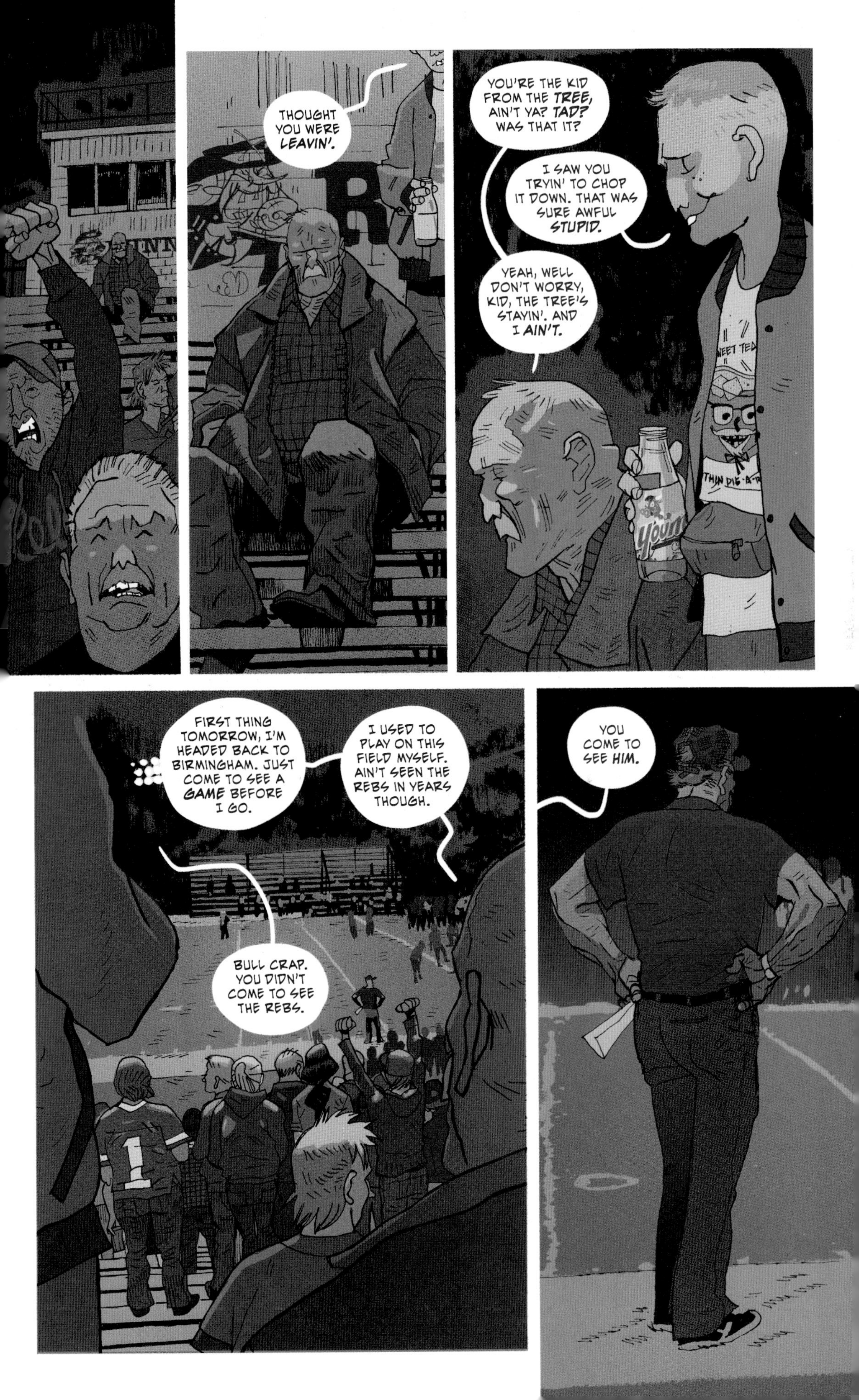
THOUGHT YOU WERE LEAVIN'.
YOU'RE THE KID FROM THE TREE, AIN'T YA? TAD? WAS THAT IT?
I SAW YOU TRYIN' TO CHOP IT DOWN. THAT WAS SURE AWFUL STUPID.
YEAH, WELL DON'T WORRY, KID, THE TREE'S STAYIN'. AND I AIN'T.
FIRST THING TOMORROW, I'M HEADED BACK TO BIRMINGHAM. JUST COME TO SEE A GAME BEFORE I GO.
I USED TO PLAY ON THIS FIELD MYSELF. AIN'T SEEN THE REBS IN YEARS THOUGH.
BULL CRAP. YOU DIDN'T COME TO SEE THE REBS.
YOU COME TO SEE HIM.

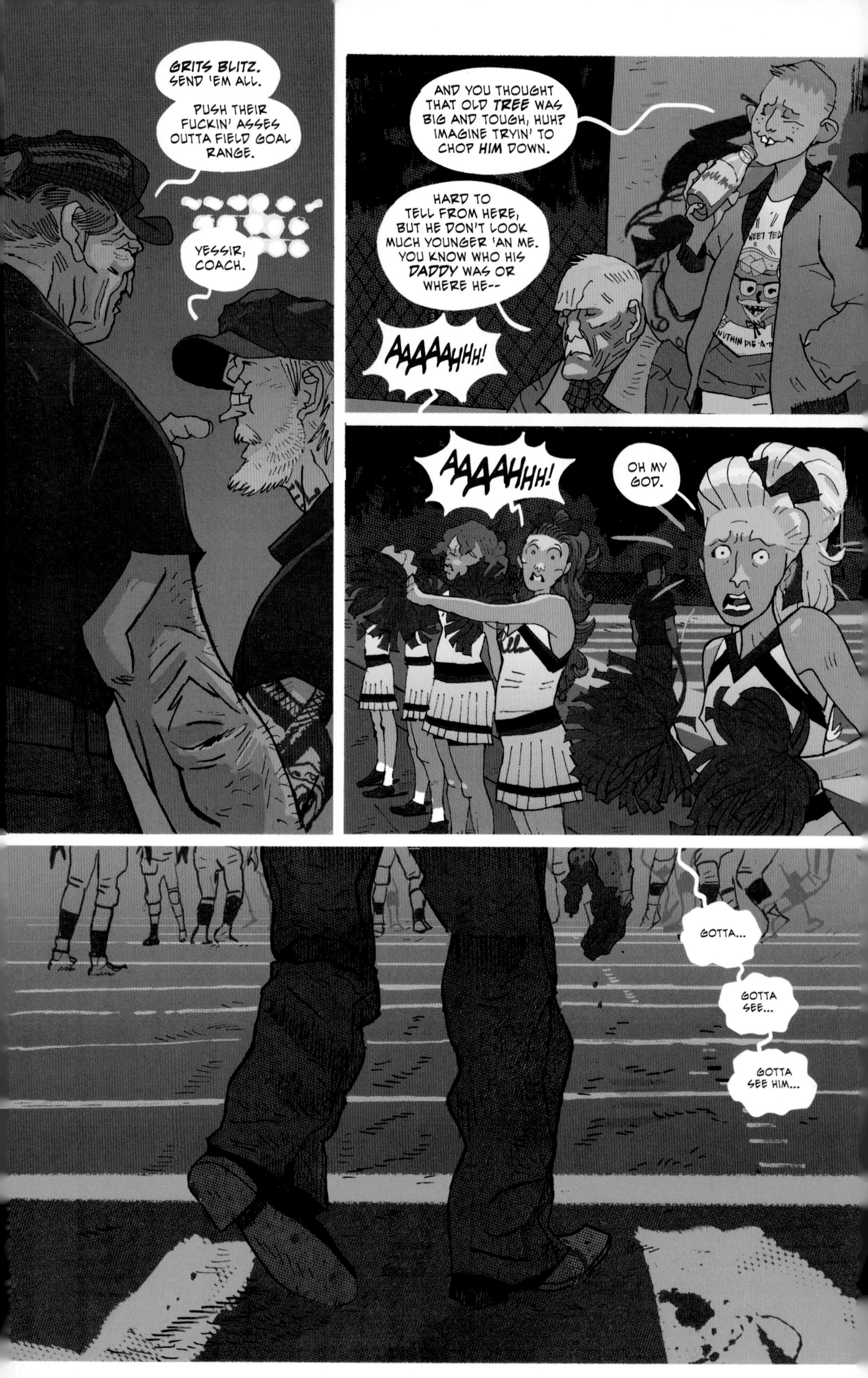
GRITS BLITZ. SEND 'EM ALL.
PUSH THEIR FUCKIN' ASSES OUTTA FIELD GOAL RANGE.
YESSIR, COACH.
AND YOU THOUGHT THAT OLD TREE WAS BIG AND TOUGH, HUH? IMAGINE TRYIN' TO CHOP HIM DOWN.
HARD TO TELL FROM HERE, BUT HE DON'T LOOK MUCH YOUNGER 'AN ME. YOU KNOW WHO HIS DADDY WAS OR WHERE HE--
AAAAAHHH!
AAAAHHH!
OH MY GOD.
GOTTA...
GOTTA SEE...
GOTTA SEE HIM...

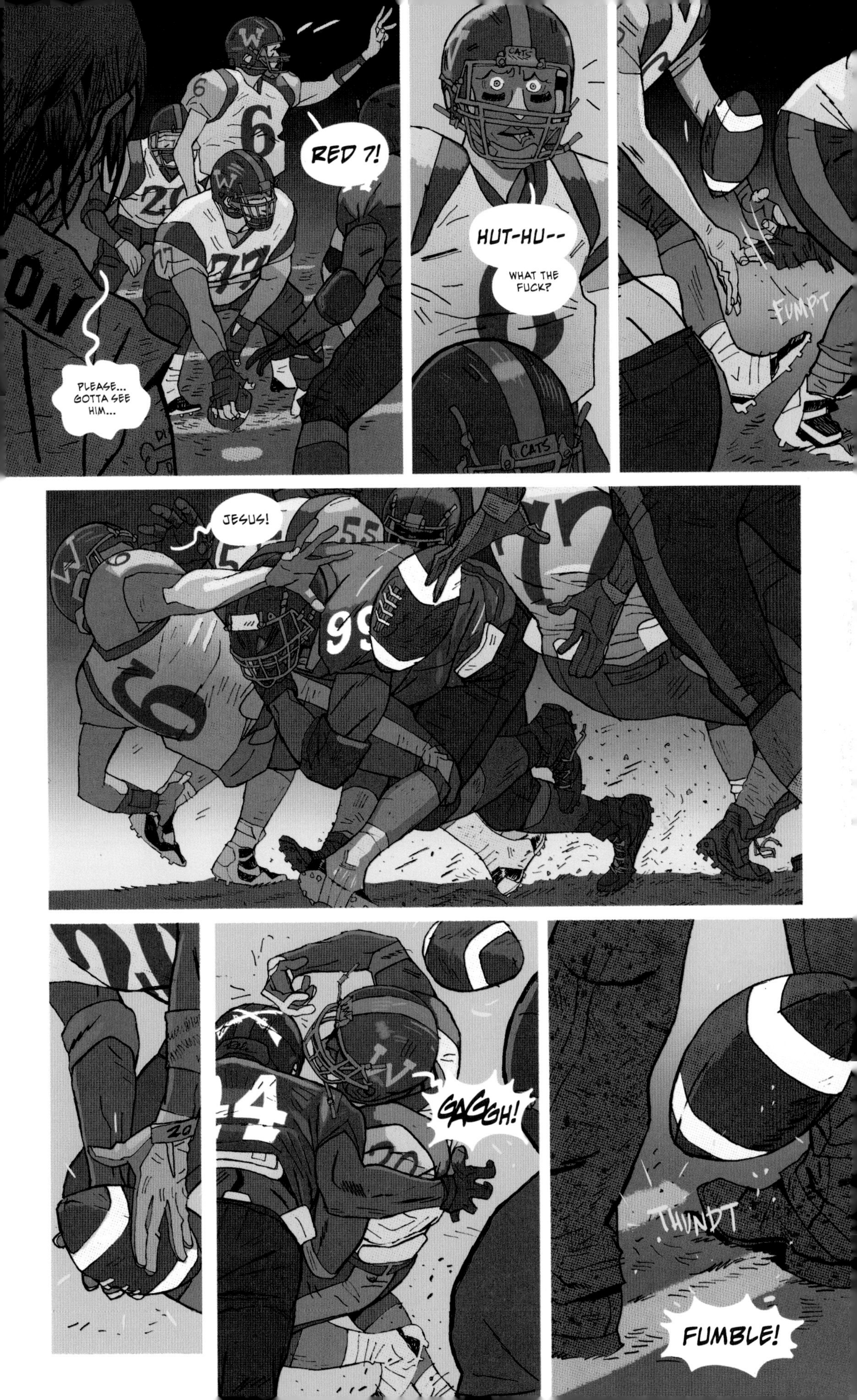
PLEASE... GOTTA SEE HIM...
RED 7!
HUT-HU--
WHAT THE FUCK?
FUMPT
JESUS!
GAGGH!
THUNDT
FUMBLE!

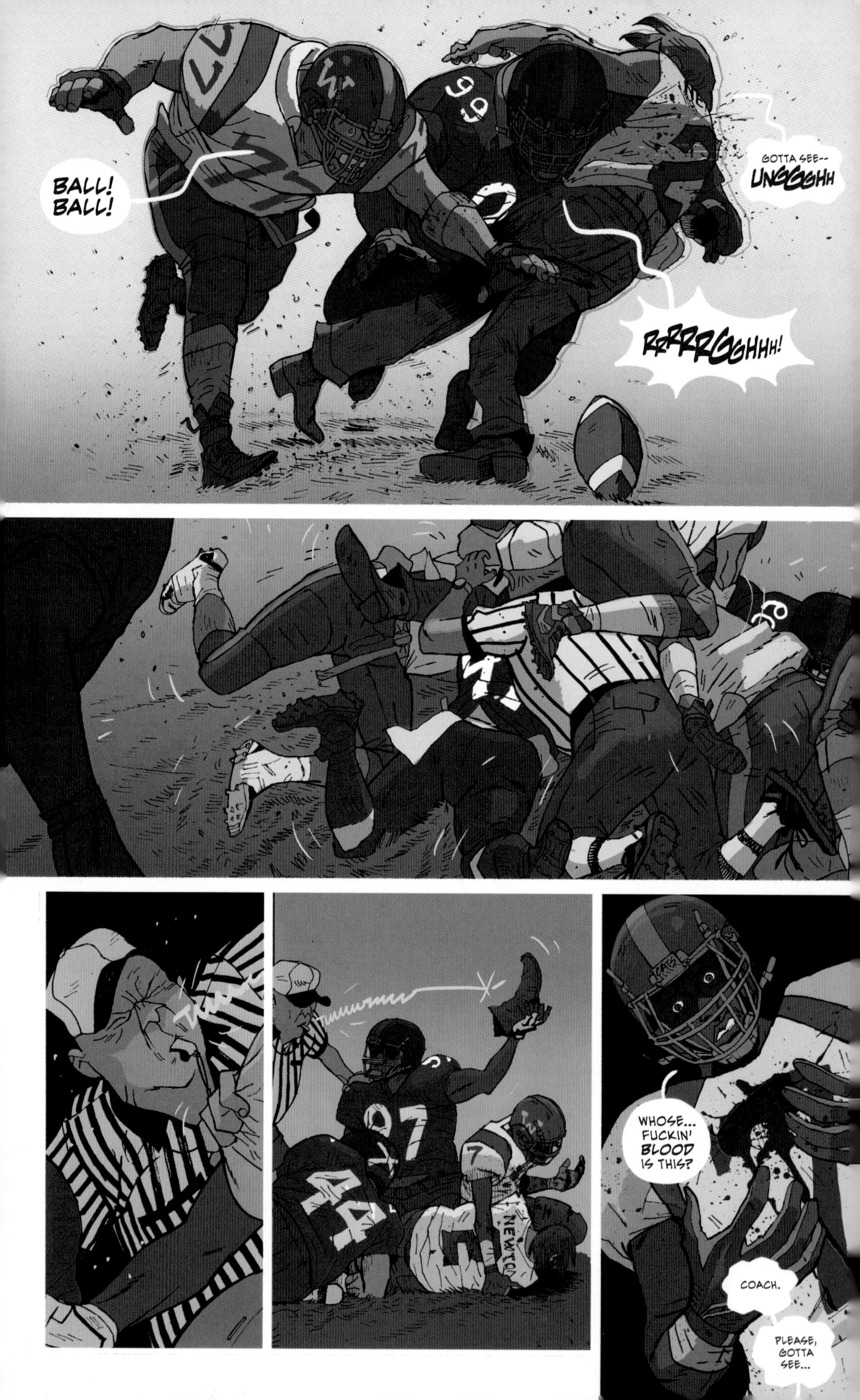
BALL! BALL!
GOTTA SEE-- UNGGGHH
RRRRRGGHHH!
WHOSE... FUCKIN' BLOOD IS THIS?
COACH.
PLEASE, GOTTA SEE...

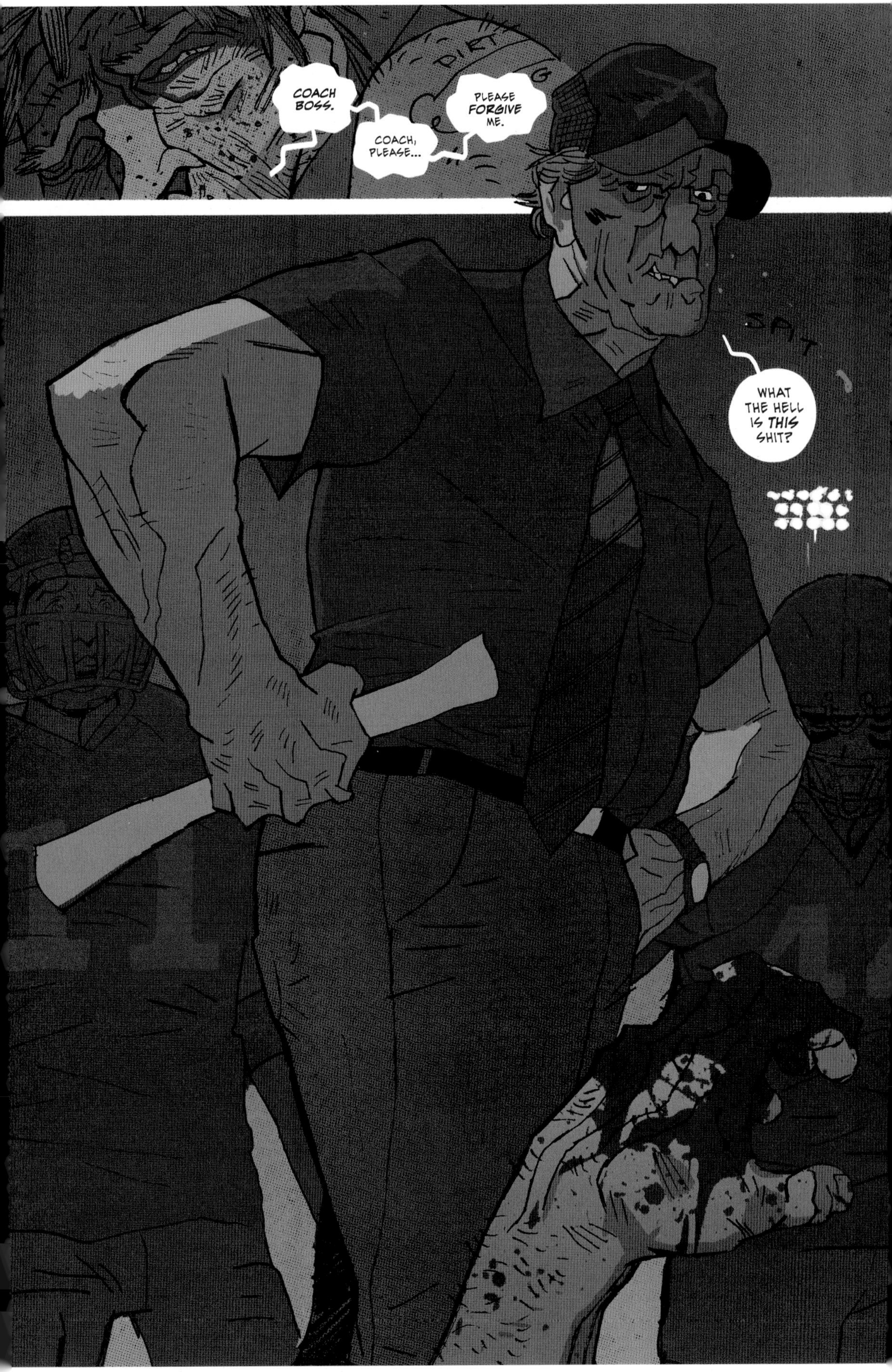
COACH BOSS.
COACH, PLEASE...
PLEASE FORGIVE ME.
SPIT
WHAT THE HELL IS THIS SHIT?

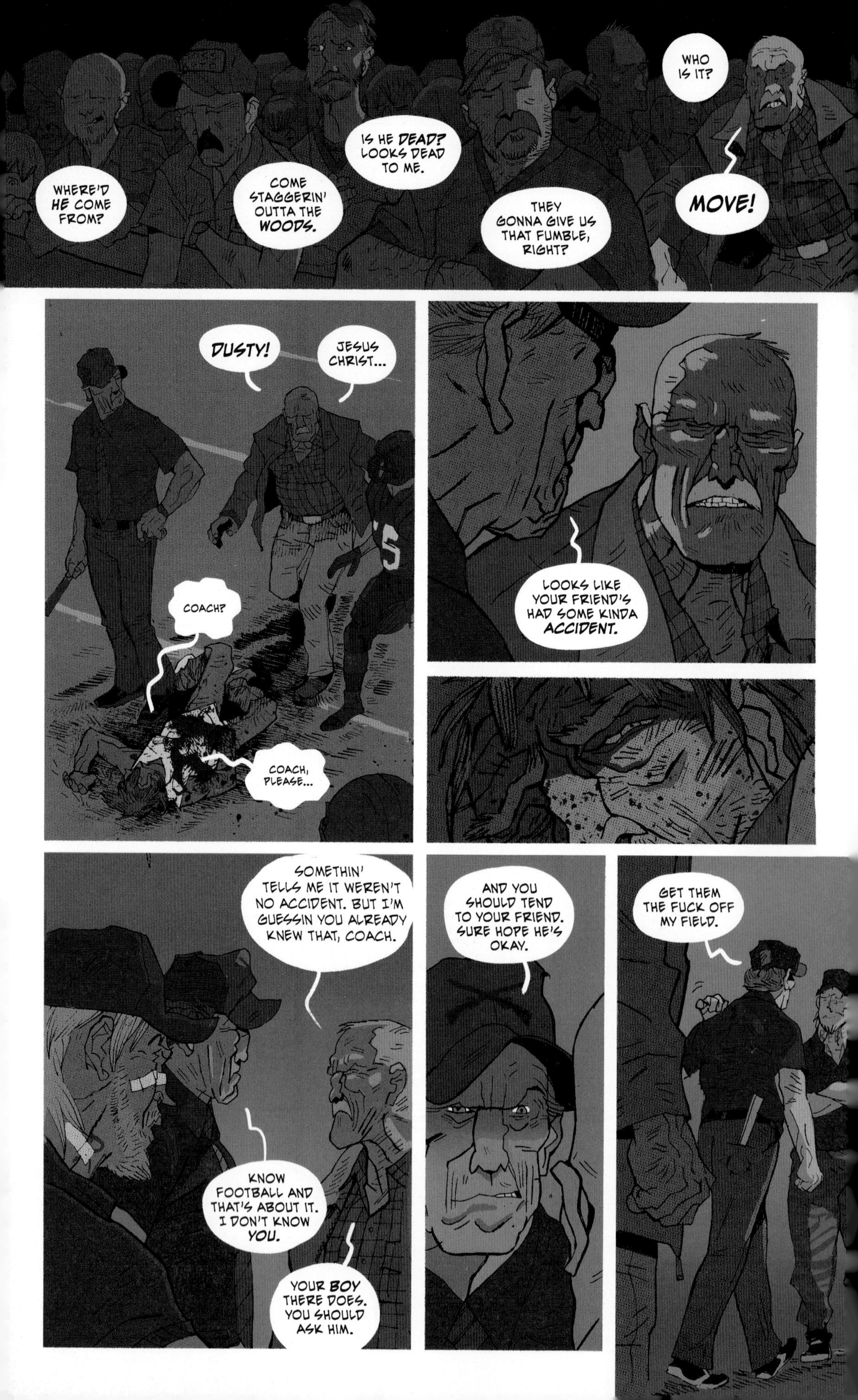

WHERE'D HE COME FROM?
COME STAGGERIN' OUTTA THE WOODS.
IS HE DEAD? LOOKS DEAD TO ME.
THEY GONNA GIVE US THAT FUMBLE, RIGHT?
WHO IS IT?
MOVE!
DUSTY!
JESUS CHRIST...
COACH?
COACH, PLEASE...
LOOKS LIKE YOUR FRIEND'S HAD SOME KINDA ACCIDENT.
SOMETHIN' TELLS ME IT WEREN'T NO ACCIDENT. BUT I'M GUESSIN YOU ALREADY KNEW THAT, COACH.
KNOW FOOTBALL AND THAT'S ABOUT IT. I DON'T KNOW YOU.
YOUR BOY THERE DOES. YOU SHOULD ASK HIM.
AND YOU SHOULD TEND TO YOUR FRIEND. SURE HOPE HE'S OKAY.
GET THEM THE FUCK OFF MY FIELD.

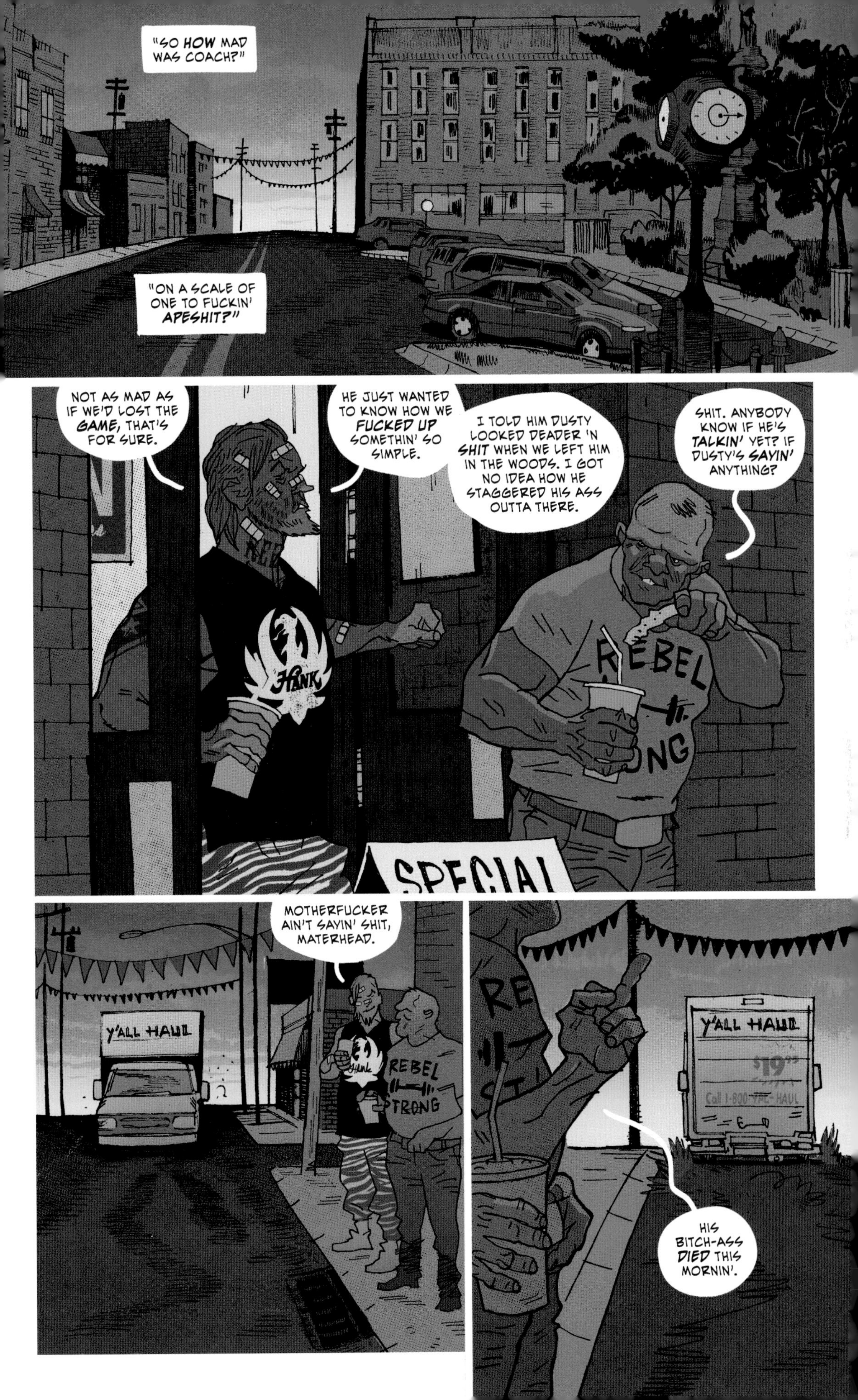
"SO HOW MAD WAS COACH?"
"ON A SCALE OF ONE TO FUCKIN' APESHIT?"
NOT AS MAD AS IF WE'D LOST THE GAME, THAT'S FOR SURE.
HE JUST WANTED TO KNOW HOW WE FUCKED UP SOMETHIN' SO SIMPLE.
I TOLD HIM DUSTY LOOKED DEADER 'N SHIT WHEN WE LEFT HIM IN THE WOODS. I GOT NO IDEA HOW HE STAGGERED HIS ASS OUTTA THERE.
SHIT. ANYBODY KNOW IF HE'S TALKIN' YET? IF DUSTY'S SAYIN' ANYTHING?
HANK
REBEL
SPECIAL
MOTHERFUCKER AIN'T SAYIN' SHIT, MATERHEAD.
Y'ALL HAUL
REBEL STRONG
Y'ALL HAUL
$19.95
HIS BITCH-ASS DIED THIS MORNIN'.

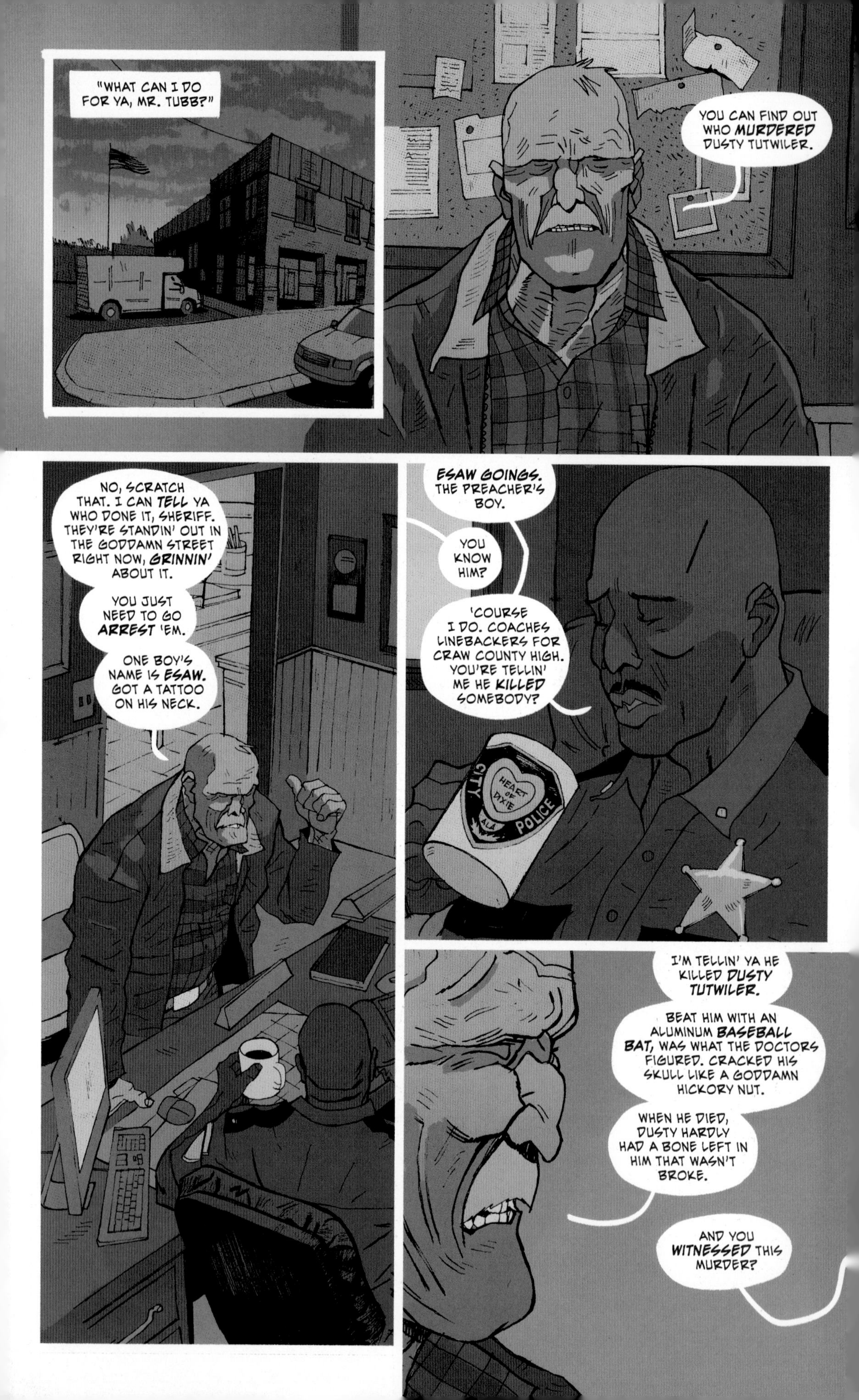
"WHAT CAN I DO FOR YA, MR. TUBB?"
YOU CAN FIND OUT WHO MURDERED DUSTY TUTWILER.
NO, SCRATCH THAT. I CAN TELL YA WHO DONE IT, SHERIFF. THEY'RE STANDIN' OUT IN THE GODDAMN STREET RIGHT NOW, GRINNIN' ABOUT IT.
YOU JUST NEED TO GO ARREST 'EM.
ONE BOY'S NAME IS ESAW. GOT A TATTOO ON HIS NECK.
ESAW GOINGS. THE PREACHER'S BOY.
YOU KNOW HIM?
'COURSE I DO. COACHES LINEBACKERS FOR CRAW COUNTY HIGH. YOU'RE TELLIN' ME HE KILLED SOMEBODY?
CITY
HEART OF DIXIE
ALA
POLICE
I'M TELLIN' YA HE KILLED DUSTY TUTWILER.
BEAT HIM WITH AN ALUMINUM BASEBALL BAT, WAS WHAT THE DOCTORS FIGURED. CRACKED HIS SKULL LIKE A GODDAMN HICKORY NUT.
WHEN HE DIED, DUSTY HARDLY HAD A BONE LEFT IN HIM THAT WASN'T BROKE.
AND YOU WITNESSED THIS MURDER?

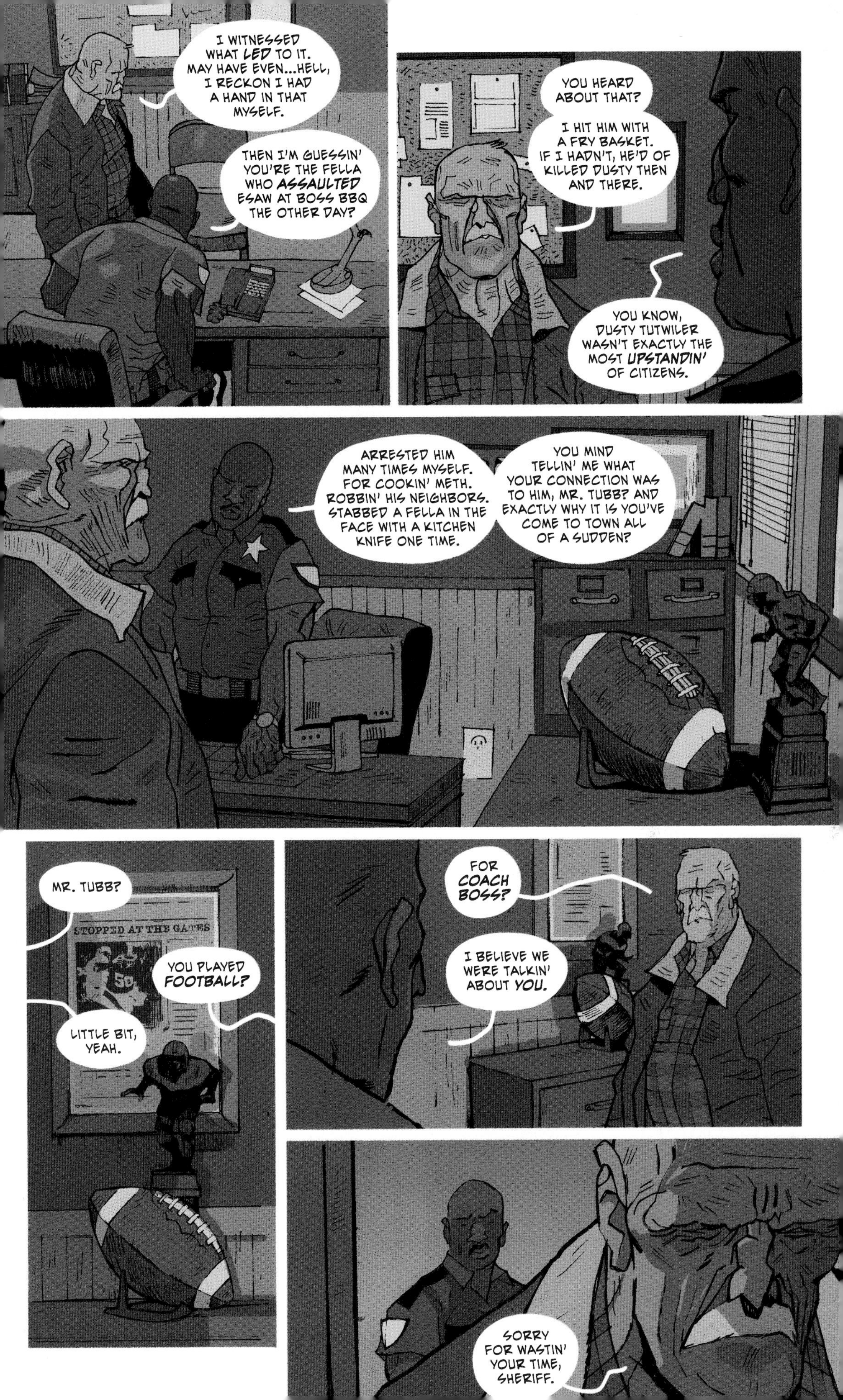
I WITNESSED WHAT LED TO IT. MAY HAVE EVEN...HELL, I RECKON I HAD A HAND IN THAT MYSELF.
THEN I'M GUESSIN' YOU'RE THE FELLA WHO ASSAULTED ESAW AT BOSS BBQ THE OTHER DAY?
YOU HEARD ABOUT THAT?
I HIT HIM WITH A FRY BASKET. IF I HADN'T, HE'D OF KILLED DUSTY THEN AND THERE.
YOU KNOW, DUSTY TUTWILER WASN'T EXACTLY THE MOST UPSTANDIN' OF CITIZENS.
ARRESTED HIM MANY TIMES MYSELF. FOR COOKIN' METH. ROBBIN' HIS NEIGHBORS. STABBED A FELLA IN THE FACE WITH A KITCHEN KNIFE ONE TIME.
YOU MIND TELLIN' ME WHAT YOUR CONNECTION WAS TO HIM, MR. TUBB? AND EXACTLY WHY IT IS YOU'VE COME TO TOWN ALL OF A SUDDEN?
MR. TUBB?
STOPPED AT THE GATES
YOU PLAYED FOOTBALL?
LITTLE BIT, YEAH.
FOR COACH BOSS?
I BELIEVE WE WERE TALKIN' ABOUT YOU.
SORRY FOR WASTIN' YOUR TIME, SHERIFF.

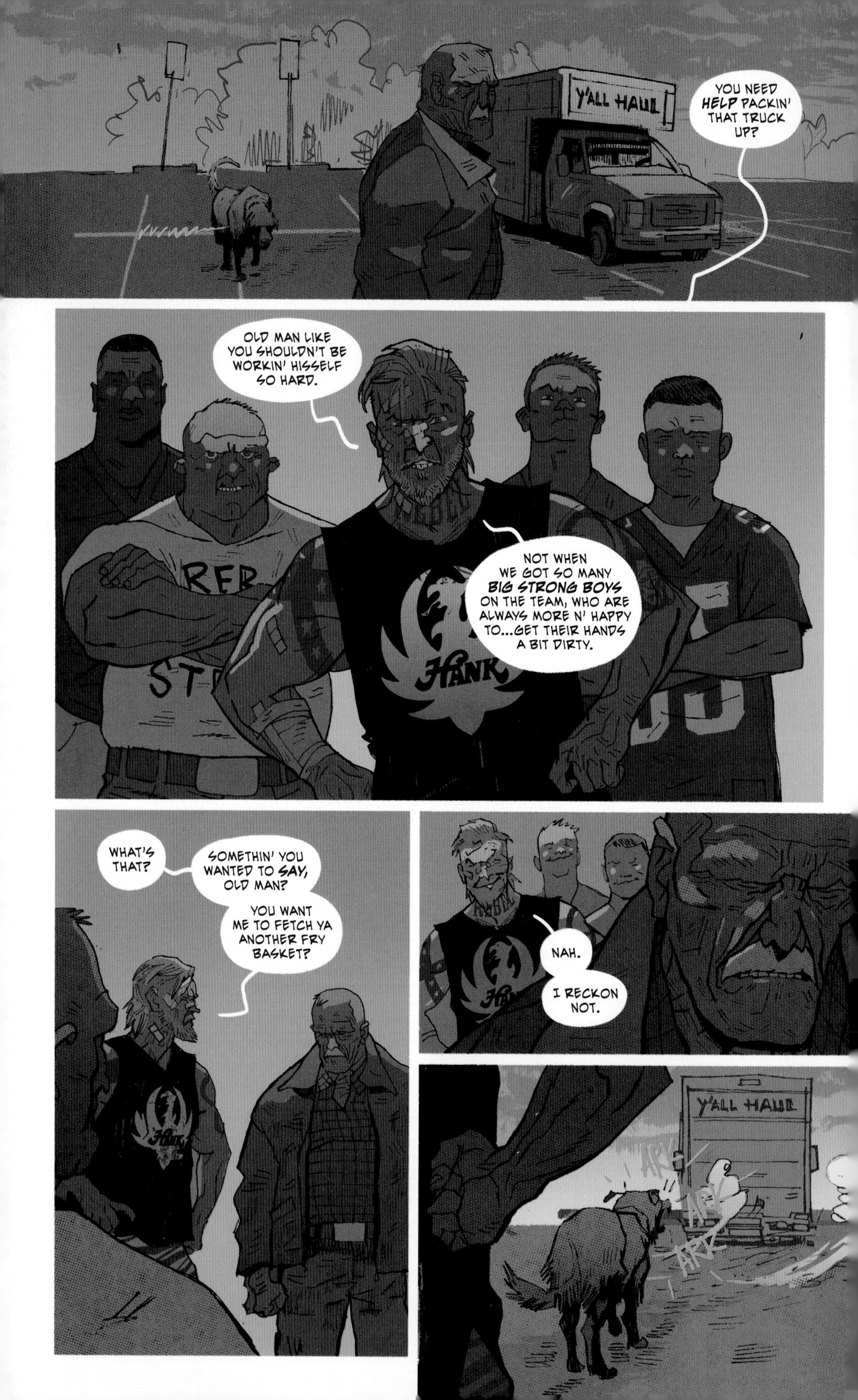
Y'ALL HAUL
YOU NEED HELP PACKIN' THAT TRUCK UP?
OLD MAN LIKE YOU SHOULDN'T BE WORKIN' HISSELF SO HARD.
NOT WHEN WE GOT SO MANY BIG STRONG BOYS ON THE TEAM, WHO ARE ALWAYS MORE N' HAPPY TO...GET THEIR HANDS A BIT DIRTY.
HANK
WHAT'S THAT?
SOMETHIN' YOU WANTED TO SAY, OLD MAN?
YOU WANT ME TO FETCH YA ANOTHER FRY BASKET?
NAH.
I RECKON NOT.
Y'ALL HAUL
ARF
ARF
ARF

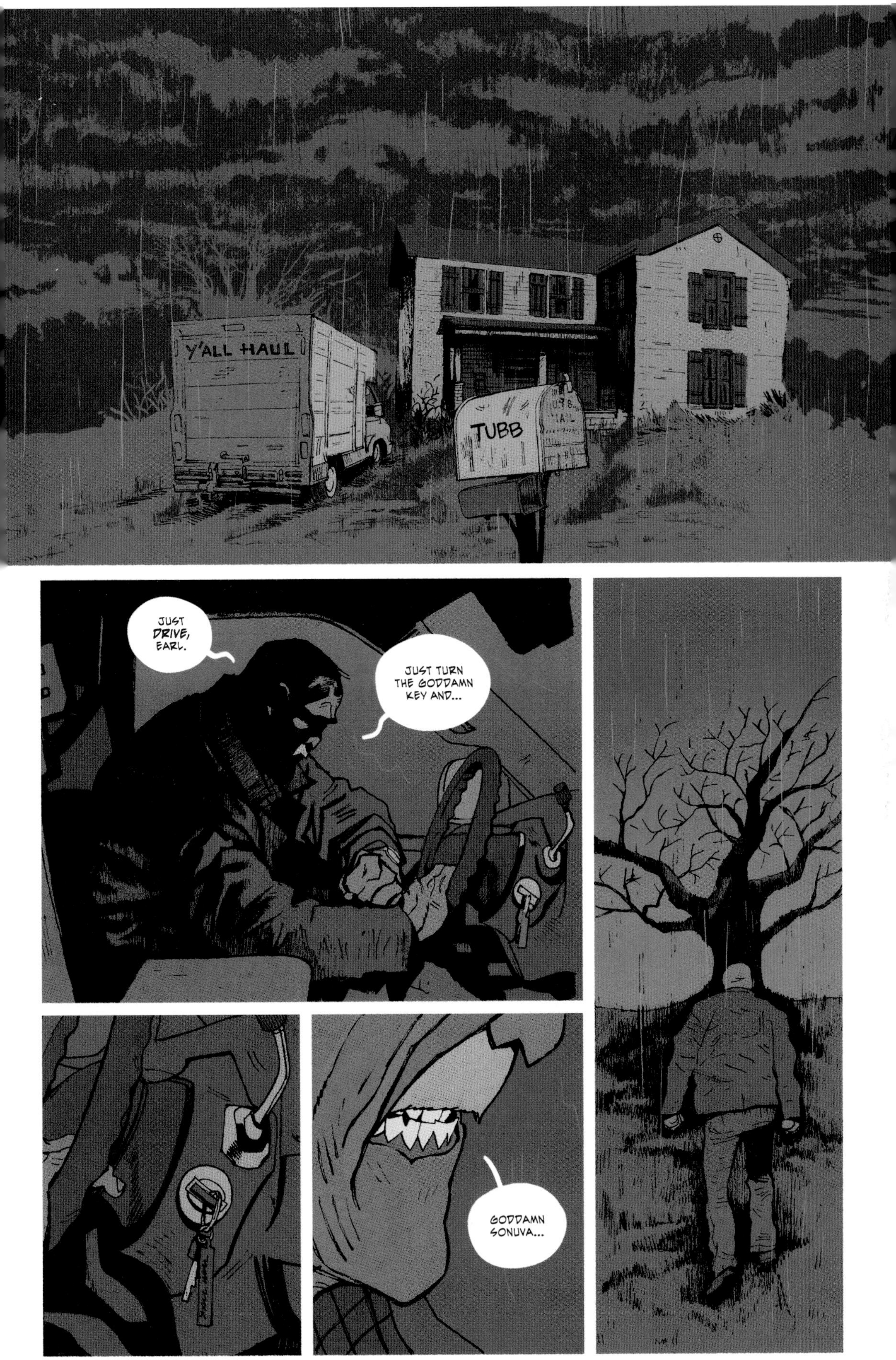
Y'ALL HAUL
TUBB
JUST DRIVE, EARL.
JUST TURN THE GODDAMN KEY AND...
GODDAMN SONUVA...

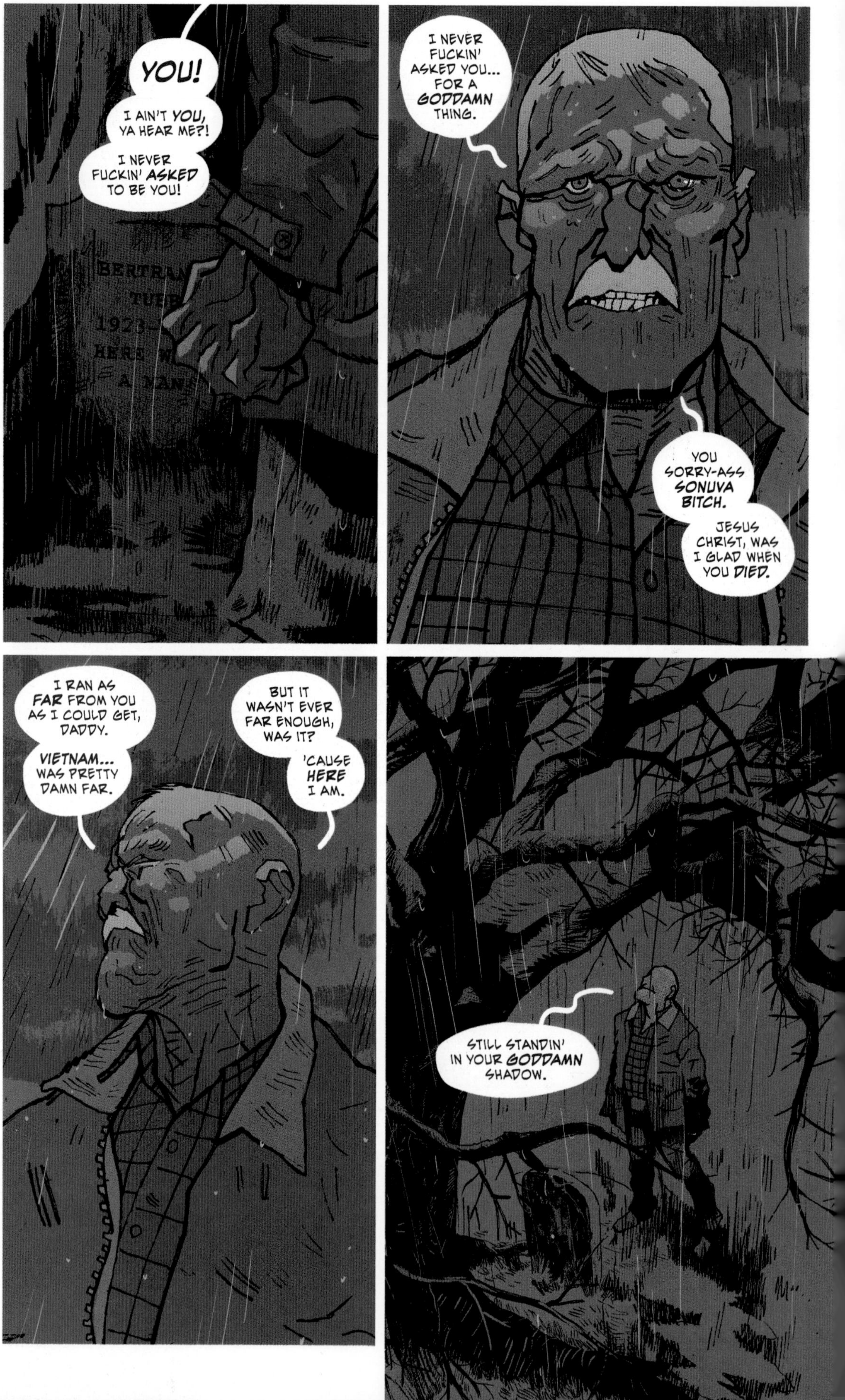
YOU!
I AIN'T YOU, YA HEAR ME?!
I NEVER FUCKIN' ASKED TO BE YOU!
I NEVER FUCKIN' ASKED YOU... FOR A GODDAMN THING.
YOU SORRY-ASS SONUVA BITCH.
JESUS CHRIST, WAS I GLAD WHEN YOU DIED.
I RAN AS FAR FROM YOU AS I COULD GET, DADDY.
VIETNAM... WAS PRETTY DAMN FAR.
BUT IT WASN'T EVER FAR ENOUGH, WAS IT?
'CAUSE HERE I AM.
STILL STANDIN' IN YOUR GODDAMN SHADOW.

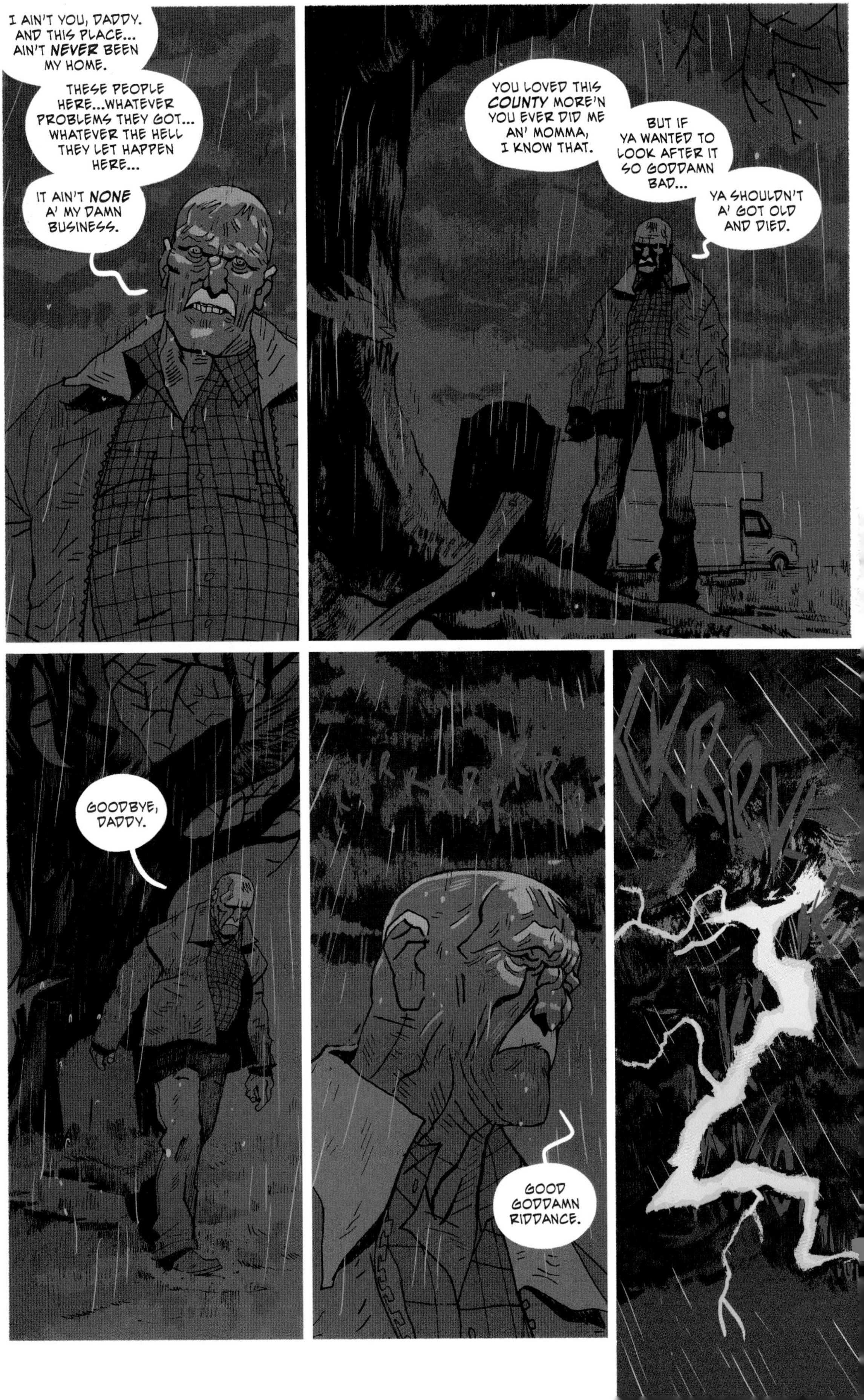

I AIN'T YOU, DADDY. AND THIS PLACE... AIN'T NEVER BEEN MY HOME.
THESE PEOPLE HERE...WHATEVER PROBLEMS THEY GOT... WHATEVER THE HELL THEY LET HAPPEN HERE...
IT AIN'T NONE A' MY DAMN BUSINESS.
YOU LOVED THIS COUNTY MORE'N YOU EVER DID ME AN' MOMMA, I KNOW THAT.
BUT IF YA WANTED TO LOOK AFTER IT SO GODDAMN BAD...
YA SHOULDN'T A' GOT OLD AND DIED.
GOODBYE, DADDY.
GOOD GODDAMN RIDDANCE.

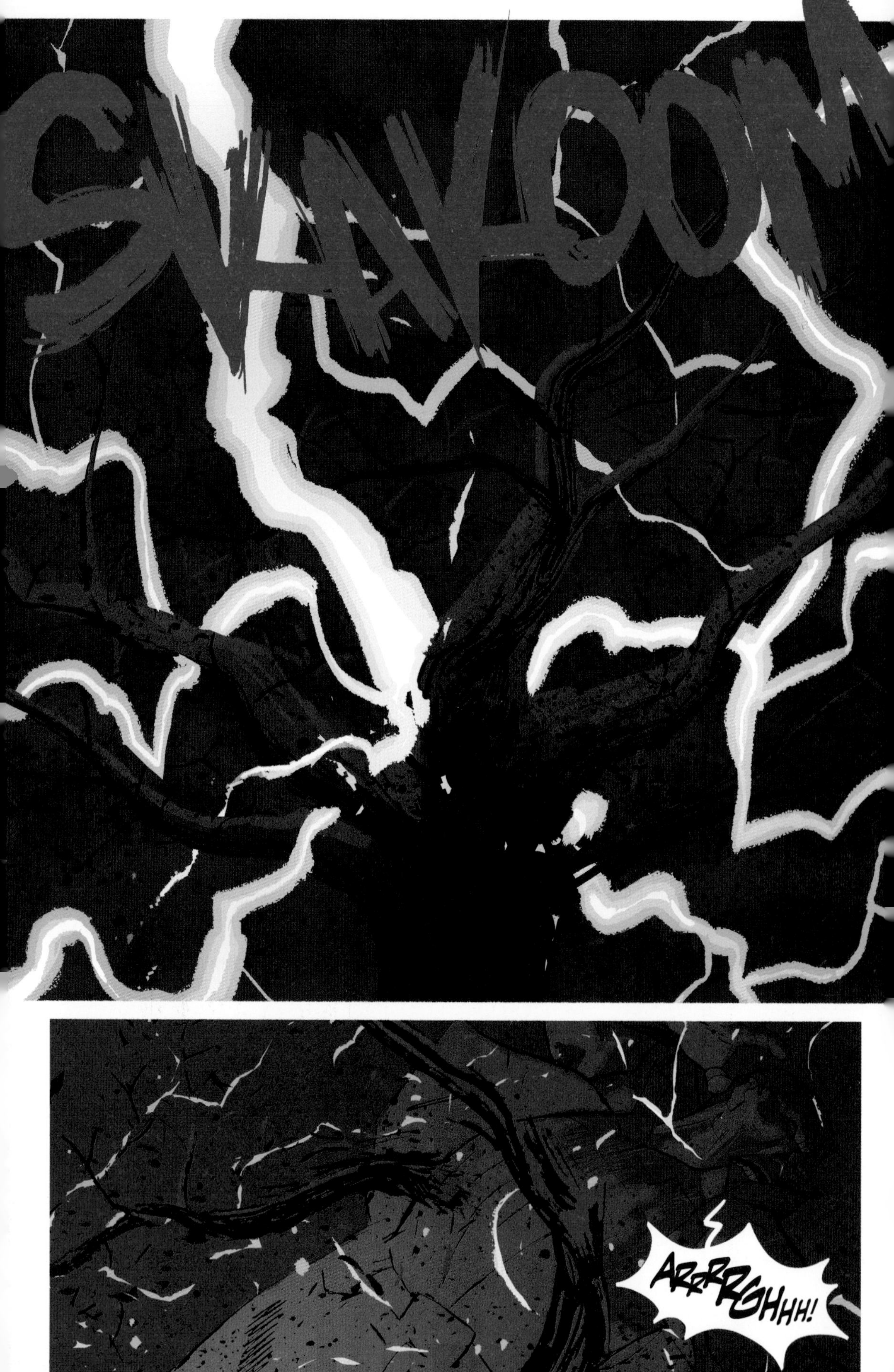
SKAKOOM
ARRRRGHHH!

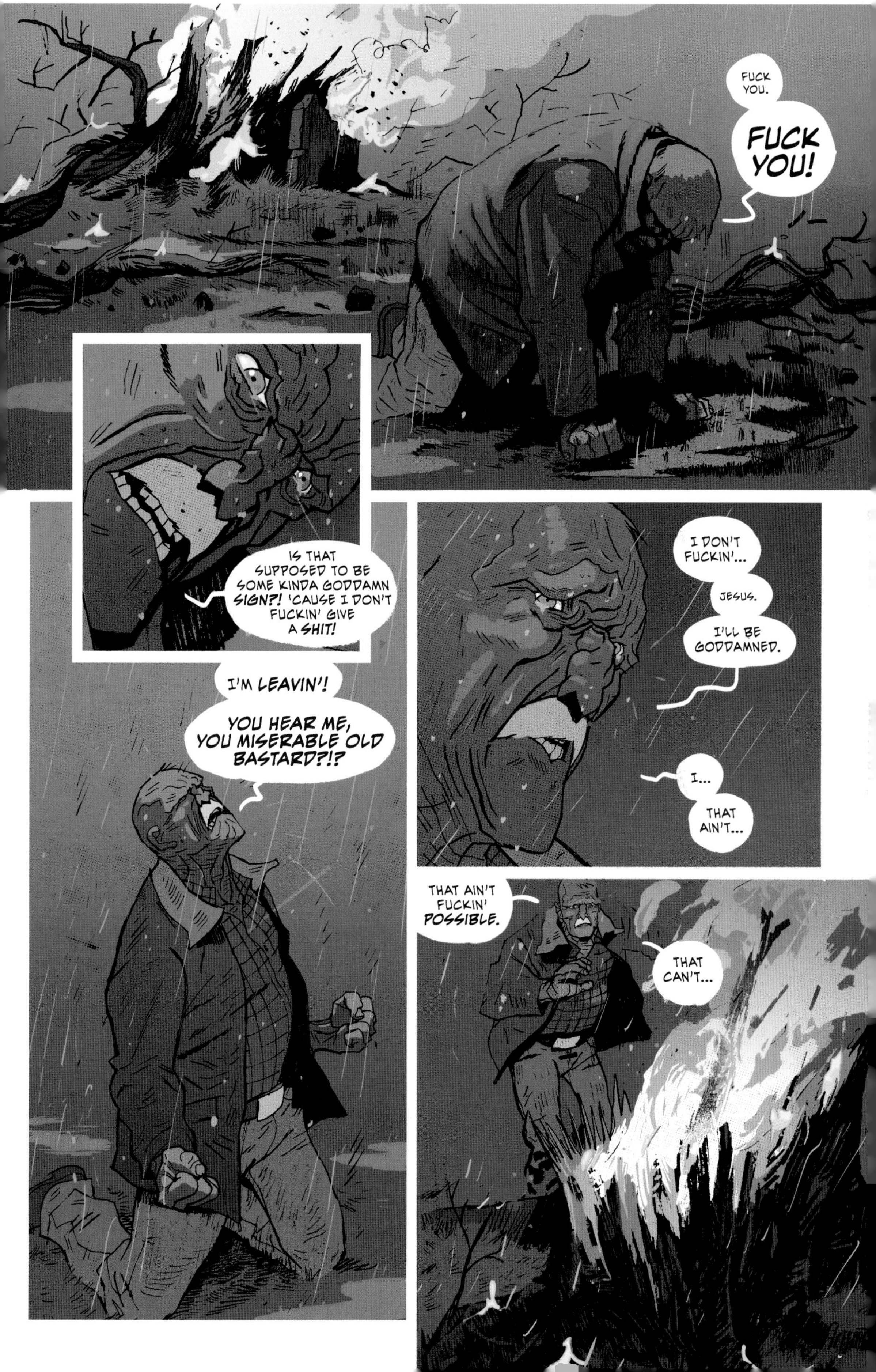
FUCK YOU.
FUCK YOU!
IS THAT SUPPOSED TO BE SOME KINDA GODDAMN SIGN?! 'CAUSE I DON'T FUCKIN' GIVE A SHIT!
I'M LEAVIN'!
YOU HEAR ME, YOU MISERABLE OLD BASTARD?!?
I DON'T FUCKIN'...
JESUS.
I'LL BE GODDAMNED.
I...
THAT AIN'T...
THAT AIN'T FUCKIN' POSSIBLE.
THAT CAN'T...

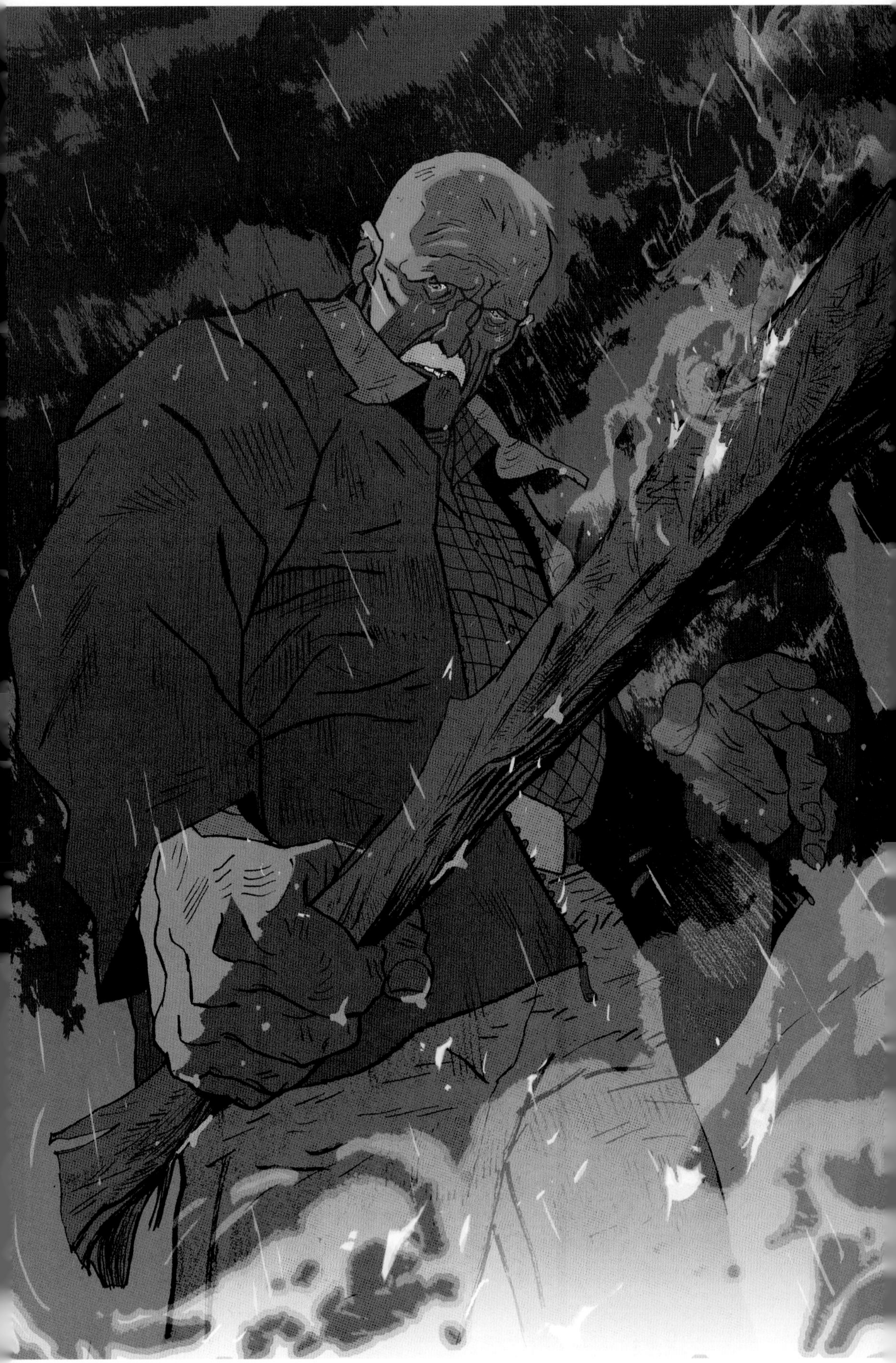

Chapter 3

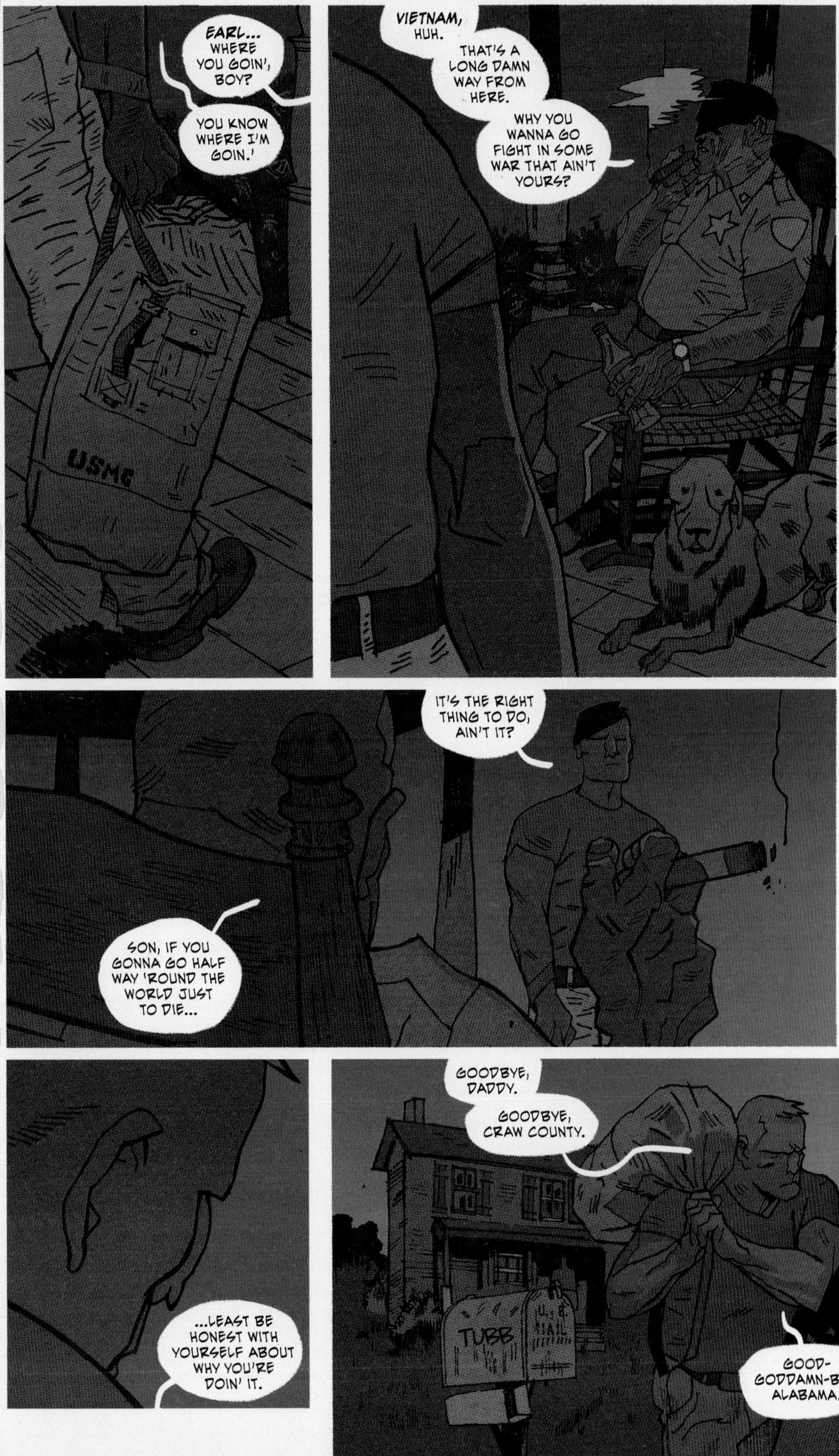
EARL... WHERE YOU GOIN', BOY?
YOU KNOW WHERE I'M GOIN.'
VIETNAM, HUH.
THAT'S A LONG DAMN WAY FROM HERE.
WHY YOU WANNA GO FIGHT IN SOME WAR THAT AIN'T YOURS?
USMC
IT'S THE RIGHT THING TO DO, AIN'T IT?
SON, IF YOU GONNA GO HALF WAY 'ROUND THE WORLD JUST TO DIE...
...LEAST BE HONEST WITH YOURSELF ABOUT WHY YOU'RE DOIN' IT.
GOODBYE, DADDY.
GOODBYE, CRAW COUNTY.
TUBB
U. S. MAIL
GOOD-GODDAMN-BYE, ALABAMA.

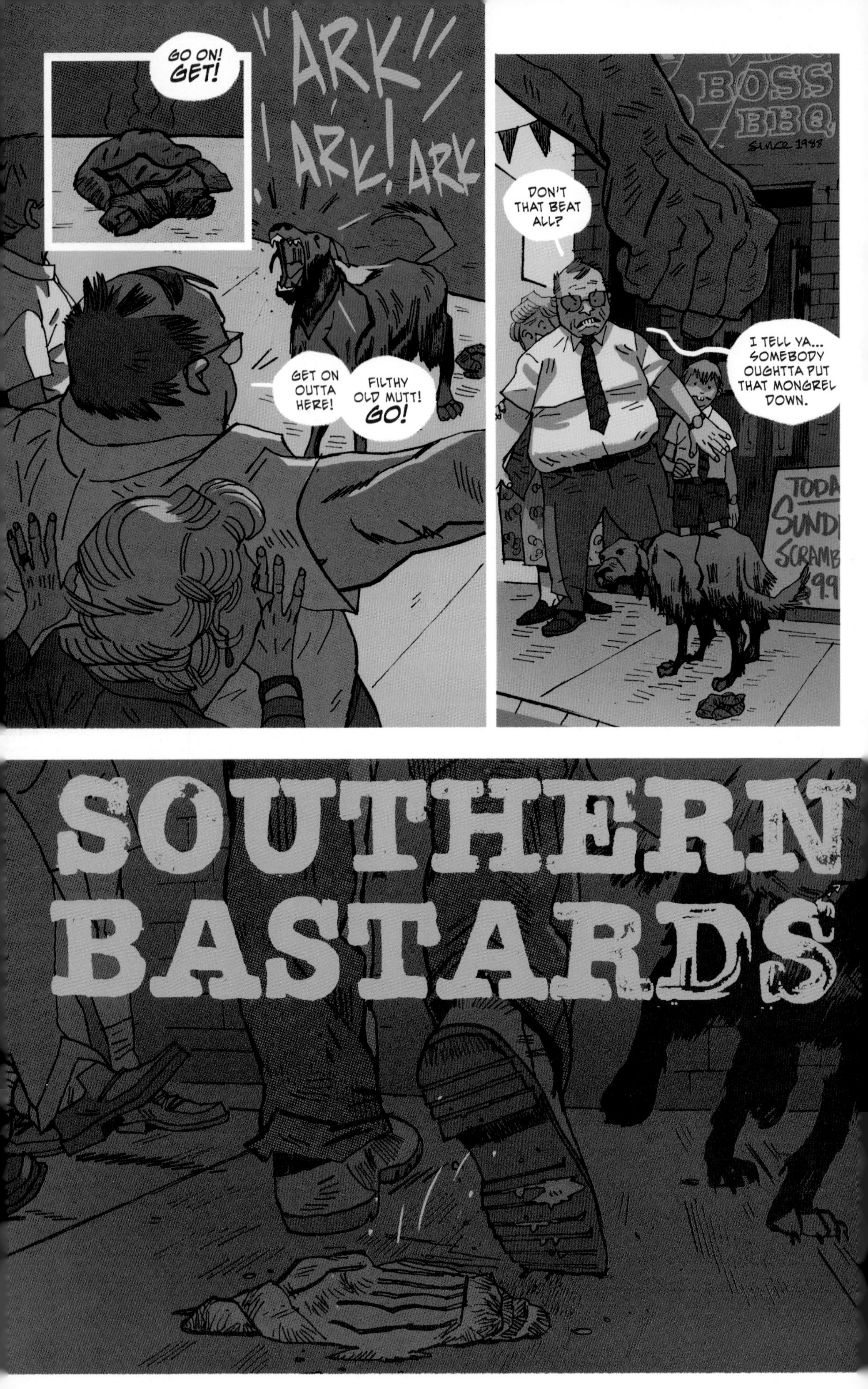
GO ON! GET!
ARK! ARK! ARK
GET ON OUTTA HERE!
FILTHY OLD MUTT! GO!
BOSS BBQ
SINCE 1988
DON'T THAT BEAT ALL?
I TELL YA... SOMEBODY OUGHTTA PUT THAT MONGREL DOWN.
SOUTHERN BASTARDS

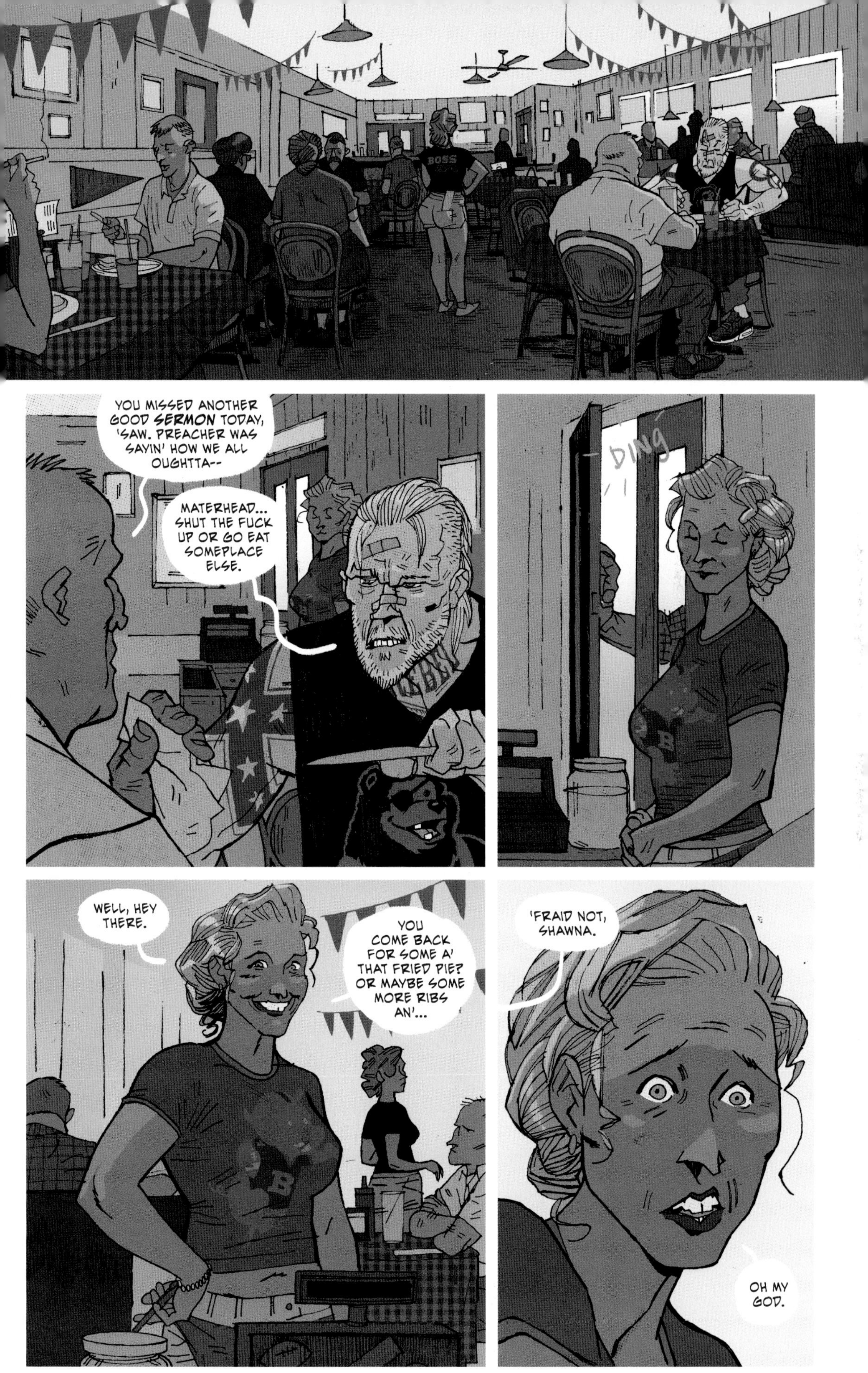
YOU MISSED ANOTHER GOOD SERMON TODAY, 'SAW. PREACHER WAS SAYIN' HOW WE ALL OUGHTTA--
MATERHEAD... SHUT THE FUCK UP OR GO EAT SOMEPLACE ELSE.
DING
WELL, HEY THERE.
YOU COME BACK FOR SOME A' THAT FRIED PIE? OR MAYBE SOME MORE RIBS AN'...
'FRAID NOT, SHAWNA.
OH MY GOD.

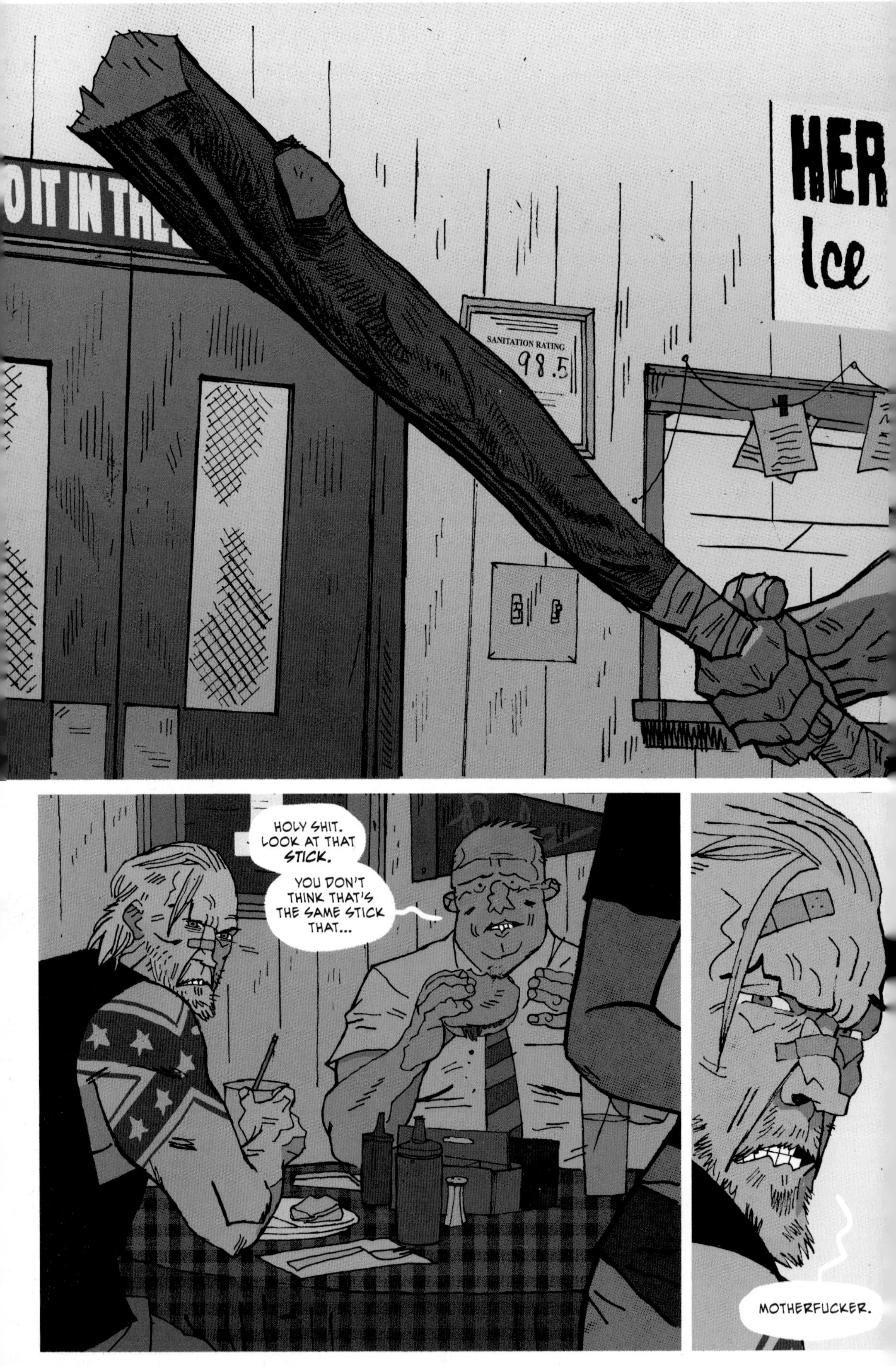
O IT IN THE
HER
Ice
SANITATION RATING
98.5
HOLY SHIT. LOOK AT THAT STICK.
YOU DON'T THINK THAT'S THE SAME STICK THAT...
MOTHERFUCKER.

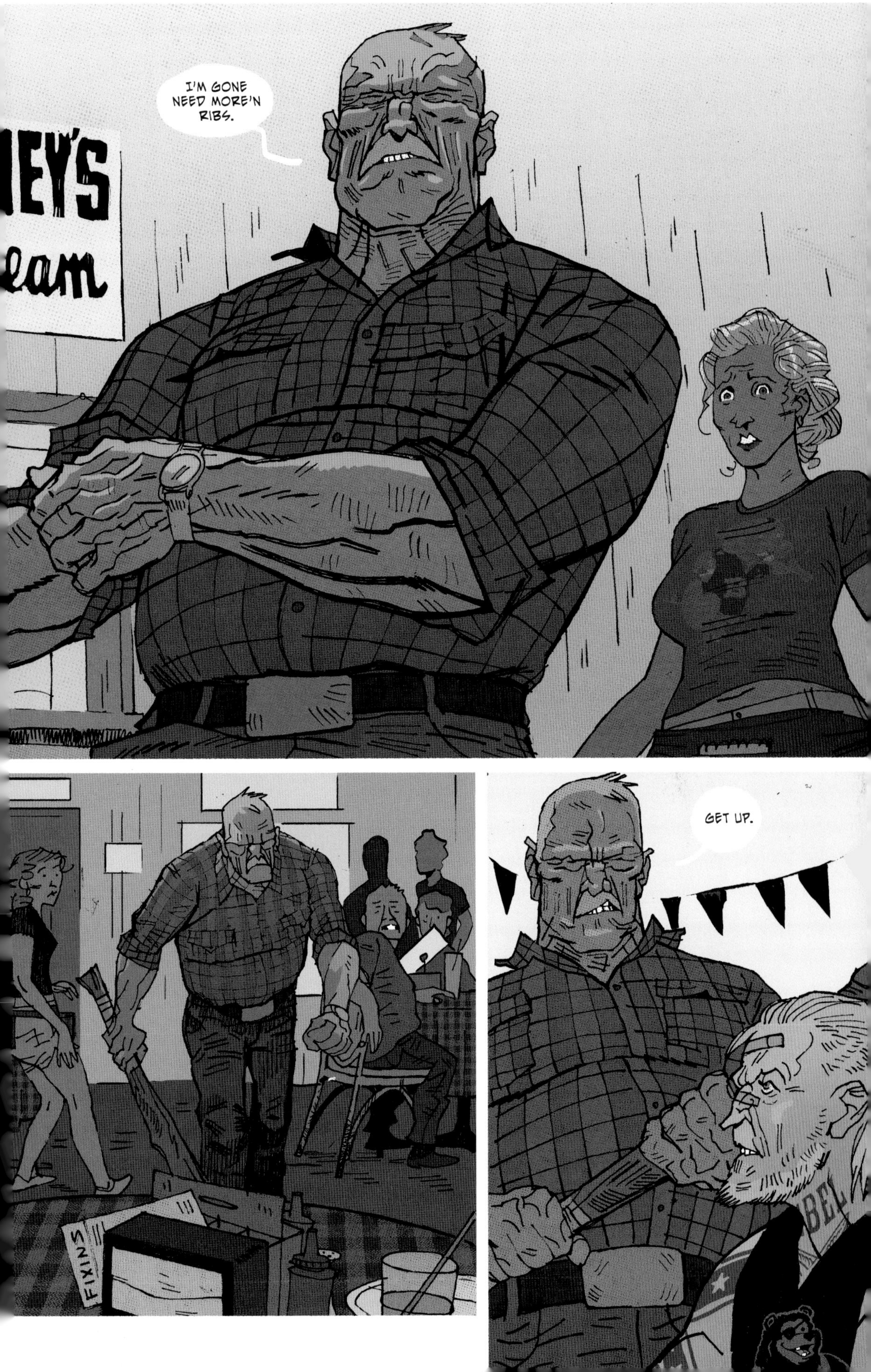
I'M GONE NEED MORE'N RIBS.
FIXINS
GET UP.

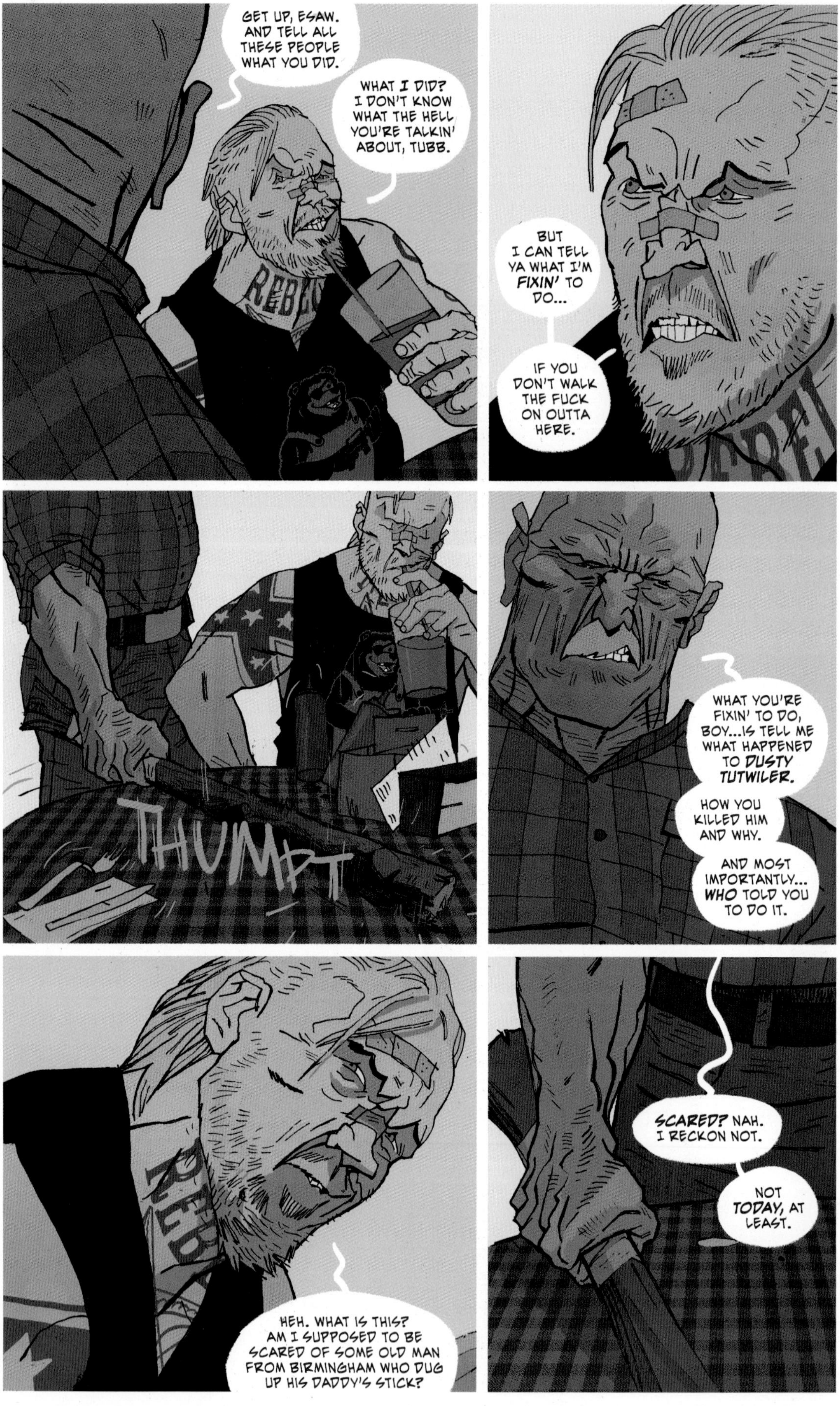
GET UP, ESAW. AND TELL ALL THESE PEOPLE WHAT YOU DID.
WHAT I DID? I DON'T KNOW WHAT THE HELL YOU'RE TALKIN' ABOUT, TUBB.
BUT I CAN TELL YA WHAT I'M FIXIN' TO DO...
IF YOU DON'T WALK THE FUCK ON OUTTA HERE.
THUMPT
WHAT YOU'RE FIXIN' TO DO, BOY...IS TELL ME WHAT HAPPENED TO DUSTY TUTWILER.
HOW YOU KILLED HIM AND WHY.
AND MOST IMPORTANTLY... WHO TOLD YOU TO DO IT.
HEH. WHAT IS THIS? AM I SUPPOSED TO BE SCARED OF SOME OLD MAN FROM BIRMINGHAM WHO DUG UP HIS DADDY'S STICK?
SCARED? NAH. I RECKON NOT.
NOT TODAY, AT LEAST.

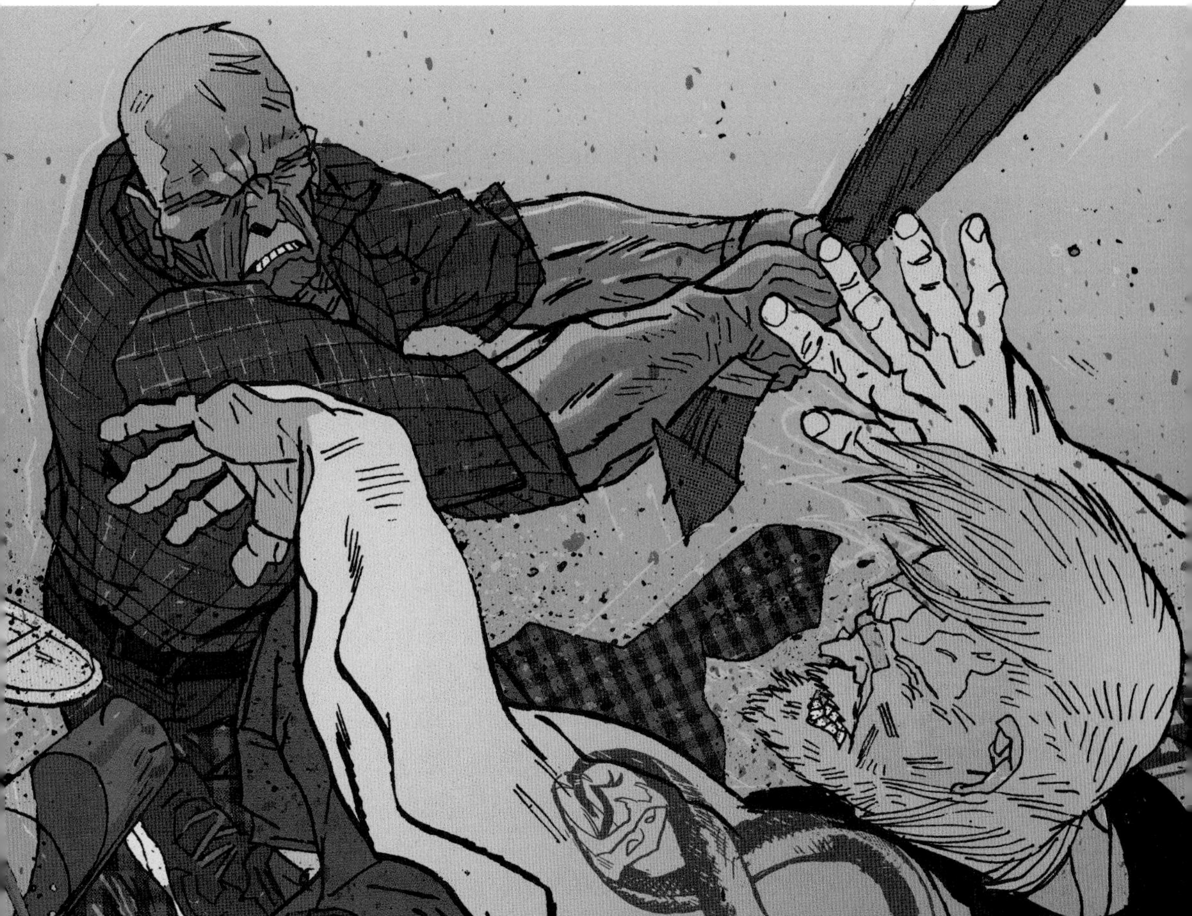

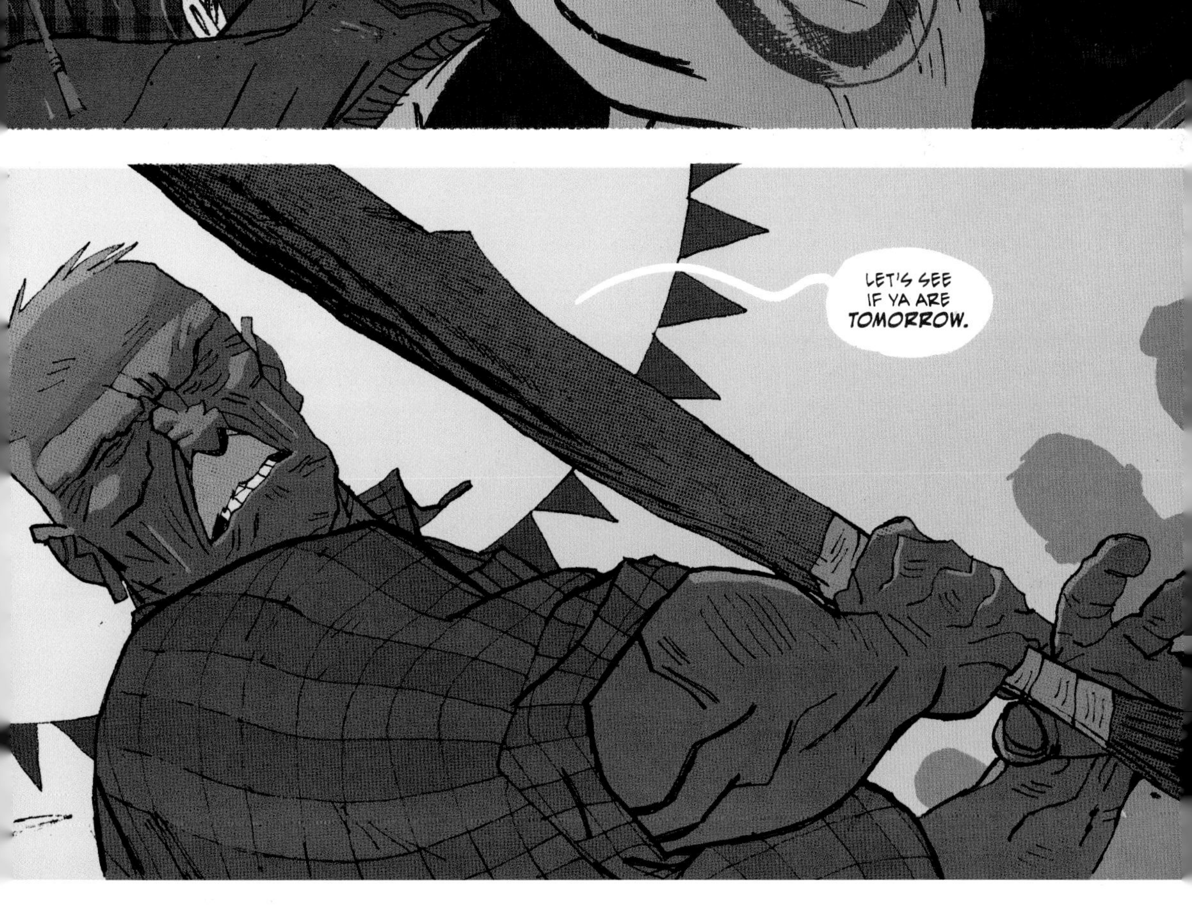
LET'S SEE
IF YA ARE
TOMORROW.

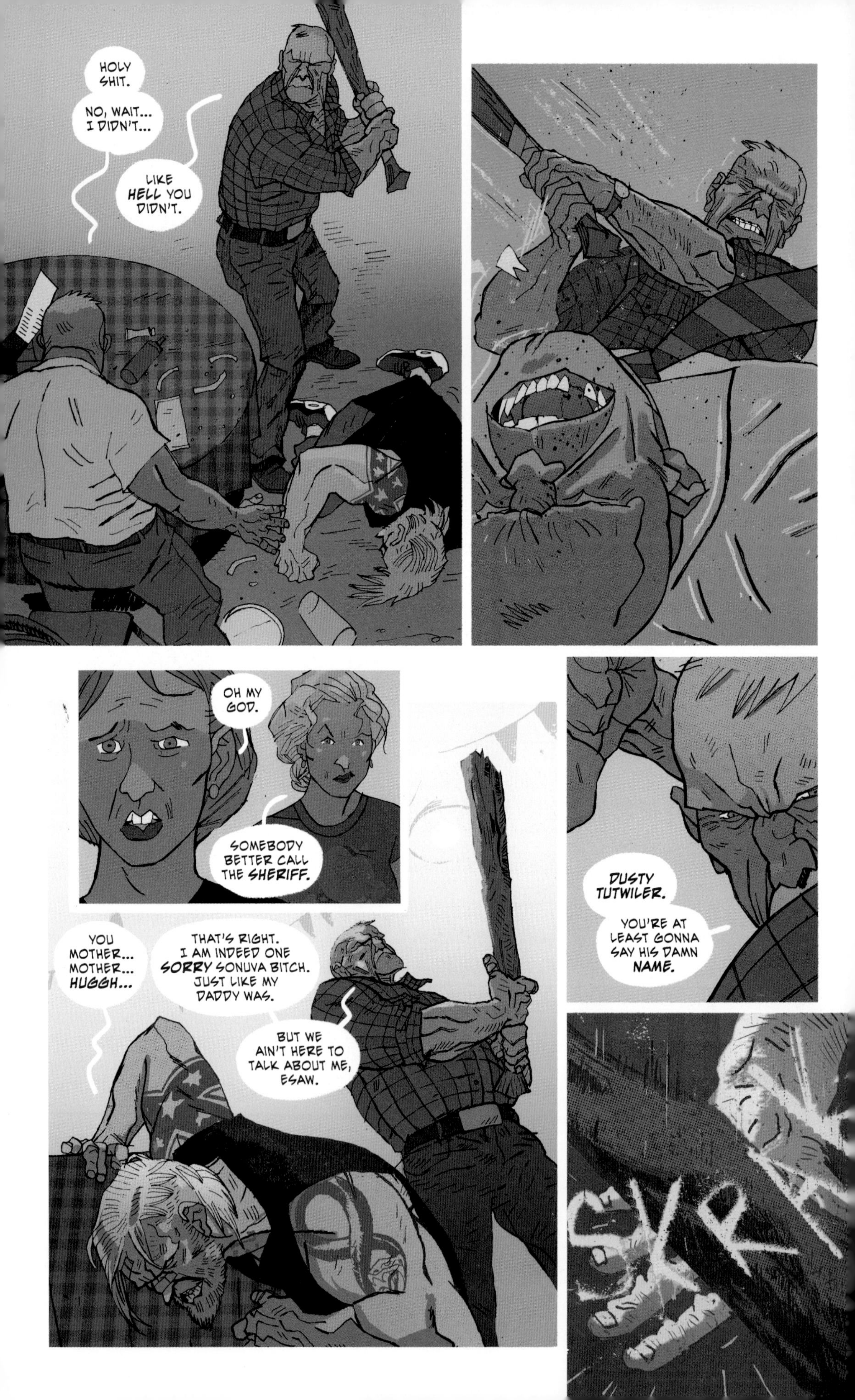
HOLY SHIT.
NO, WAIT... I DIDN'T...
LIKE HELL YOU DIDN'T.
OH MY GOD.
SOMEBODY BETTER CALL THE SHERIFF.
YOU MOTHER... MOTHER... HUGGH...
THAT'S RIGHT. I AM INDEED ONE SORRY SONUVA BITCH. JUST LIKE MY DADDY WAS.
BUT WE AIN'T HERE TO TALK ABOUT ME, ESAW.
DUSTY TUTWILER.
YOU'RE AT LEAST GONNA SAY HIS DAMN NAME.

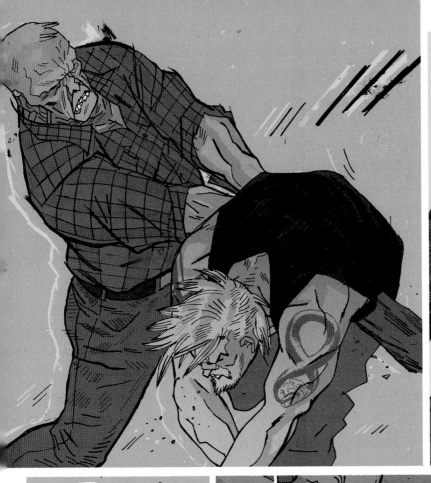

I DON'T KNOW WHAT THE HELL HE WAS MIXED UP IN WITH YOU.

WHATEVER IT WAS, HE DIDN'T DESERVE TO DIE LIKE THAT.

A *DOG* DON'T DESERVE TO DIE LIKE THAT.

SOMEBODY'S GONNA ANSWER FOR WHAT HAPPENED TO DUSTY.

FOR WHAT'S HAPPENED TO THIS WHOLE DAMN COUNTY.

YOU...

YOU'RE DEAD.

NAH. FOR THE FIRST TIME IN FOREVER...

I DON'T THINK I AM.

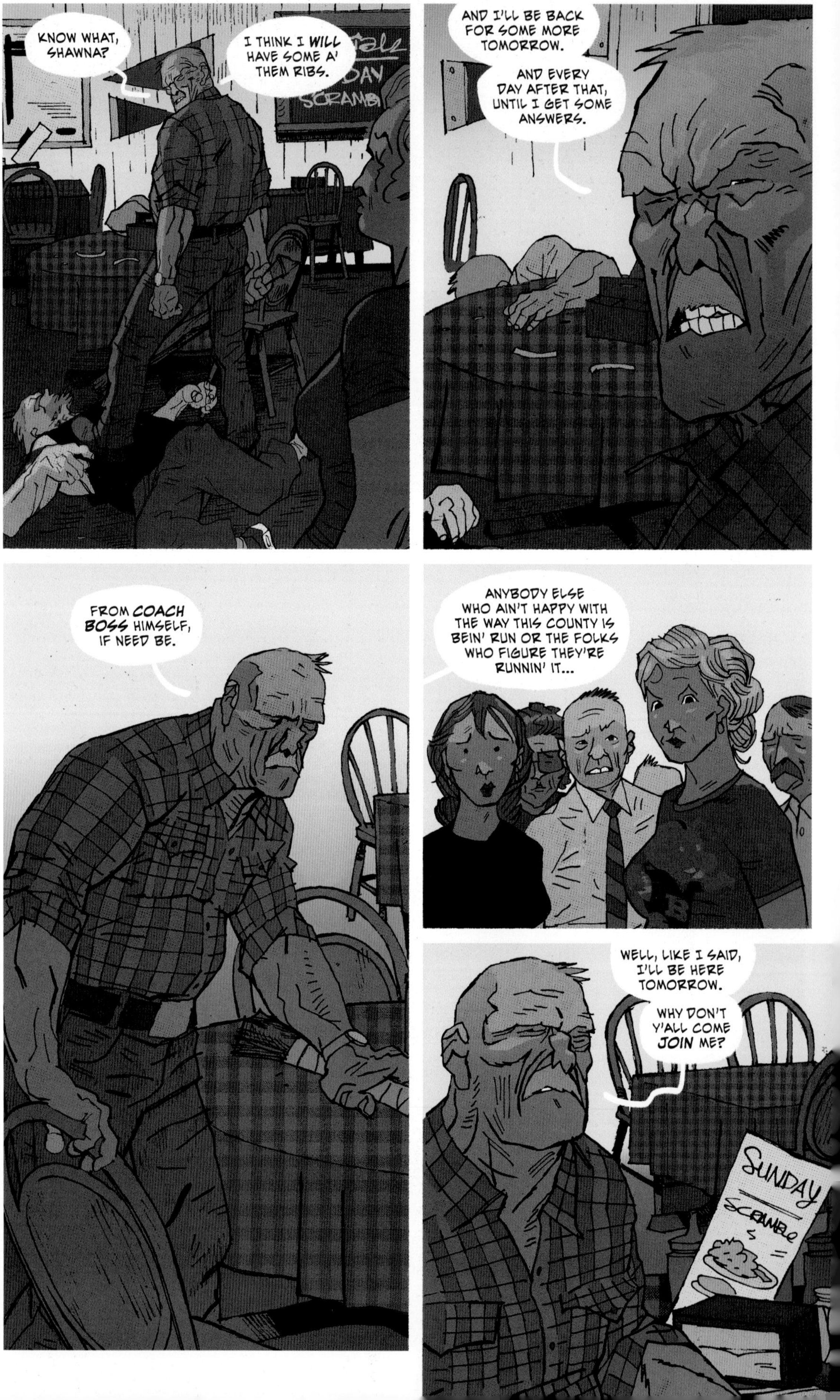
KNOW WHAT, SHAWNA?
I THINK I *WILL* HAVE SOME A' THEM RIBS.
AND I'LL BE BACK FOR SOME MORE TOMORROW.
AND EVERY DAY AFTER THAT, UNTIL I GET SOME ANSWERS.
FROM *COACH BOSS* HIMSELF, IF NEED BE.
ANYBODY ELSE WHO AIN'T HAPPY WITH THE WAY THIS COUNTY IS BEIN' RUN OR THE FOLKS WHO FIGURE THEY'RE RUNNIN' IT...
WELL, LIKE I SAID, I'LL BE HERE TOMORROW.
WHY DON'T Y'ALL COME *JOIN* ME?
SUNDAY
SCRAMBLE

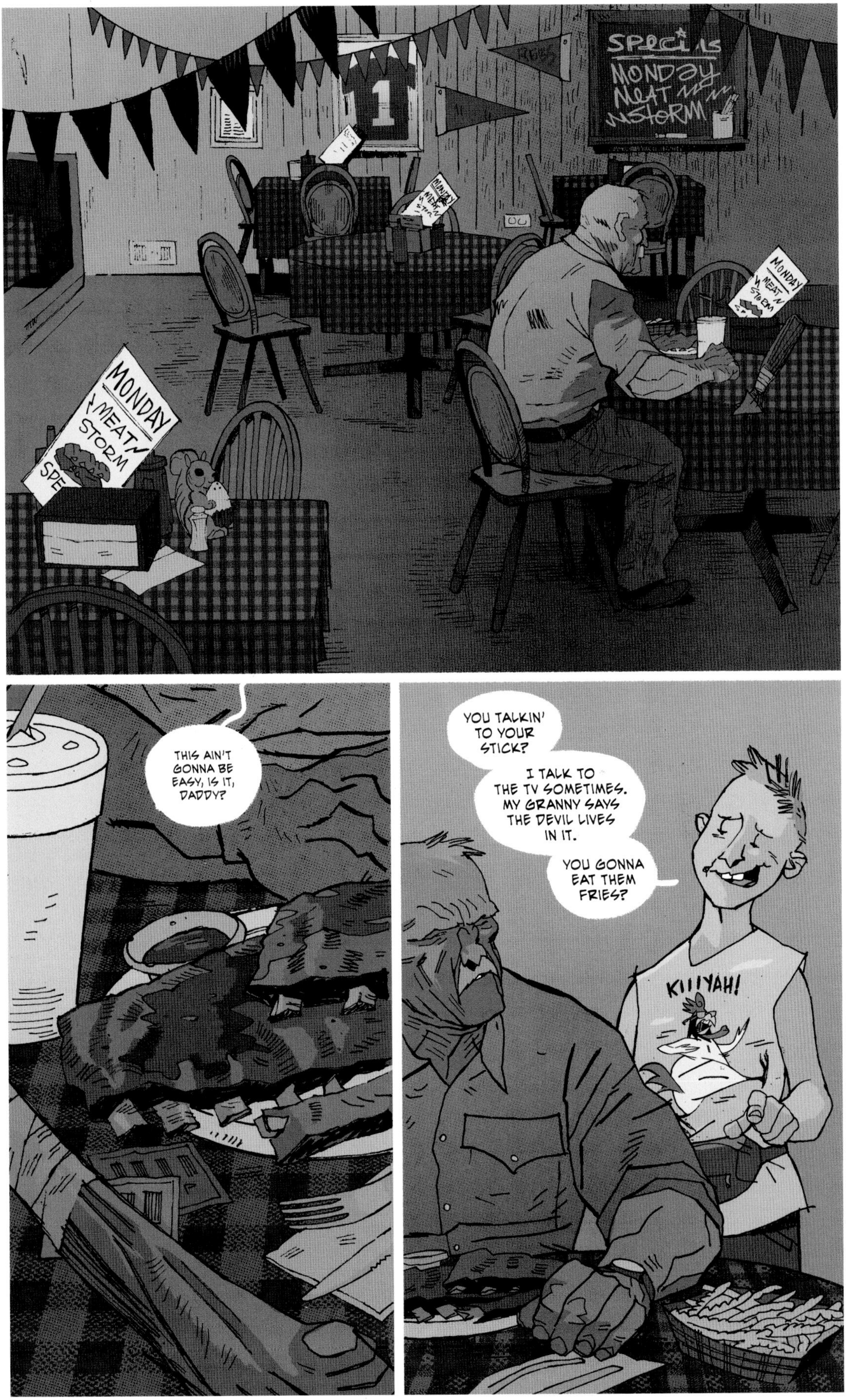
MONDAY MEAT STORM
MONDAY MEAT STORM
THIS AIN'T GONNA BE EASY, IS IT, DADDY?
YOU TALKIN' TO YOUR STICK?
I TALK TO THE TV SOMETIMES. MY GRANNY SAYS THE DEVIL LIVES IN IT.
YOU GONNA EAT THEM FRIES?
KIIYAH!

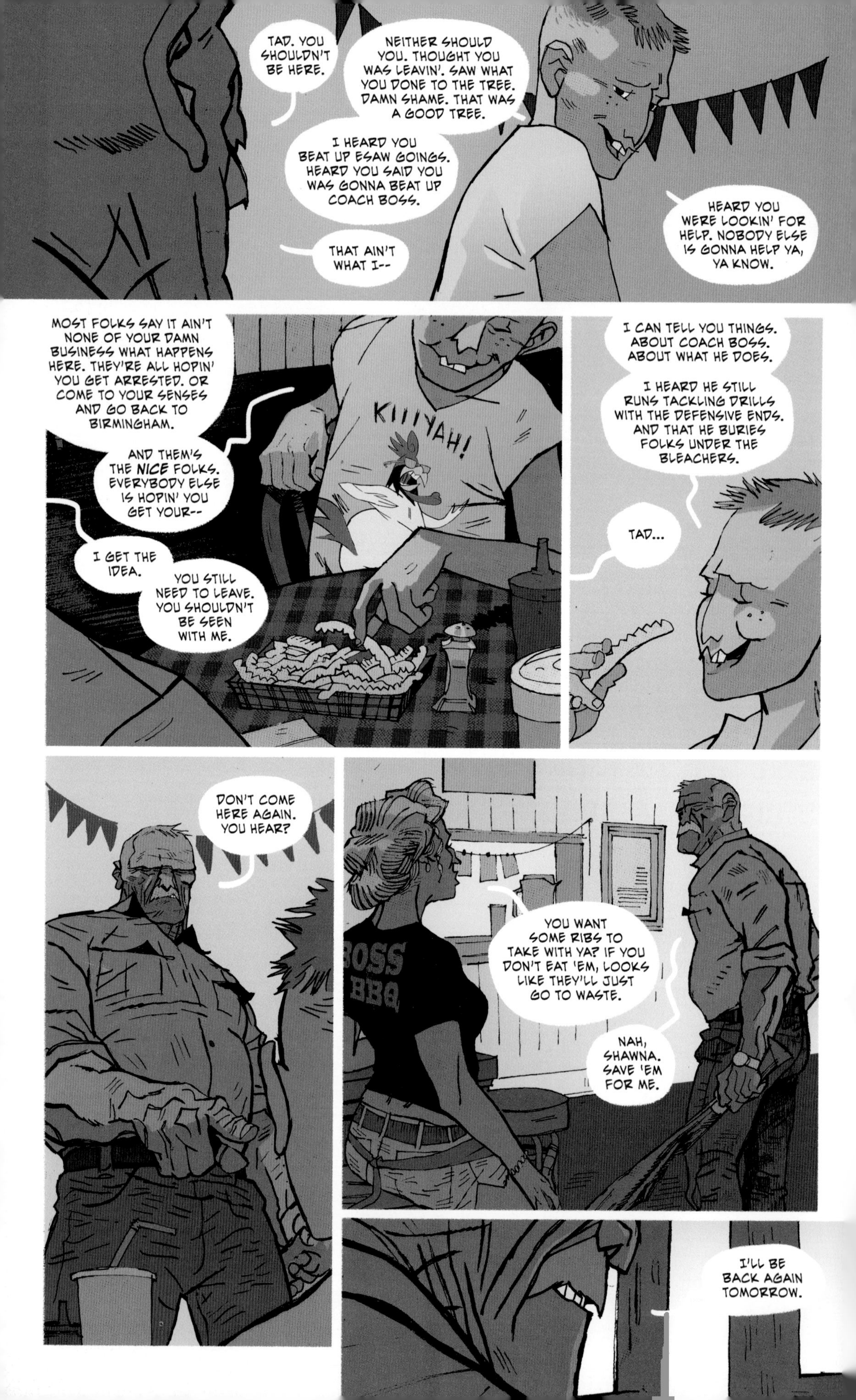
TAD. YOU SHOULDN'T BE HERE.
NEITHER SHOULD YOU. THOUGHT YOU WAS LEAVIN'. SAW WHAT YOU DONE TO THE TREE. DAMN SHAME. THAT WAS A GOOD TREE.
I HEARD YOU BEAT UP ESAW GOINGS. HEARD YOU SAID YOU WAS GONNA BEAT UP COACH BOSS.
THAT AIN'T WHAT I--
HEARD YOU WERE LOOKIN' FOR HELP. NOBODY ELSE IS GONNA HELP YA, YA KNOW.
MOST FOLKS SAY IT AIN'T NONE OF YOUR DAMN BUSINESS WHAT HAPPENS HERE. THEY'RE ALL HOPIN' YOU GET ARRESTED. OR COME TO YOUR SENSES AND GO BACK TO BIRMINGHAM.
AND THEM'S THE NICE FOLKS. EVERYBODY ELSE IS HOPIN' YOU GET YOUR--
I GET THE IDEA.
YOU STILL NEED TO LEAVE. YOU SHOULDN'T BE SEEN WITH ME.
KIIIYAH!
I CAN TELL YOU THINGS. ABOUT COACH BOSS. ABOUT WHAT HE DOES.
I HEARD HE STILL RUNS TACKLING DRILLS WITH THE DEFENSIVE ENDS. AND THAT HE BURIES FOLKS UNDER THE BLEACHERS.
TAD...
DON'T COME HERE AGAIN. YOU HEAR?
BOSS BBQ
YOU WANT SOME RIBS TO TAKE WITH YA? IF YOU DON'T EAT 'EM, LOOKS LIKE THEY'LL JUST GO TO WASTE.
NAH, SHAWNA. SAVE 'EM FOR ME.
I'LL BE BACK AGAIN TOMORROW.

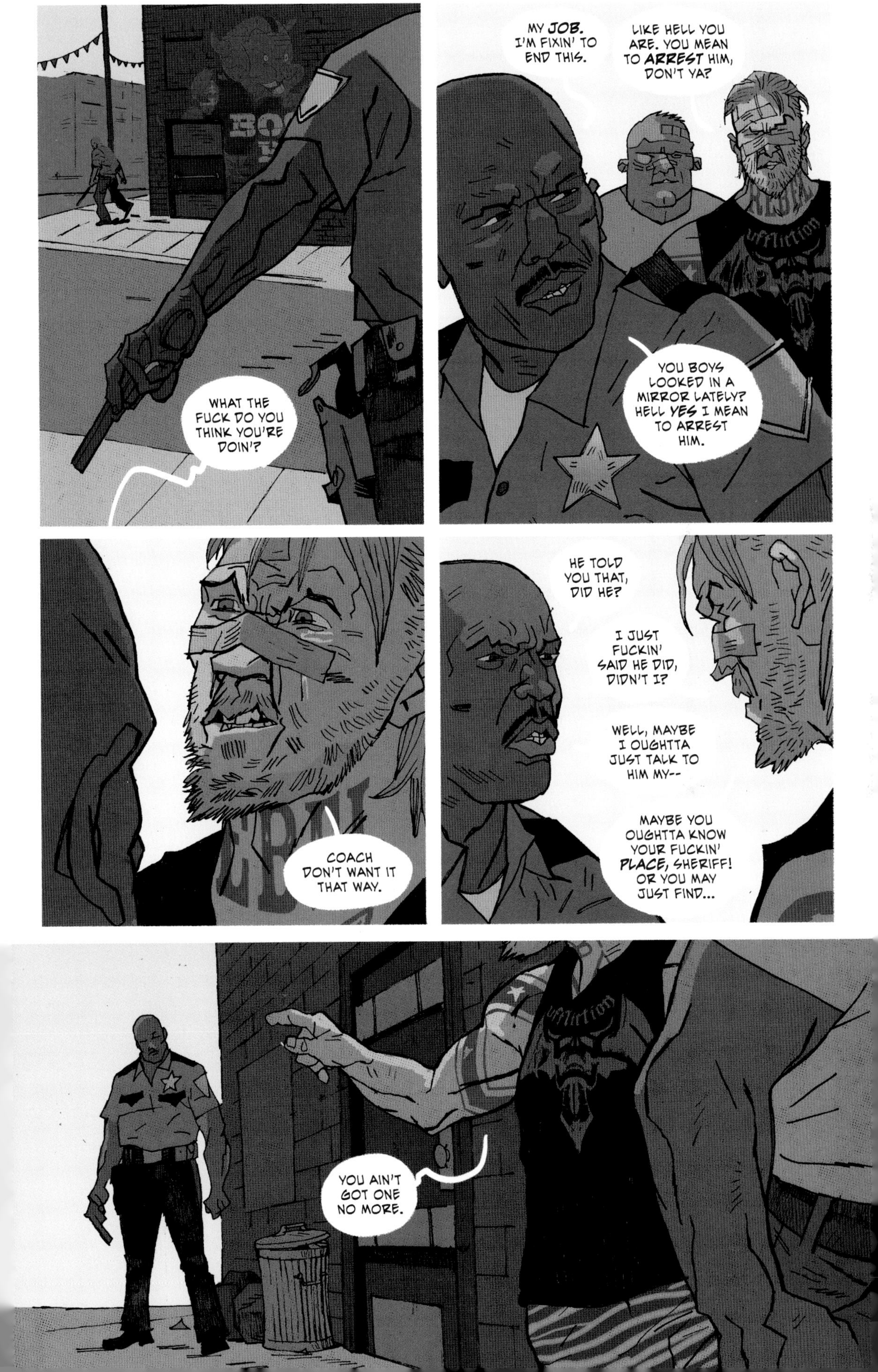
WHAT THE FUCK DO YOU THINK YOU'RE DOIN'?
MY JOB. I'M FIXIN' TO END THIS.
LIKE HELL YOU ARE. YOU MEAN TO ARREST HIM, DON'T YA?
YOU BOYS LOOKED IN A MIRROR LATELY? HELL YES I MEAN TO ARREST HIM.
COACH DON'T WANT IT THAT WAY.
HE TOLD YOU THAT, DID HE?
I JUST FUCKIN' SAID HE DID, DIDN'T I?
WELL, MAYBE I OUGHTTA JUST TALK TO HIM MY--
MAYBE YOU OUGHTTA KNOW YOUR FUCKIN' PLACE, SHERIFF! OR YOU MAY JUST FIND...
YOU AIN'T GOT ONE NO MORE.

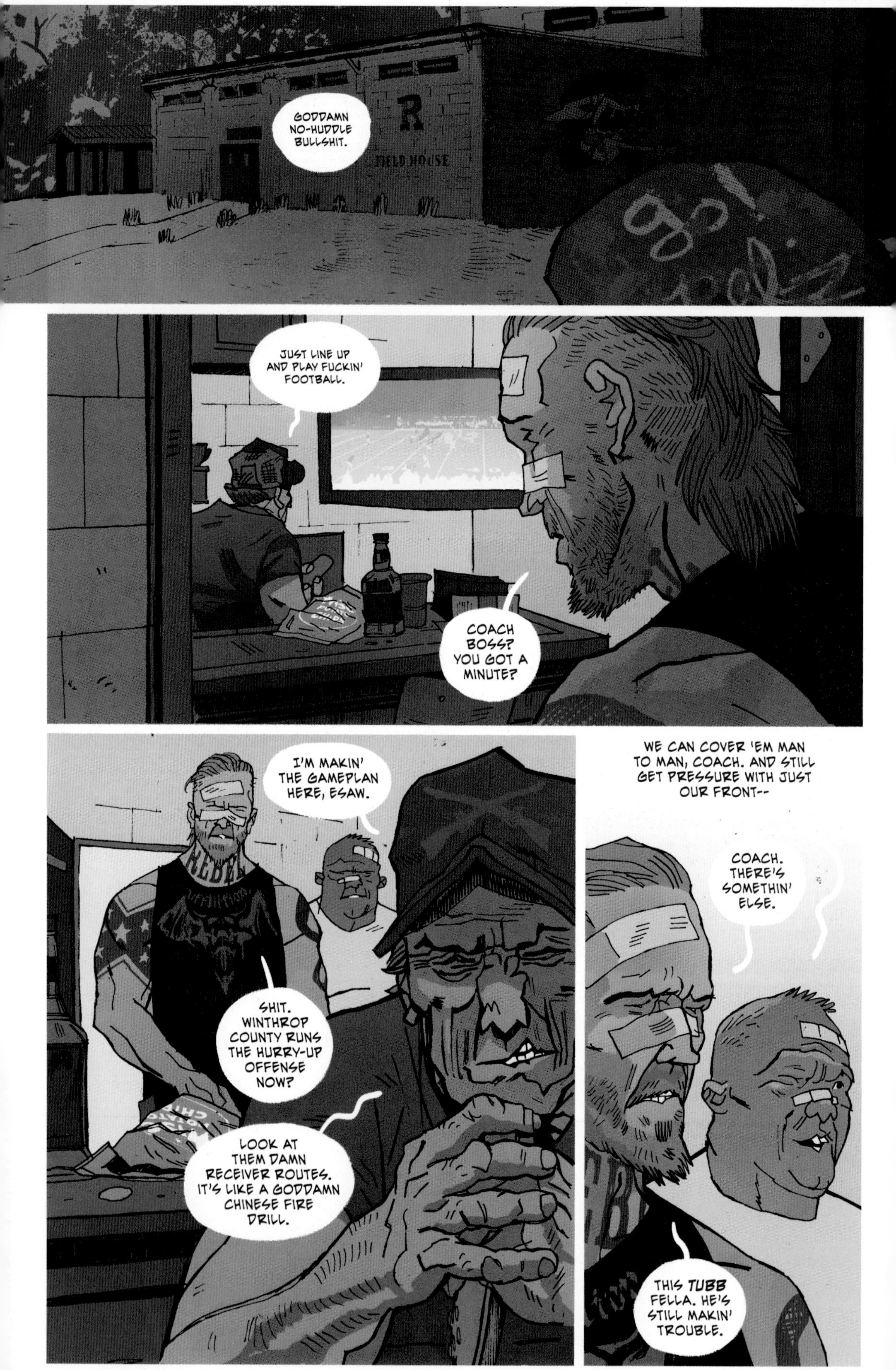
GODDAMN NO-HUDDLE BULLSHIT.
FIELD HOUSE
JUST LINE UP AND PLAY FUCKIN' FOOTBALL.
COACH BOSS? YOU GOT A MINUTE?
I'M MAKIN' THE GAMEPLAN HERE, ESAW.
SHIT. WINTHROP COUNTY RUNS THE HURRY-UP OFFENSE NOW?
LOOK AT THEM DAMN RECEIVER ROUTES. IT'S LIKE A GODDAMN CHINESE FIRE DRILL.
WE CAN COVER 'EM MAN TO MAN, COACH. AND STILL GET PRESSURE WITH JUST OUR FRONT--
COACH. THERE'S SOMETHIN' ELSE.
THIS TUBB FELLA. HE'S STILL MAKIN' TROUBLE.

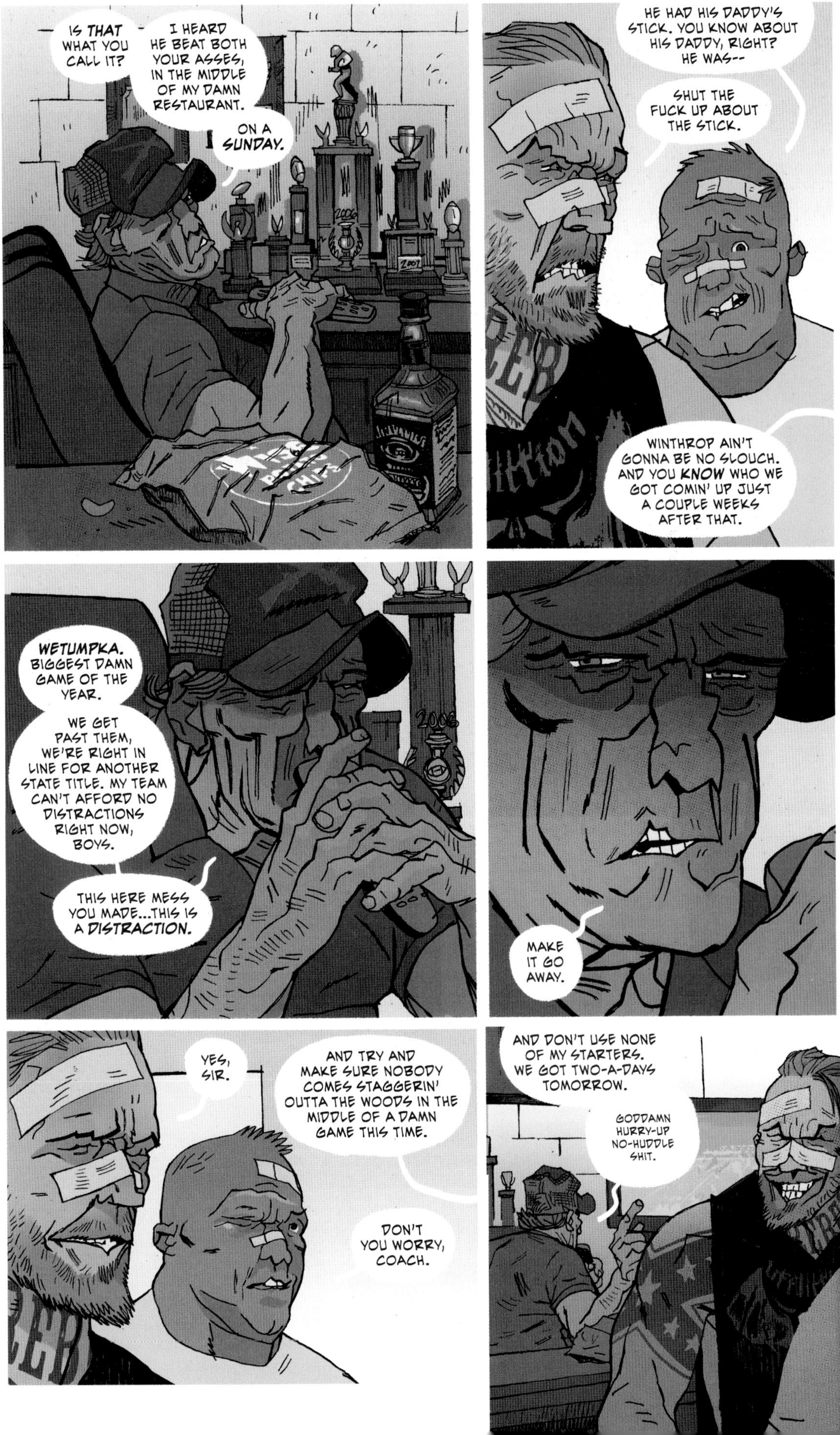
IS THAT WHAT YOU CALL IT?
I HEARD HE BEAT BOTH YOUR ASSES, IN THE MIDDLE OF MY DAMN RESTAURANT.
ON A SUNDAY.
HE HAD HIS DADDY'S STICK. YOU KNOW ABOUT HIS DADDY, RIGHT? HE WAS--
SHUT THE FUCK UP ABOUT THE STICK.
WINTHROP AIN'T GONNA BE NO SLOUCH. AND YOU KNOW WHO WE GOT COMIN' UP JUST A COUPLE WEEKS AFTER THAT.
WETUMPKA. BIGGEST DAMN GAME OF THE YEAR.
WE GET PAST THEM, WE'RE RIGHT IN LINE FOR ANOTHER STATE TITLE. MY TEAM CAN'T AFFORD NO DISTRACTIONS RIGHT NOW, BOYS.
THIS HERE MESS YOU MADE...THIS IS A DISTRACTION.
MAKE IT GO AWAY.
YES, SIR.
AND TRY AND MAKE SURE NOBODY COMES STAGGERIN' OUTTA THE WOODS IN THE MIDDLE OF A DAMN GAME THIS TIME.
DON'T YOU WORRY, COACH.
AND DON'T USE NONE OF MY STARTERS. WE GOT TWO-A-DAYS TOMORROW.
GODDAMN HURRY-UP NO-HUDDLE SHIT.

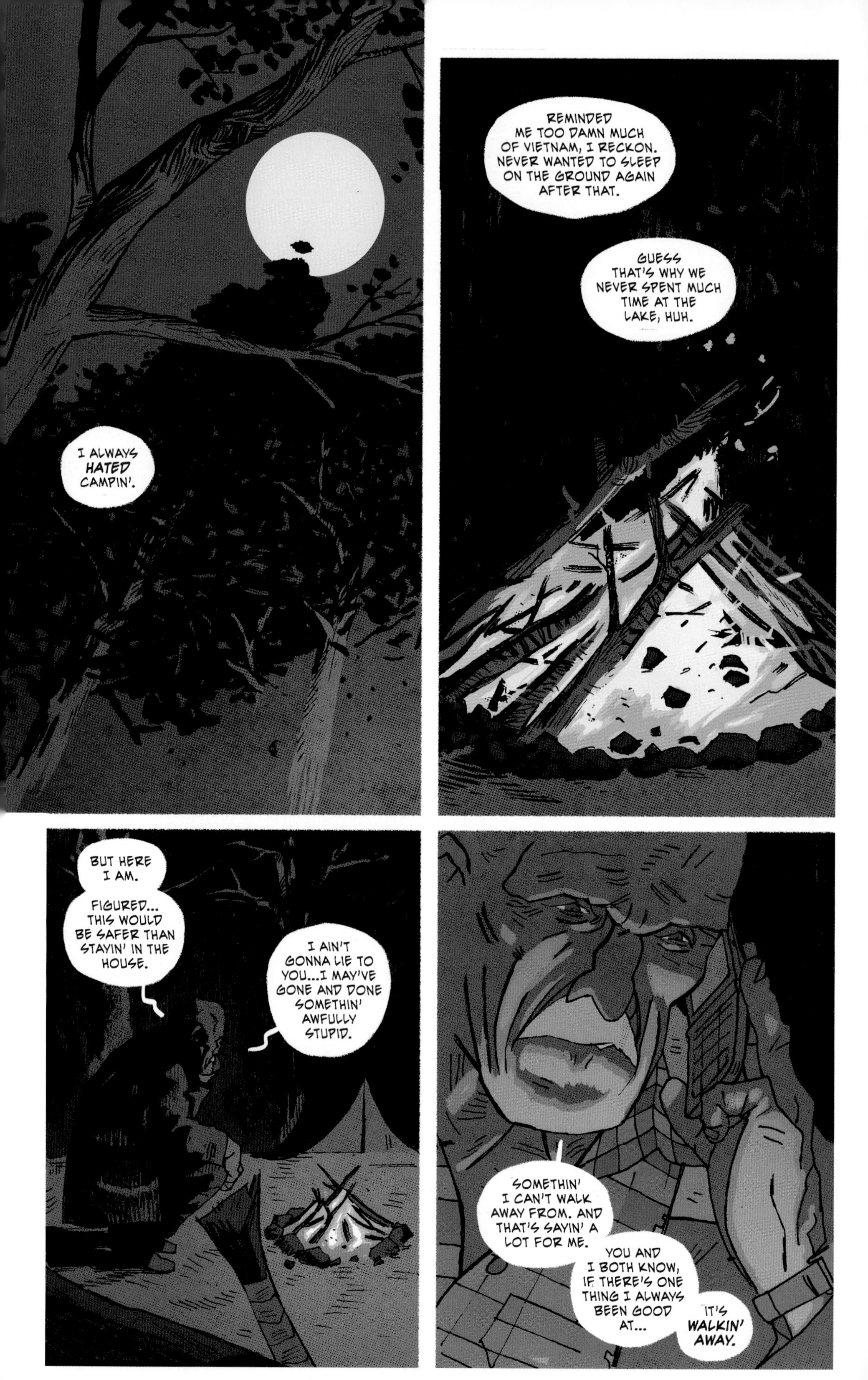
I ALWAYS HATED CAMPIN'.
REMINDED ME TOO DAMN MUCH OF VIETNAM, I RECKON. NEVER WANTED TO SLEEP ON THE GROUND AGAIN AFTER THAT.
GUESS THAT'S WHY WE NEVER SPENT MUCH TIME AT THE LAKE, HUH.
BUT HERE I AM.
FIGURED... THIS WOULD BE SAFER THAN STAYIN' IN THE HOUSE.
I AIN'T GONNA LIE TO YOU...I MAY'VE GONE AND DONE SOMETHIN' AWFULLY STUPID.
SOMETHIN' I CAN'T WALK AWAY FROM. AND THAT'S SAYIN' A LOT FOR ME.
YOU AND I BOTH KNOW, IF THERE'S ONE THING I ALWAYS BEEN GOOD AT...
IT'S WALKIN' AWAY.

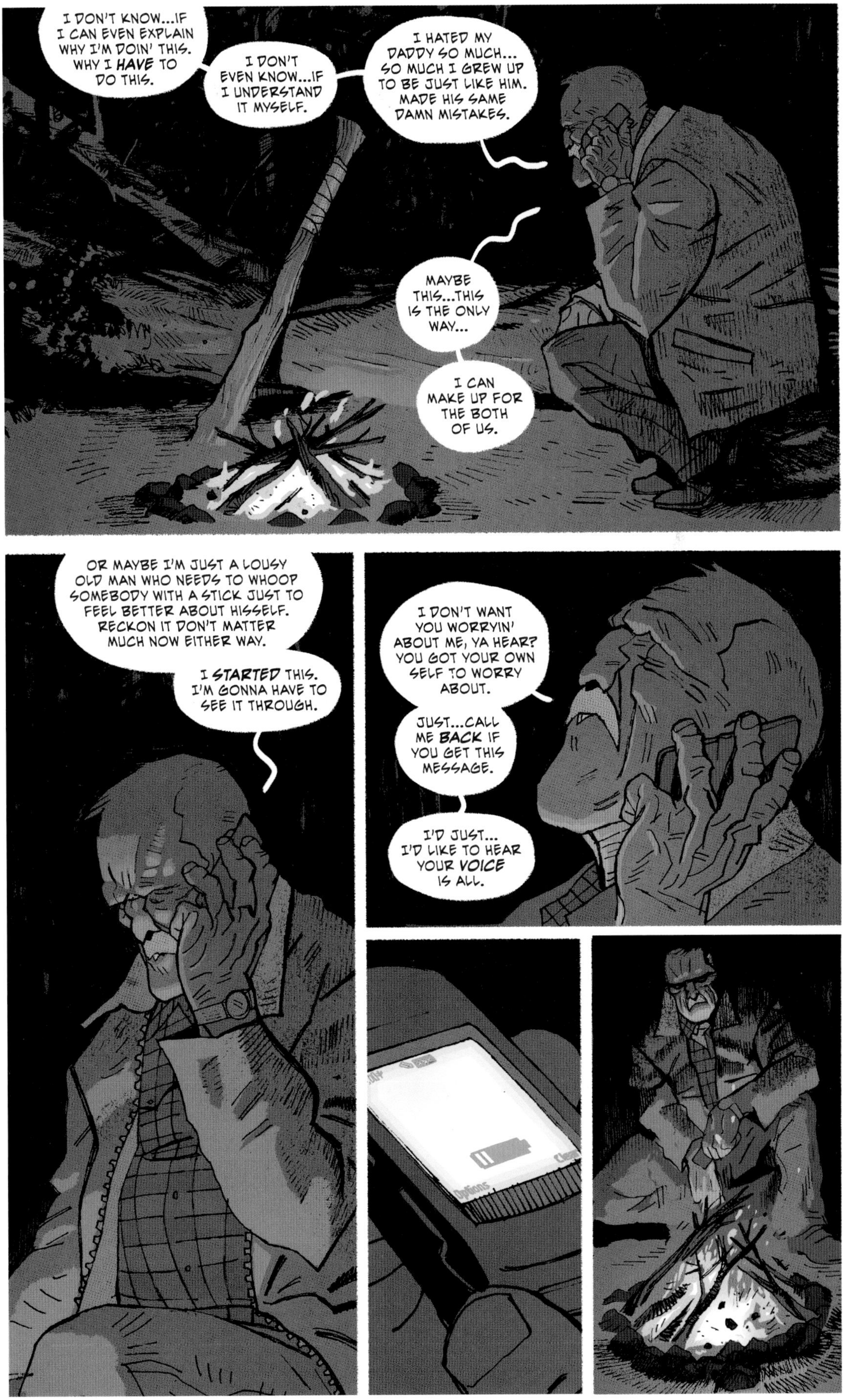
I DON'T KNOW...IF I CAN EVEN EXPLAIN WHY I'M DOIN' THIS. WHY I **HAVE** TO DO THIS.
I DON'T EVEN KNOW...IF I UNDERSTAND IT MYSELF.
I HATED MY DADDY SO MUCH... SO MUCH I GREW UP TO BE JUST LIKE HIM. MADE HIS SAME DAMN MISTAKES.
MAYBE THIS...THIS IS THE ONLY WAY...
I CAN MAKE UP FOR THE BOTH OF US.
OR MAYBE I'M JUST A LOUSY OLD MAN WHO NEEDS TO WHOOP SOMEBODY WITH A STICK JUST TO FEEL BETTER ABOUT HISSELF. RECKON IT DON'T MATTER MUCH NOW EITHER WAY.
I **STARTED** THIS. I'M GONNA HAVE TO SEE IT THROUGH.
I DON'T WANT YOU WORRYIN' ABOUT ME, YA HEAR? YOU GOT YOUR OWN SELF TO WORRY ABOUT.
JUST...CALL ME **BACK** IF YOU GET THIS MESSAGE.
I'D JUST... I'D LIKE TO HEAR YOUR **VOICE** IS ALL.

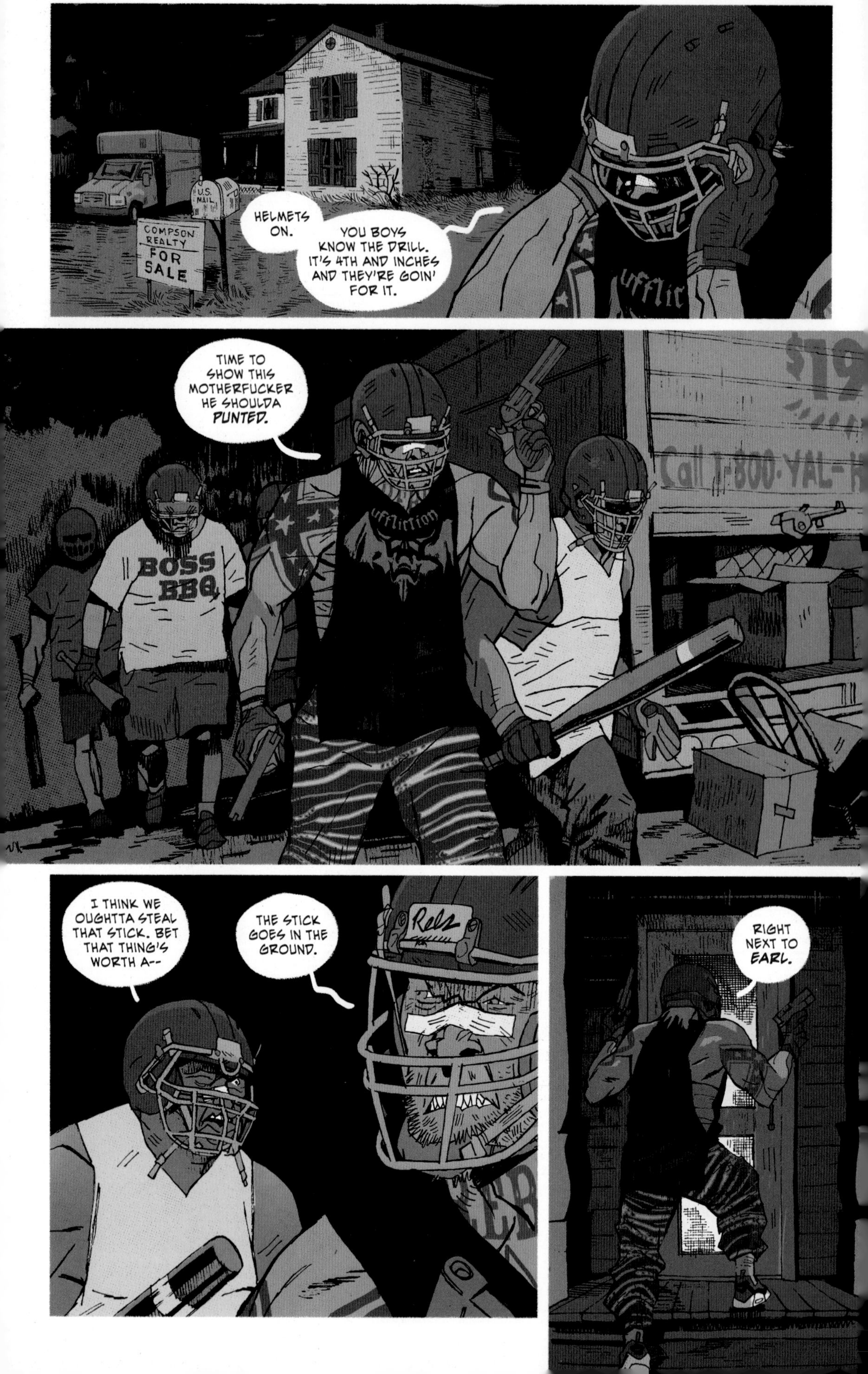
U.S. MAIL
COMPSON REALTY FOR SALE
HELMETS ON.
YOU BOYS KNOW THE DRILL. IT'S 4TH AND INCHES AND THEY'RE GOIN' FOR IT.
TIME TO SHOW THIS MOTHERFUCKER HE SHOULDA PUNTED.
BOSS BBQ
Call 1-800-YAL-
I THINK WE OUGHTTA STEAL THAT STICK. BET THAT THING'S WORTH A--
THE STICK GOES IN THE GROUND.
RIGHT NEXT TO EARL.

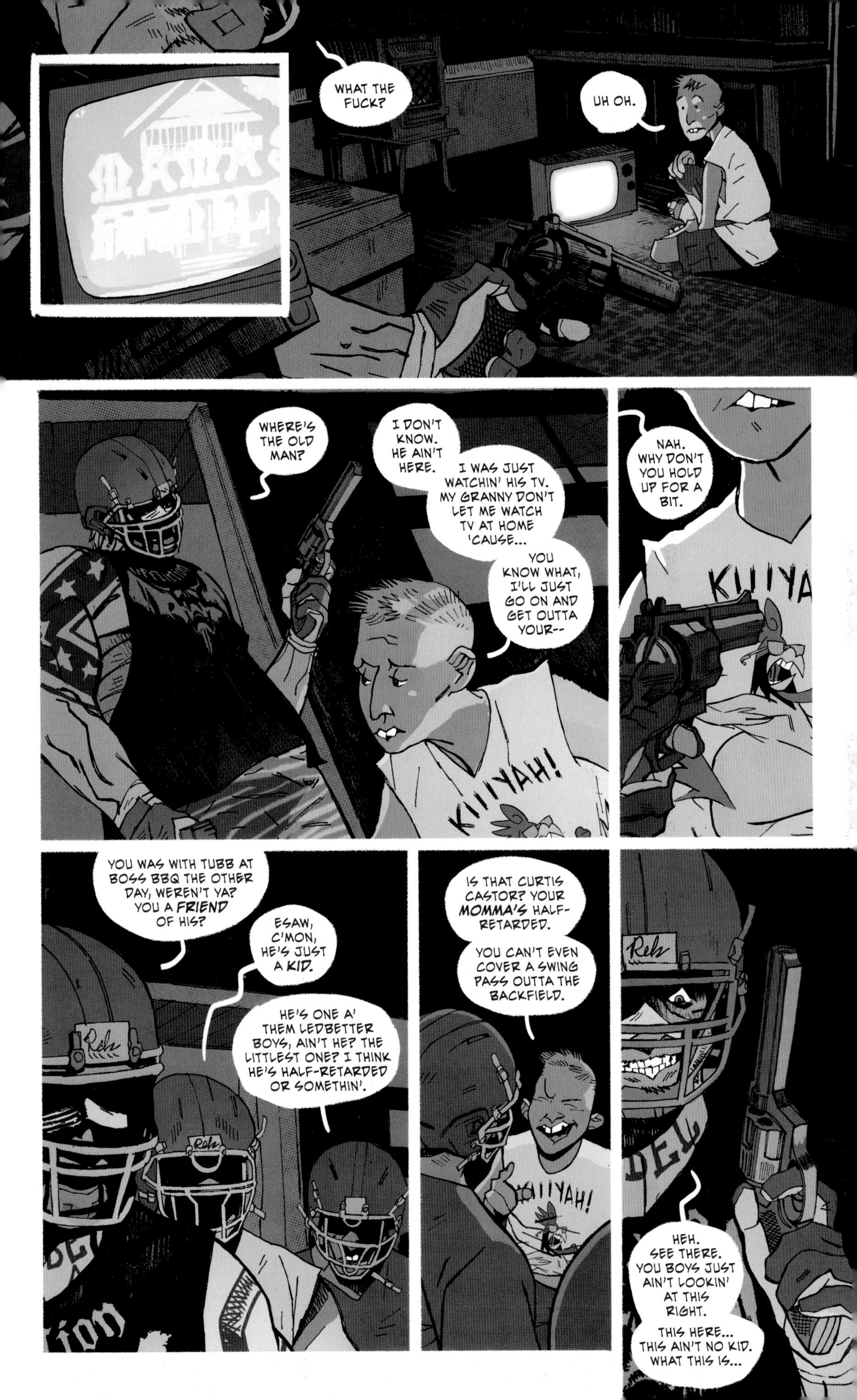

WHAT THE FUCK?
UH OH.
WHERE'S THE OLD MAN?
I DON'T KNOW. HE AIN'T HERE.
I WAS JUST WATCHIN' HIS TV. MY GRANNY DON'T LET ME WATCH TV AT HOME 'CAUSE...
YOU KNOW WHAT, I'LL JUST GO ON AND GET OUTTA YOUR--
KIIIYAH!
NAH. WHY DON'T YOU HOLD UP FOR A BIT.
KIIIYA
YOU WAS WITH TUBB AT BOSS BBQ THE OTHER DAY, WEREN'T YA? YOU A **FRIEND** OF HIS?
ESAW, C'MON, HE'S JUST A **KID**.
HE'S ONE A' THEM LEDBETTER BOYS, AIN'T HE? THE LITTLEST ONE? I THINK HE'S HALF-RETARDED OR SOMETHIN'.
IS THAT CURTIS CASTOR? YOUR **MOMMA'S** HALF-RETARDED.
YOU CAN'T EVEN COVER A SWING PASS OUTTA THE BACKFIELD.
KIIIYAH!
HEH. SEE THERE. YOU BOYS JUST AIN'T LOOKIN' AT THIS RIGHT.
THIS HERE... THIS AIN'T NO KID. WHAT THIS IS...

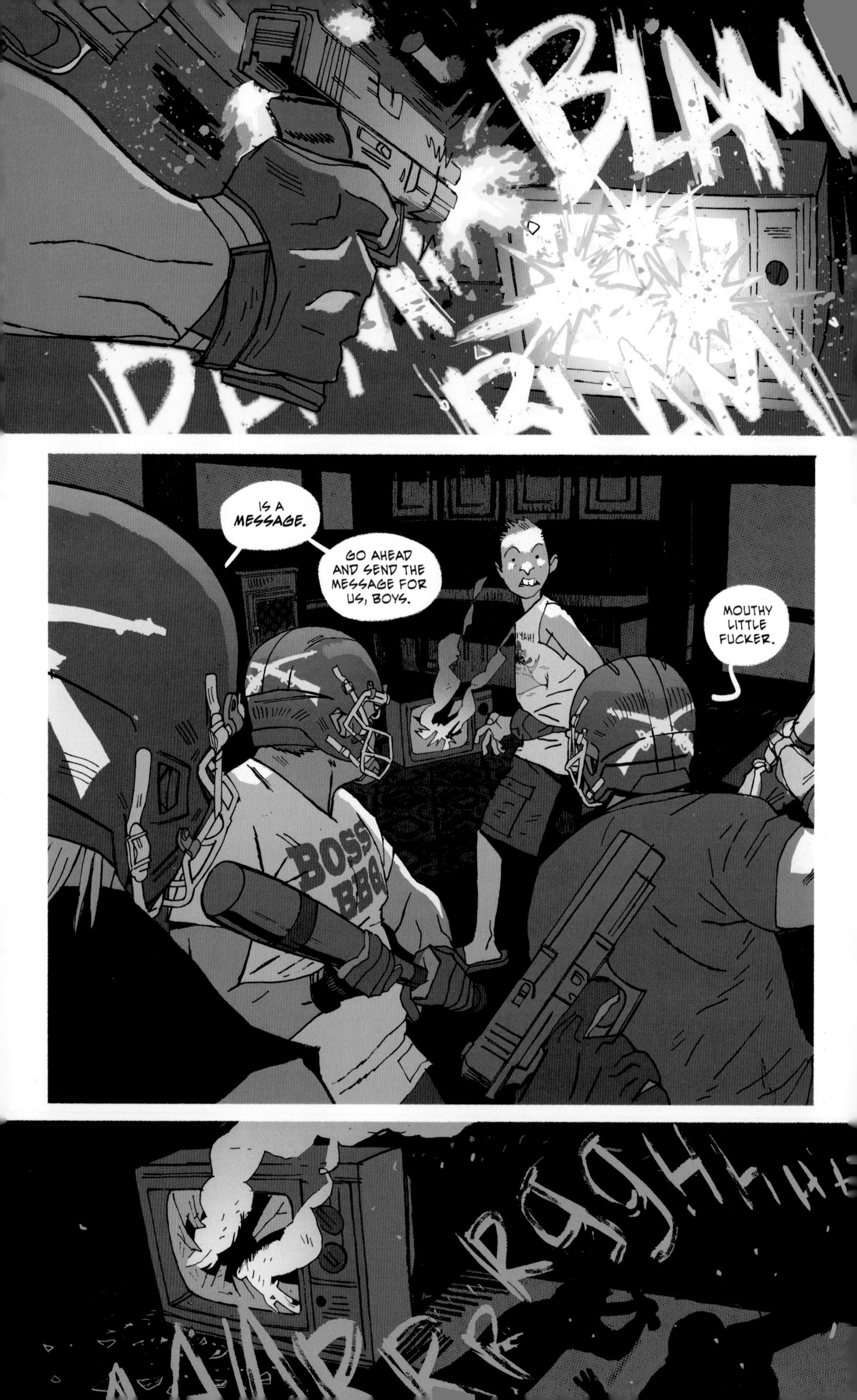
BLAM
IS A MESSAGE.
GO AHEAD AND SEND THE MESSAGE FOR US, BOYS.
MOUTHY LITTLE FUCKER.
BOSS BBQ

Chapter 4

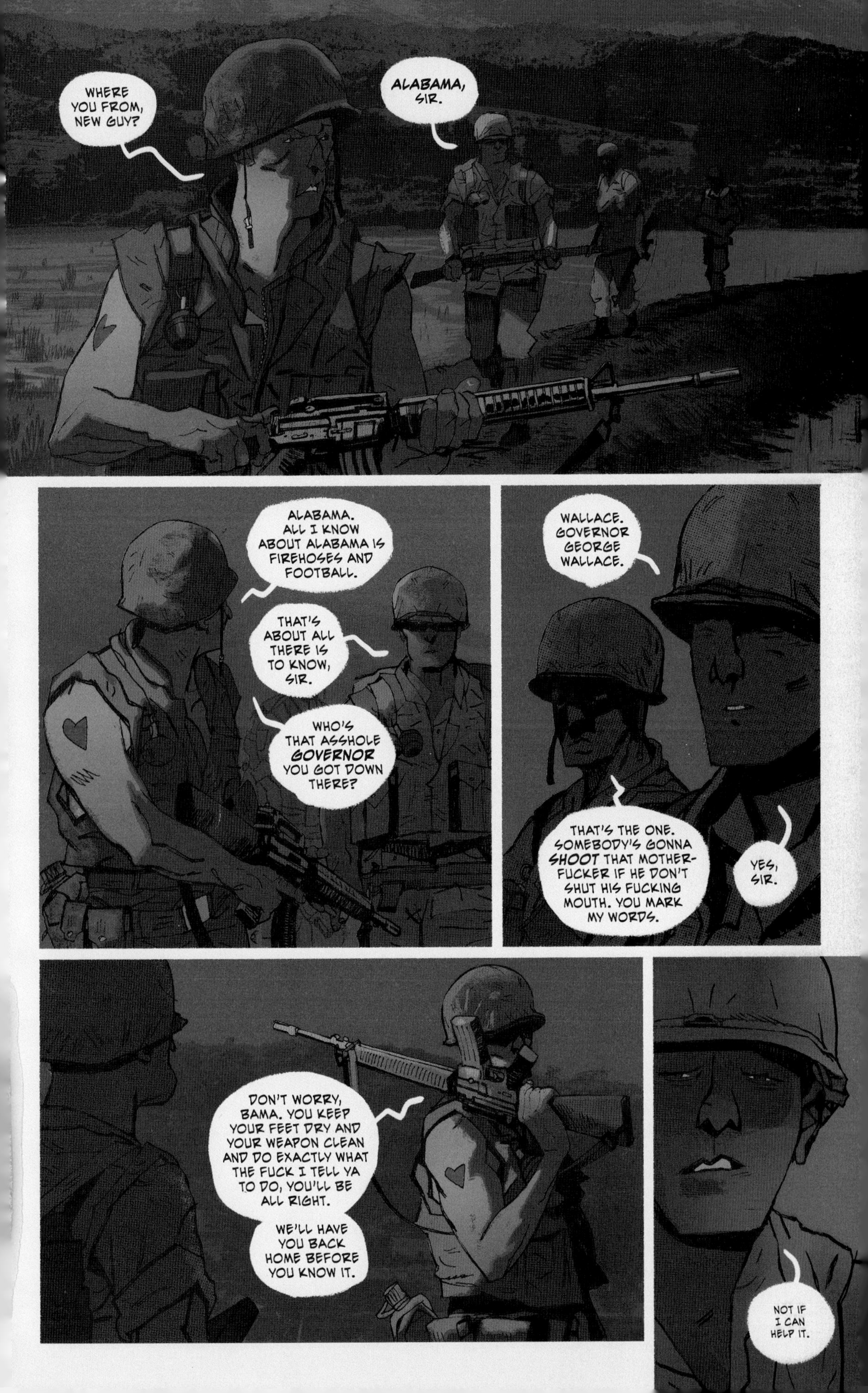

WHERE YOU FROM, NEW GUY?
ALABAMA, SIR.
ALABAMA. ALL I KNOW ABOUT ALABAMA IS FIREHOSES AND FOOTBALL.
THAT'S ABOUT ALL THERE IS TO KNOW, SIR.
WHO'S THAT ASSHOLE GOVERNOR YOU GOT DOWN THERE?
WALLACE. GOVERNOR GEORGE WALLACE.
THAT'S THE ONE. SOMEBODY'S GONNA SHOOT THAT MOTHER-FUCKER IF HE DON'T SHUT HIS FUCKING MOUTH. YOU MARK MY WORDS.
YES, SIR.
DON'T WORRY, BAMA. YOU KEEP YOUR FEET DRY AND YOUR WEAPON CLEAN AND DO EXACTLY WHAT THE FUCK I TELL YA TO DO, YOU'LL BE ALL RIGHT.
WE'LL HAVE YOU BACK HOME BEFORE YOU KNOW IT.
NOT IF I CAN HELP IT.

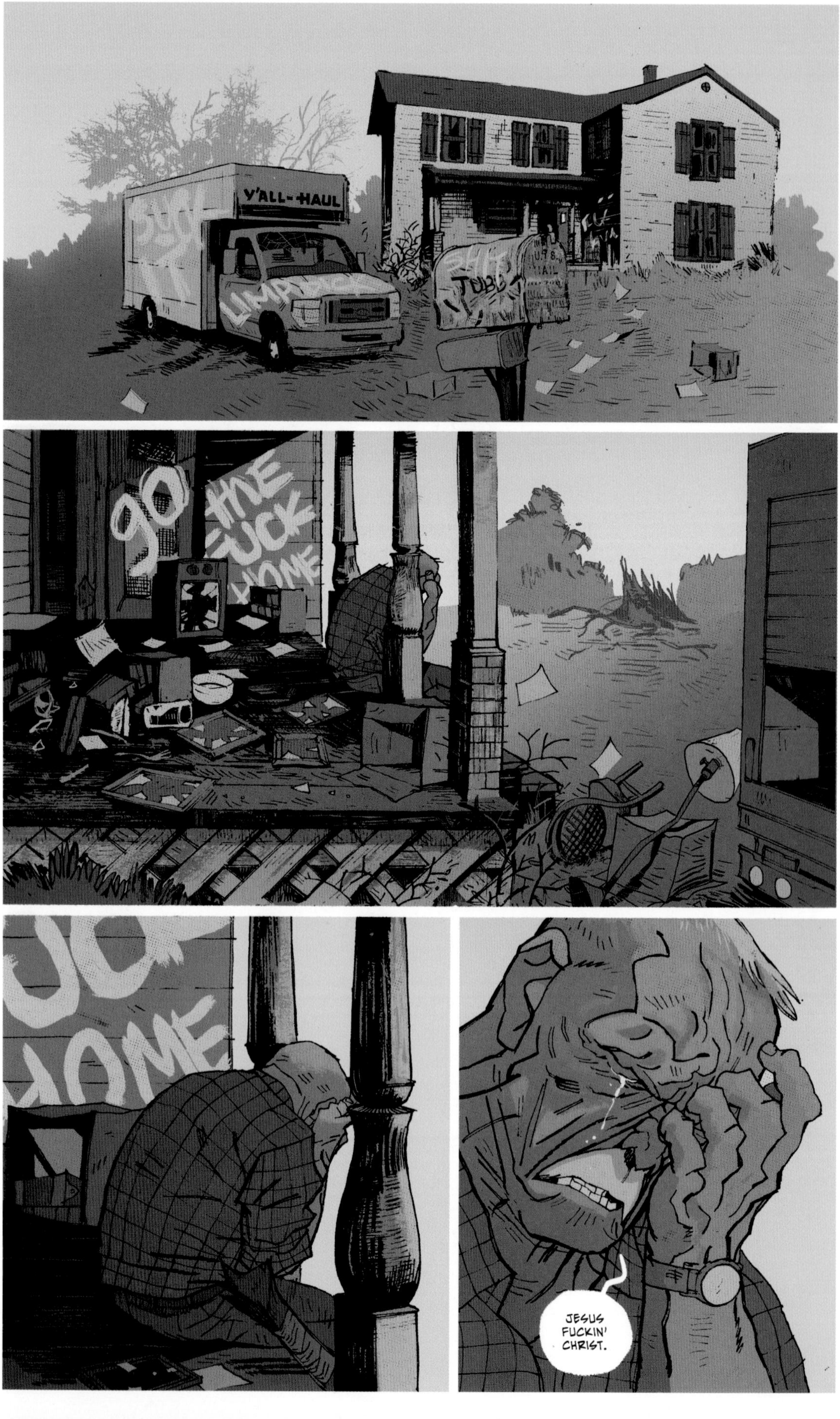
Y'ALL-HAUL
JESUS FUCKIN' CHRIST.

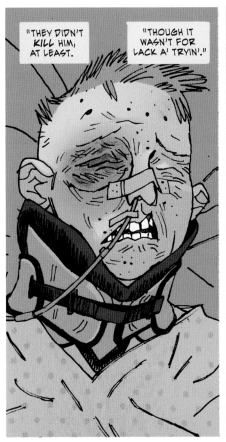

"THEY DIDN'T KILL HIM, AT LEAST."

"THOUGH IT WASN'T FOR LACK A' TRYIN'."

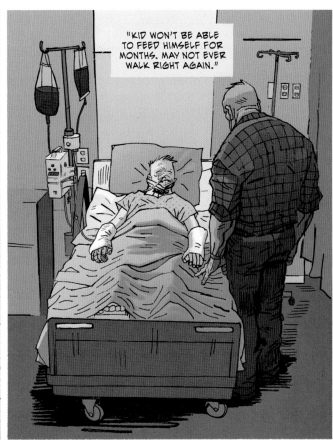

"KID WON'T BE ABLE TO FEED HIMSELF FOR MONTHS. MAY NOT EVER WALK RIGHT AGAIN."

"CERTAINLY WON'T BE CLIMBIN' NO MORE TREES."

"THIS HAS ALL GONE WAY TOO FAR. I SHOULDA LEFT WHEN I HAD THE CHANCE. SHOULDA PACKED UP AND BEEN GONE.

"SHOULDA..."

BUT I DIDN'T.

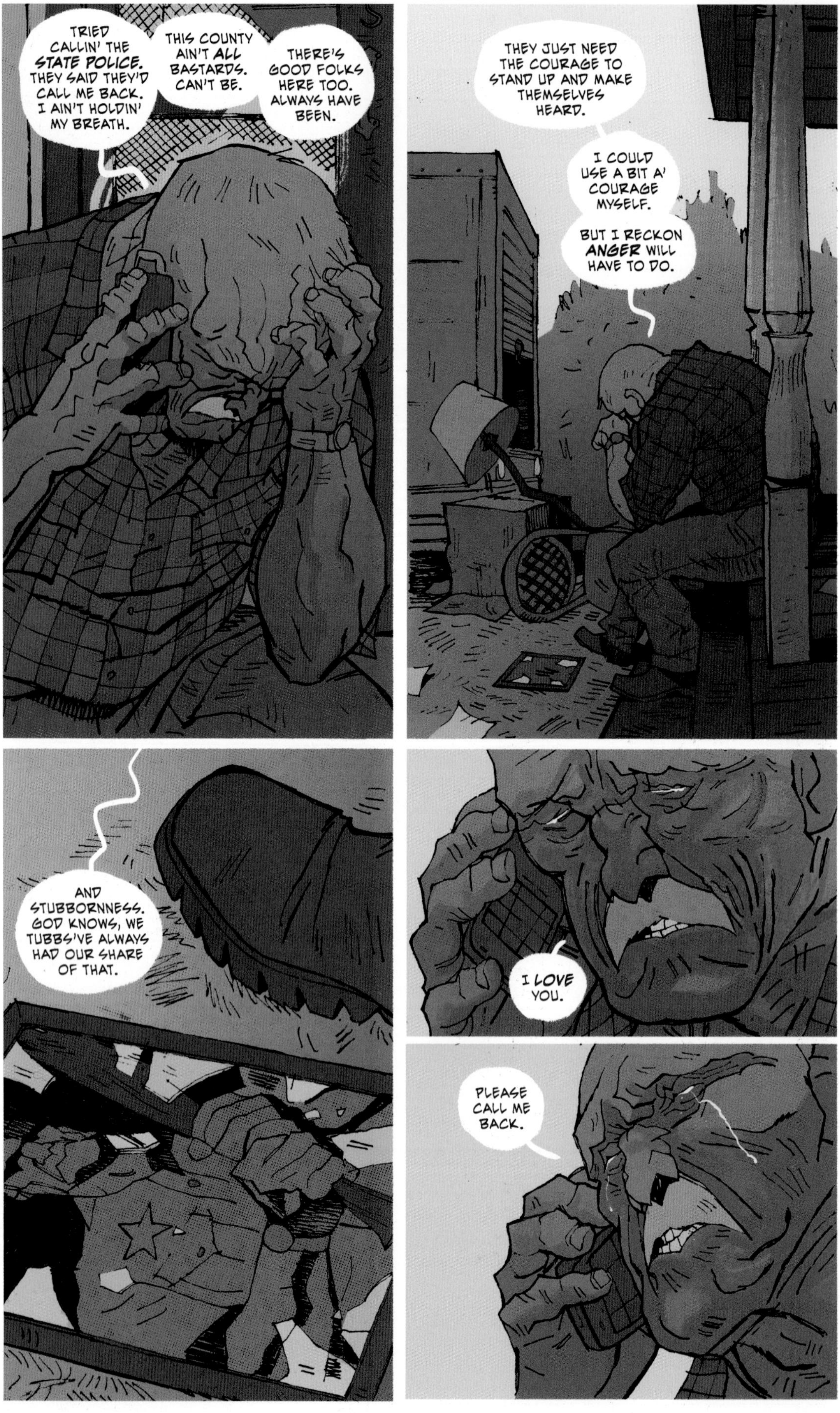
TRIED CALLIN' THE STATE POLICE. THEY SAID THEY'D CALL ME BACK. I AIN'T HOLDIN' MY BREATH.
THIS COUNTY AIN'T ALL BASTARDS. CAN'T BE.
THERE'S GOOD FOLKS HERE TOO. ALWAYS HAVE BEEN.
THEY JUST NEED THE COURAGE TO STAND UP AND MAKE THEMSELVES HEARD.
I COULD USE A BIT A' COURAGE MYSELF.
BUT I RECKON ANGER WILL HAVE TO DO.
AND STUBBORNNESS. GOD KNOWS, WE TUBBS'VE ALWAYS HAD OUR SHARE OF THAT.
I LOVE YOU.
PLEASE CALL ME BACK.

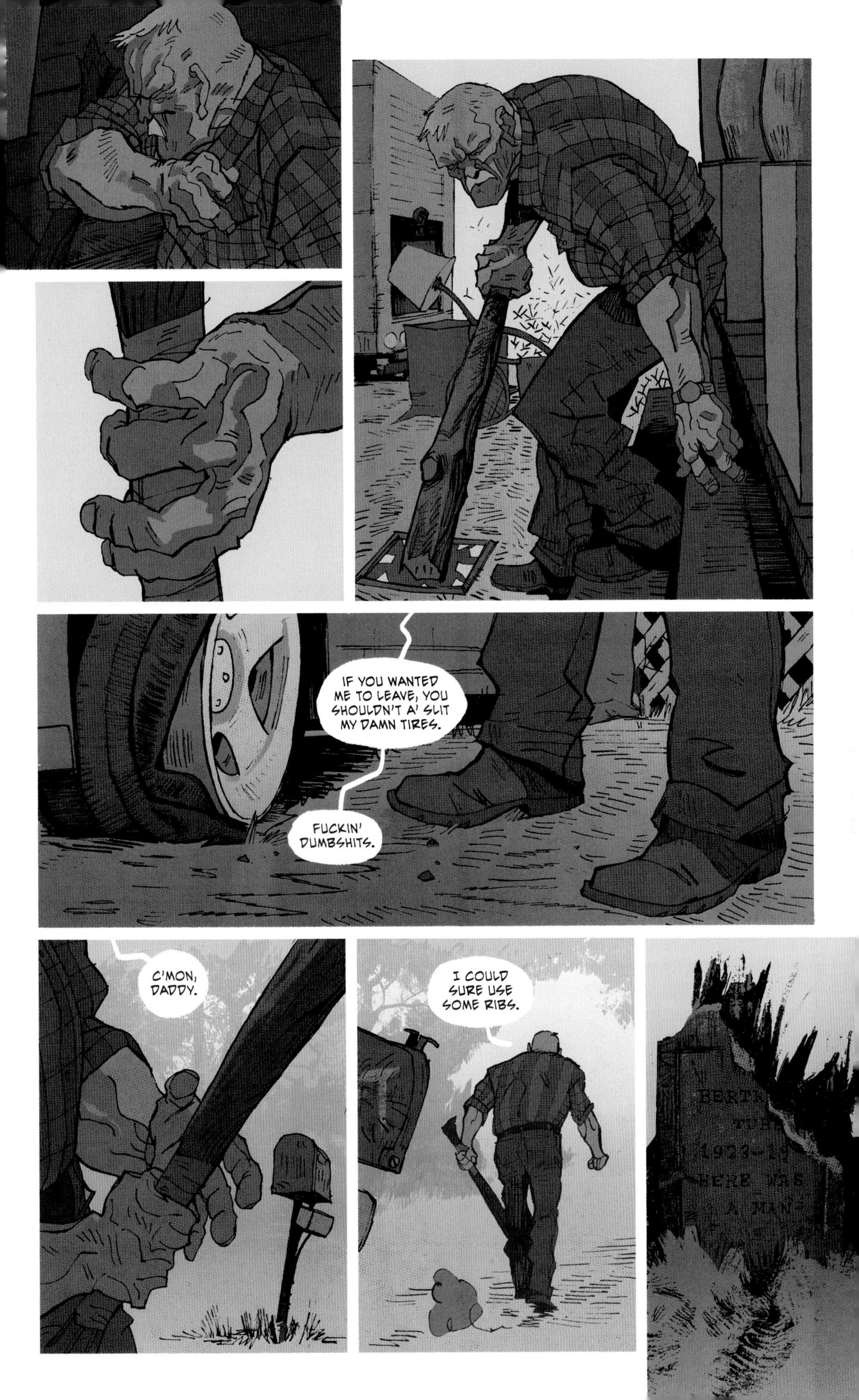
IF YOU WANTED ME TO LEAVE, YOU SHOULDN'T A' SLIT MY DAMN TIRES.
FUCKIN' DUMBSHITS.
C'MON, DADDY.
I COULD SURE USE SOME RIBS.

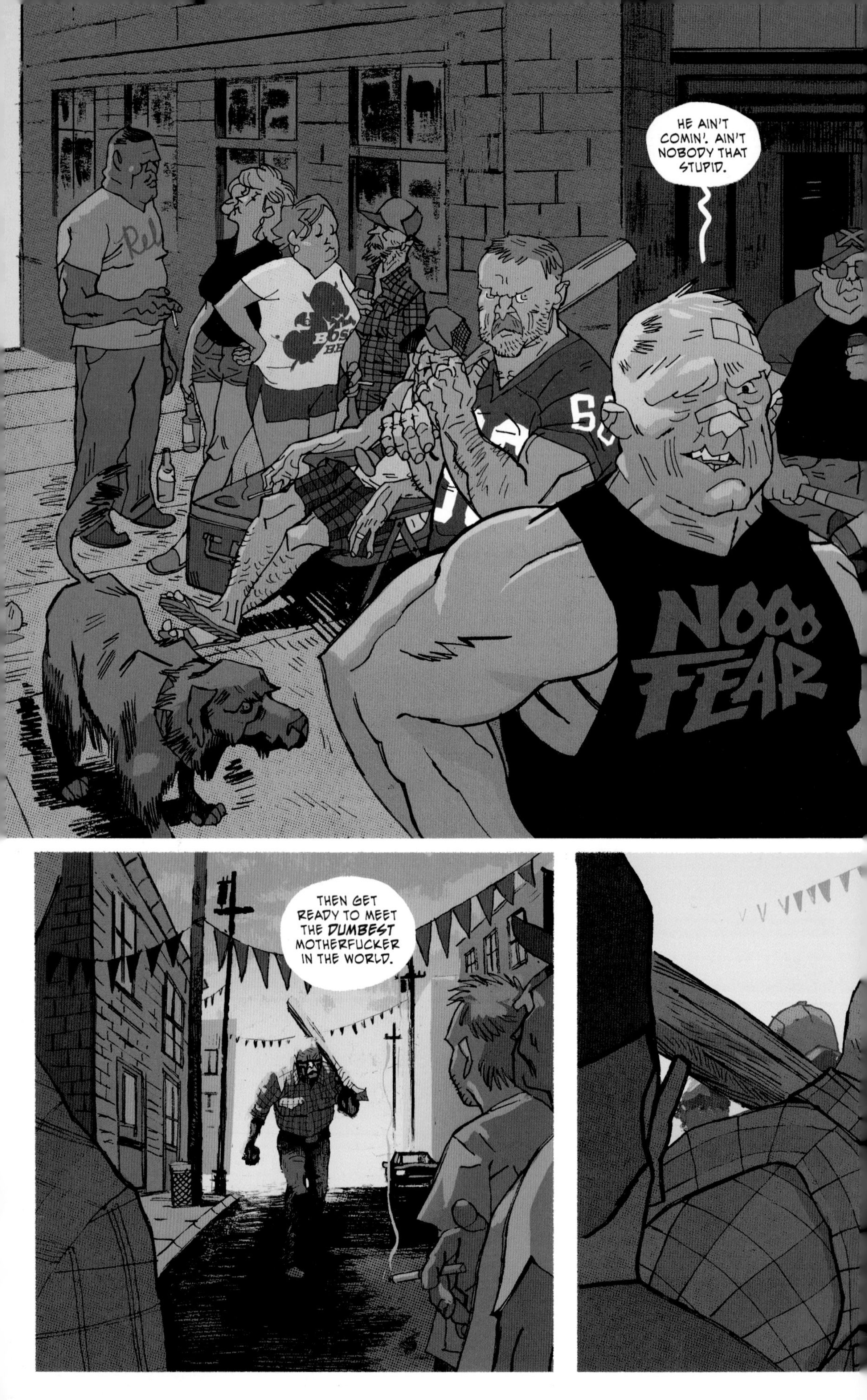
HE AIN'T COMIN'. AIN'T NOBODY THAT STUPID.
NO FEAR
THEN GET READY TO MEET THE *DUMBEST* MOTHERFUCKER IN THE WORLD.

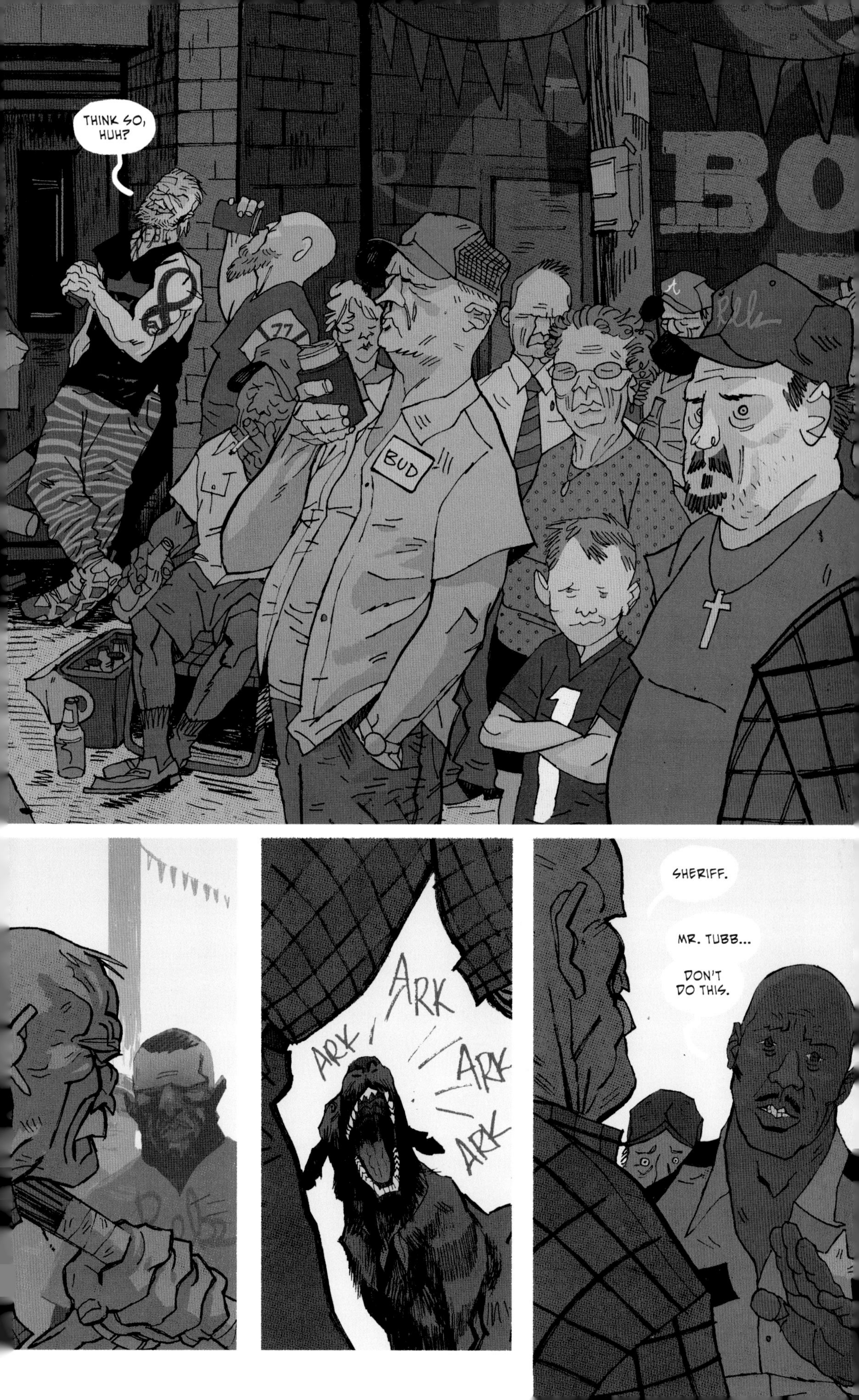
THINK SO,
HUH?
BUD
ARK
ARK
ARK
ARK
SHERIFF.
MR. TUBB...
DON'T
DO THIS.

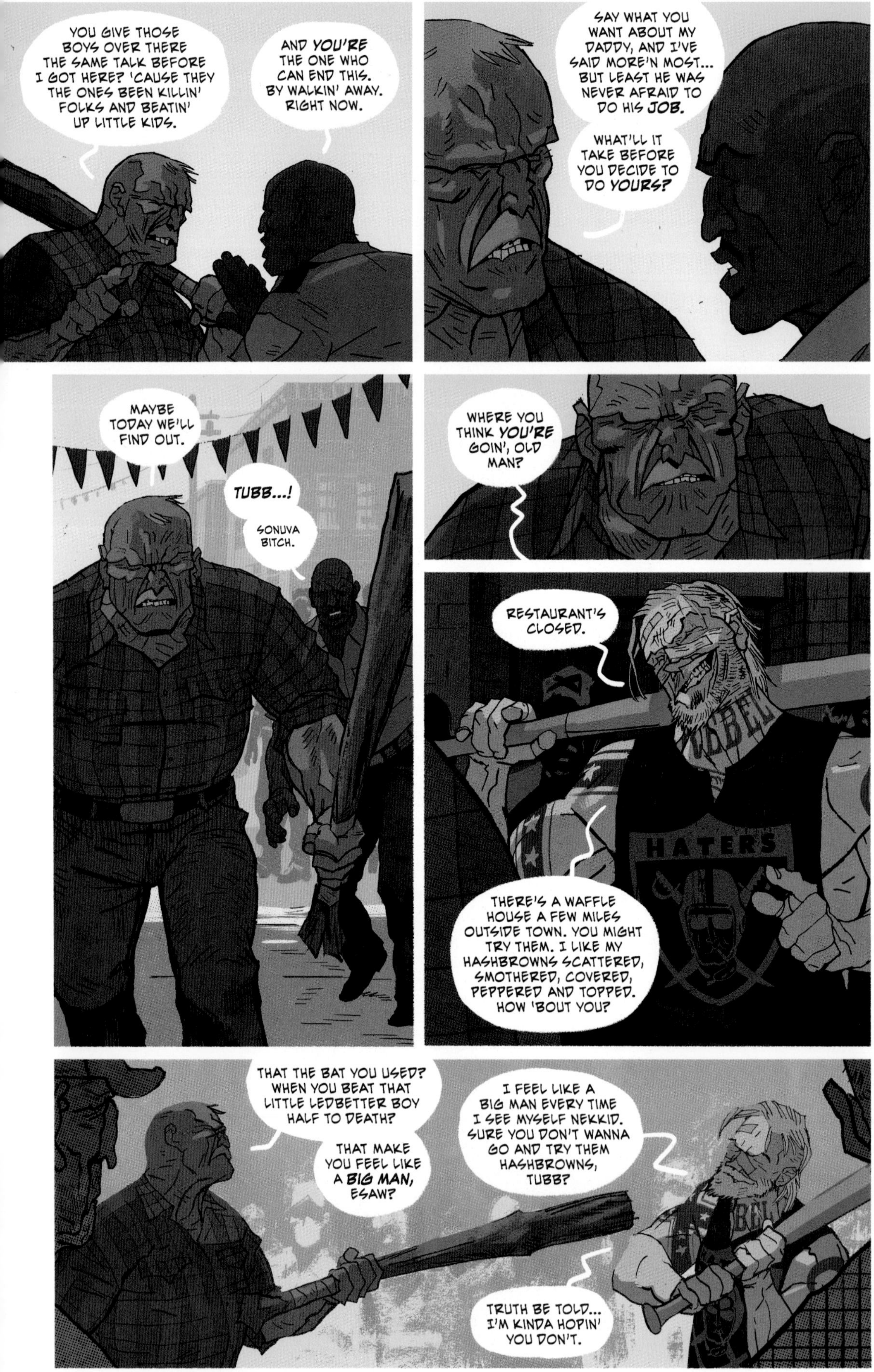
YOU GIVE THOSE BOYS OVER THERE THE SAME TALK BEFORE I GOT HERE? 'CAUSE THEY THE ONES BEEN KILLIN' FOLKS AND BEATIN' UP LITTLE KIDS.
AND *YOU'RE* THE ONE WHO CAN END THIS. BY WALKIN' AWAY. RIGHT NOW.
SAY WHAT YOU WANT ABOUT MY DADDY, AND I'VE SAID MORE'N MOST... BUT LEAST HE WAS NEVER AFRAID TO DO HIS **JOB.**
WHAT'LL IT TAKE BEFORE YOU DECIDE TO DO ***YOURS?***
MAYBE TODAY WE'LL FIND OUT.
***TUBB...!***
SONUVA BITCH.
WHERE YOU THINK ***YOU'RE*** GOIN', OLD MAN?
RESTAURANT'S CLOSED.
HATERS
THERE'S A WAFFLE HOUSE A FEW MILES OUTSIDE TOWN. YOU MIGHT TRY THEM. I LIKE MY HASHBROWNS SCATTERED, SMOTHERED, COVERED, PEPPERED AND TOPPED. HOW 'BOUT YOU?
THAT THE BAT YOU USED? WHEN YOU BEAT THAT LITTLE LEDBETTER BOY HALF TO DEATH?
THAT MAKE YOU FEEL LIKE A ***BIG MAN,*** ESAW?
I FEEL LIKE A BIG MAN EVERY TIME I SEE MYSELF NEKKID. SURE YOU DON'T WANNA GO AND TRY THEM HASHBROWNS, TUBB?
TRUTH BE TOLD... I'M KINDA HOPIN' YOU DON'T.

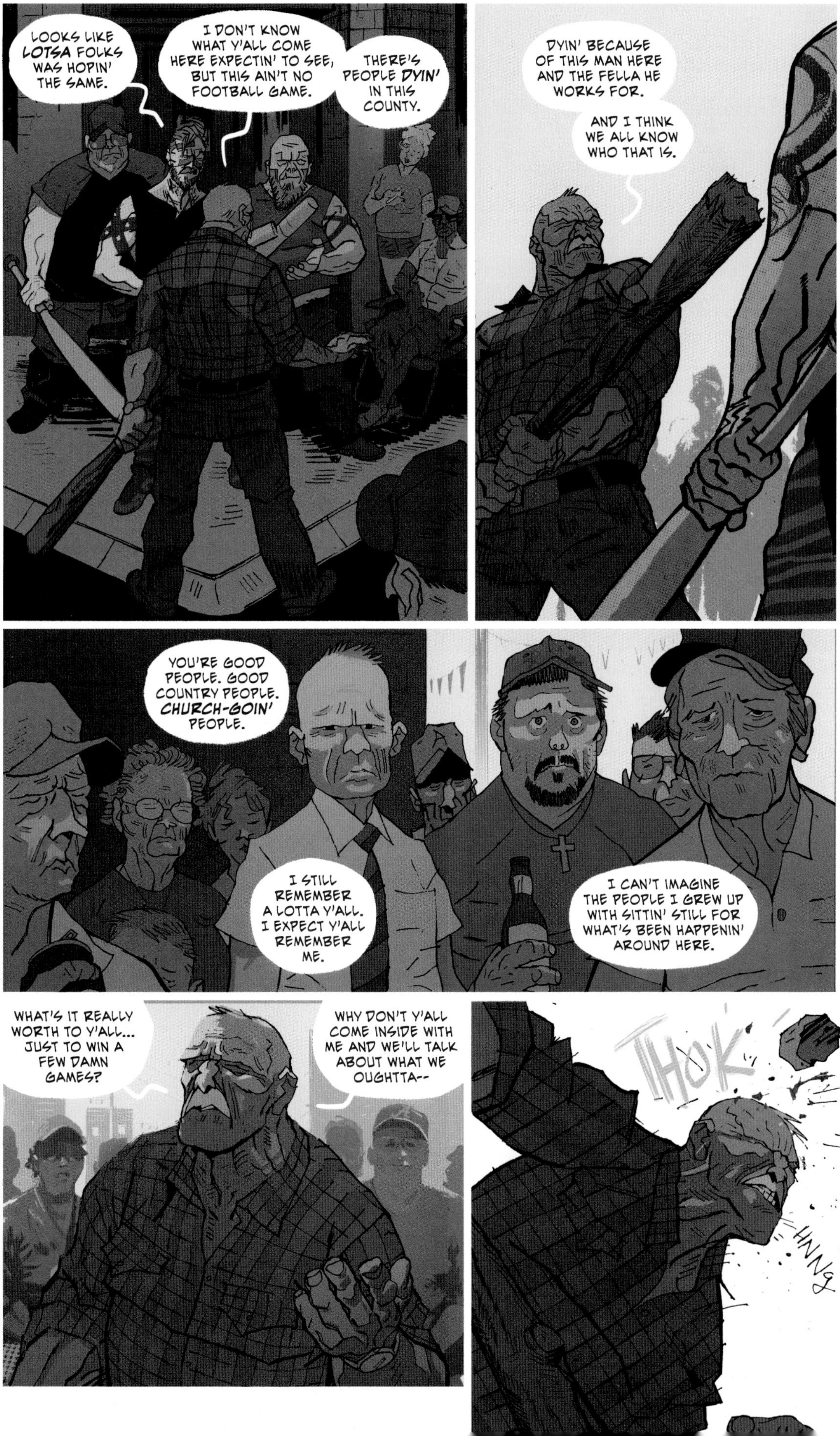
LOOKS LIKE LOTSA FOLKS WAS HOPIN' THE SAME.
I DON'T KNOW WHAT Y'ALL COME HERE EXPECTIN' TO SEE, BUT THIS AIN'T NO FOOTBALL GAME.
THERE'S PEOPLE DYIN' IN THIS COUNTY.
DYIN' BECAUSE OF THIS MAN HERE AND THE FELLA HE WORKS FOR.
AND I THINK WE ALL KNOW WHO THAT IS.
YOU'RE GOOD PEOPLE. GOOD COUNTRY PEOPLE. CHURCH-GOIN' PEOPLE.
I STILL REMEMBER A LOTTA Y'ALL. I EXPECT Y'ALL REMEMBER ME.
I CAN'T IMAGINE THE PEOPLE I GREW UP WITH SITTIN' STILL FOR WHAT'S BEEN HAPPENIN' AROUND HERE.
WHAT'S IT REALLY WORTH TO Y'ALL... JUST TO WIN A FEW DAMN GAMES?
WHY DON'T Y'ALL COME INSIDE WITH ME AND WE'LL TALK ABOUT WHAT WE OUGHTTA--
THOK
HNNg

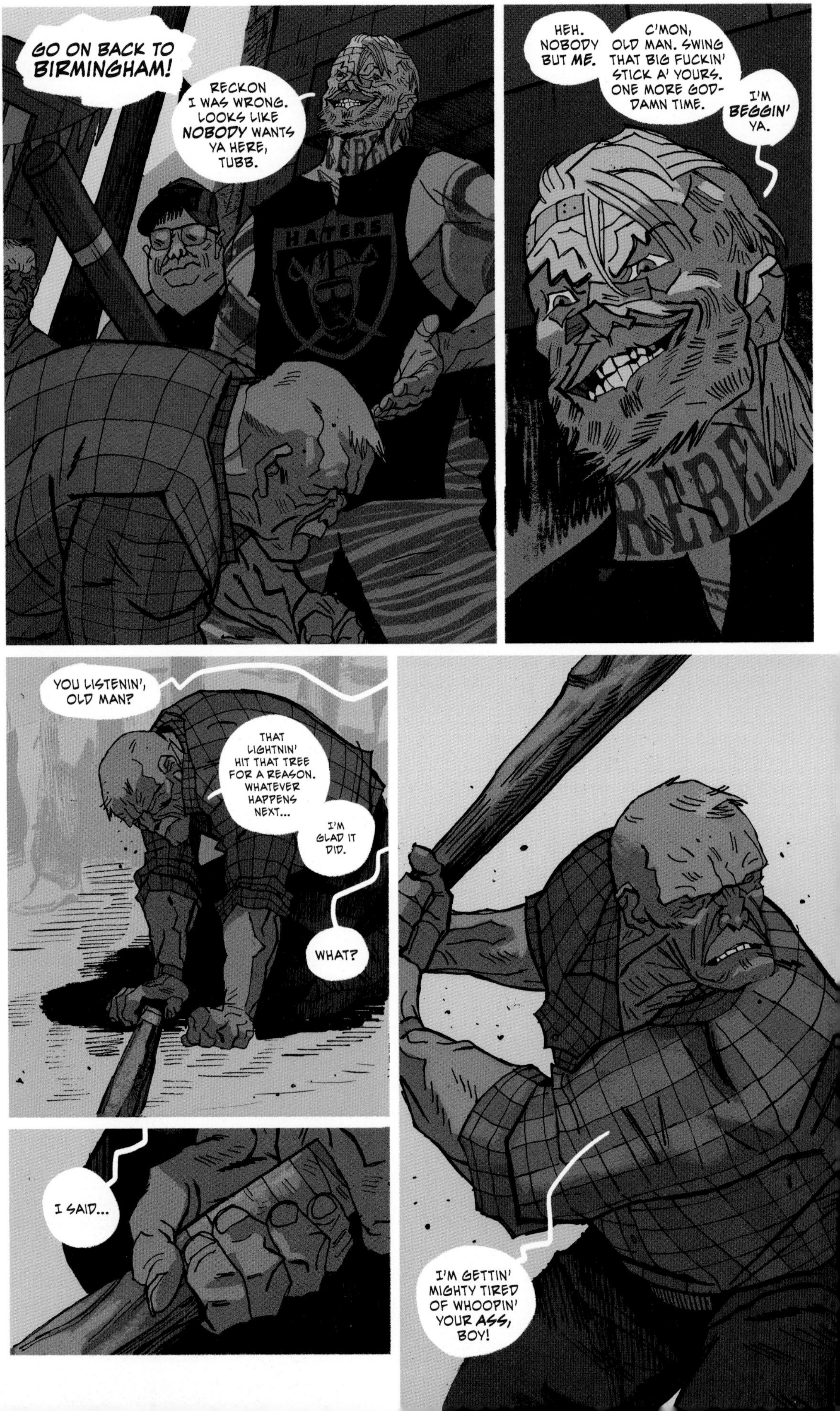
GO ON BACK TO BIRMINGHAM!
RECKON I WAS WRONG. LOOKS LIKE NOBODY WANTS YA HERE, TUBB.
HEH. NOBODY BUT ME.
C'MON, OLD MAN. SWING THAT BIG FUCKIN' STICK A' YOURS. ONE MORE GOD-DAMN TIME.
I'M BEGGIN' YA.
YOU LISTENIN', OLD MAN?
THAT LIGHTNIN' HIT THAT TREE FOR A REASON. WHATEVER HAPPENS NEXT...
I'M GLAD IT DID.
WHAT?
I SAID...
I'M GETTIN' MIGHTY TIRED OF WHOOPIN' YOUR ASS, BOY!

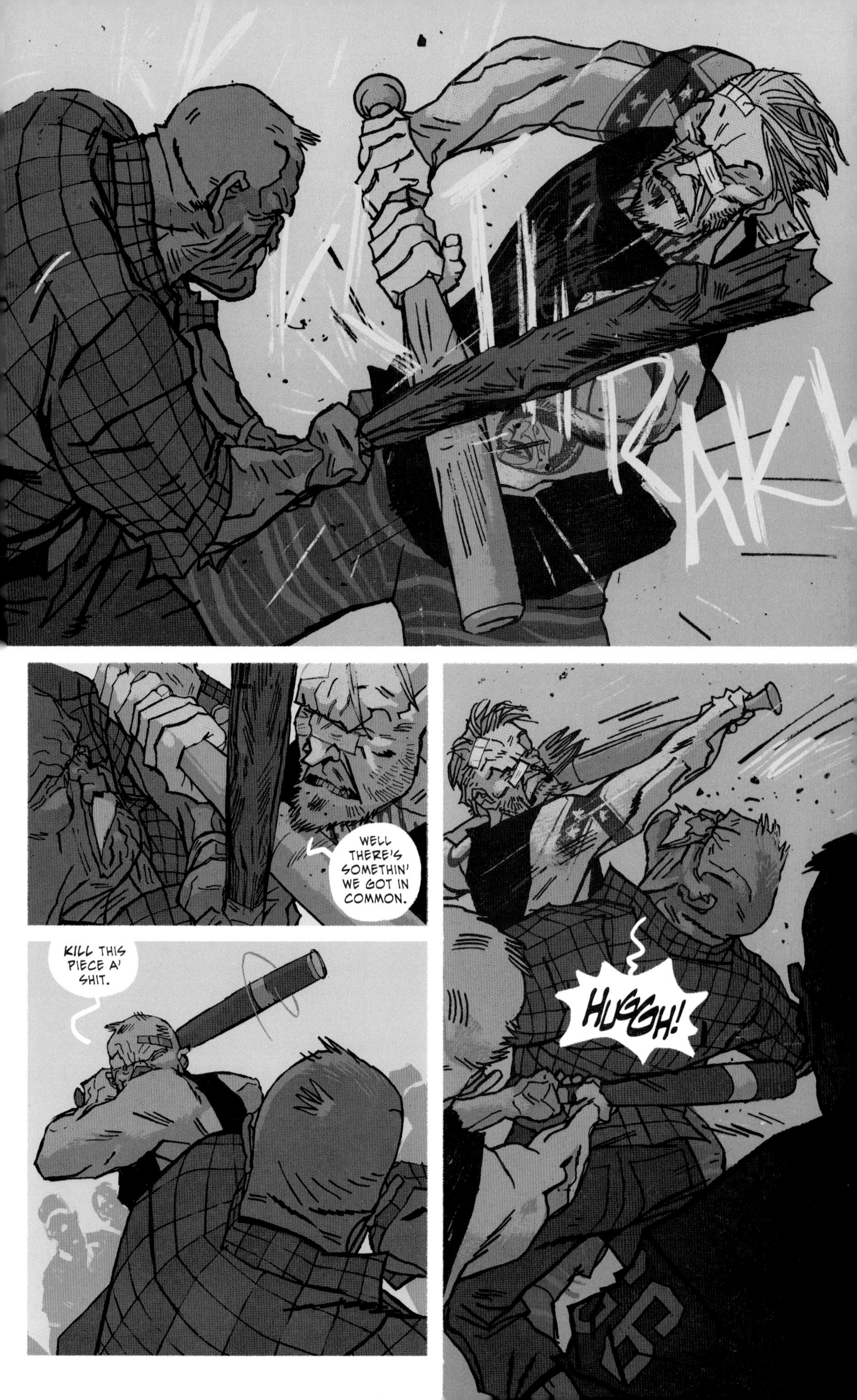
RAK
WELL THERE'S SOMETHIN' WE GOT IN COMMON.
KILL THIS PIECE A' SHIT.
HUGGH!

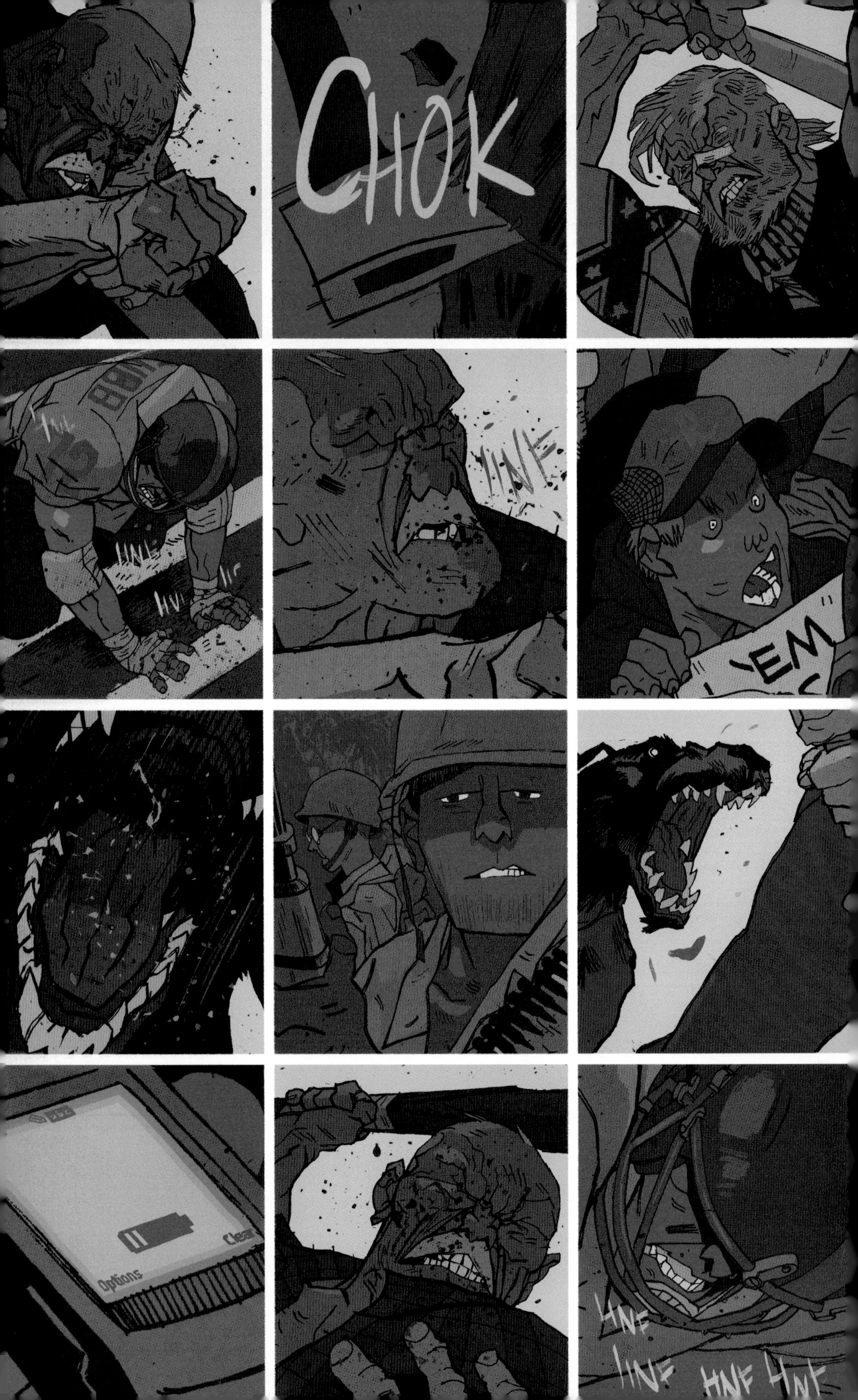
CHOK
HNF
EM
Options
Clear
HNF
HNF
HNF HNF

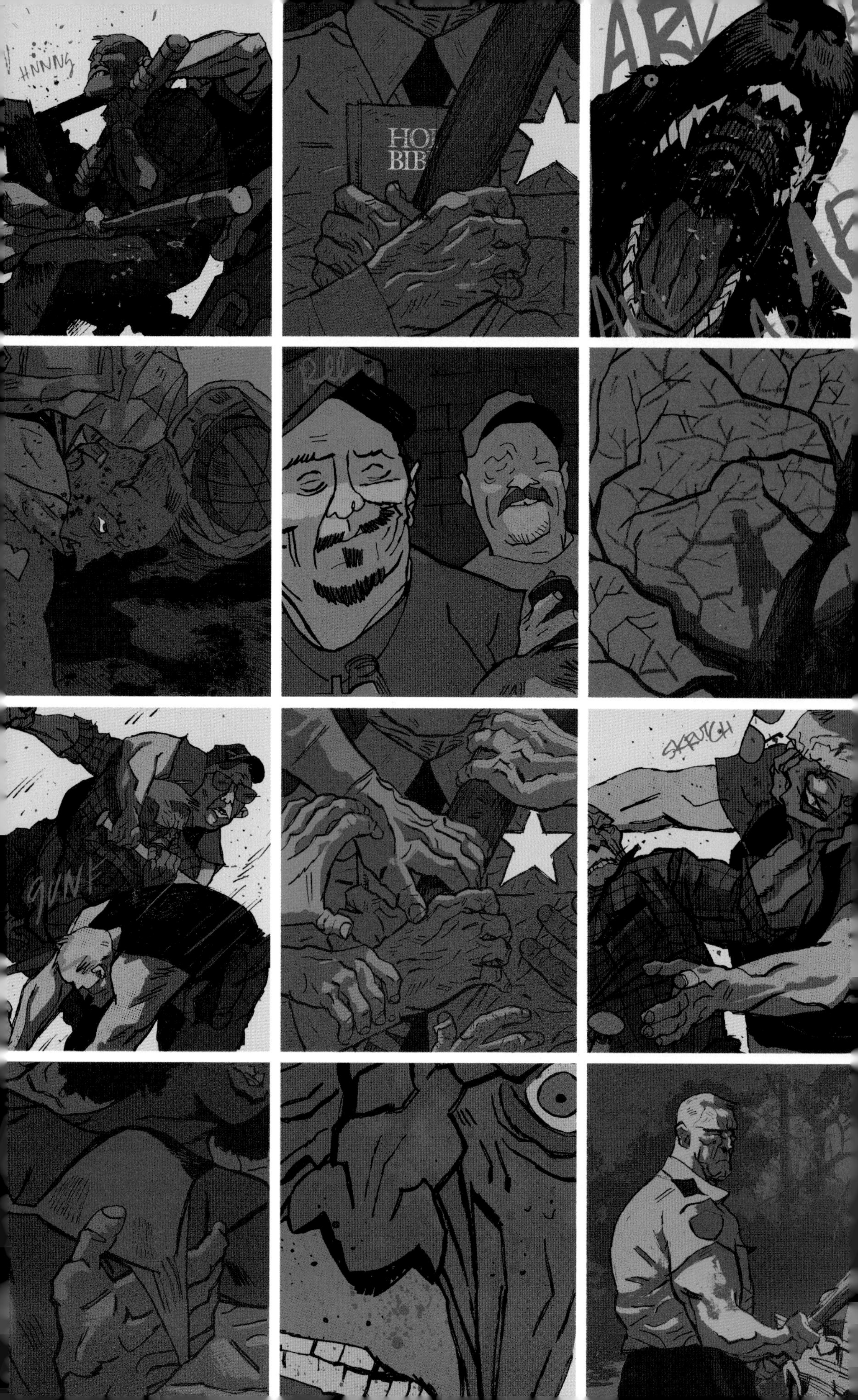
HNNNG
HOL
BIB
SKRUTCH
GUNK

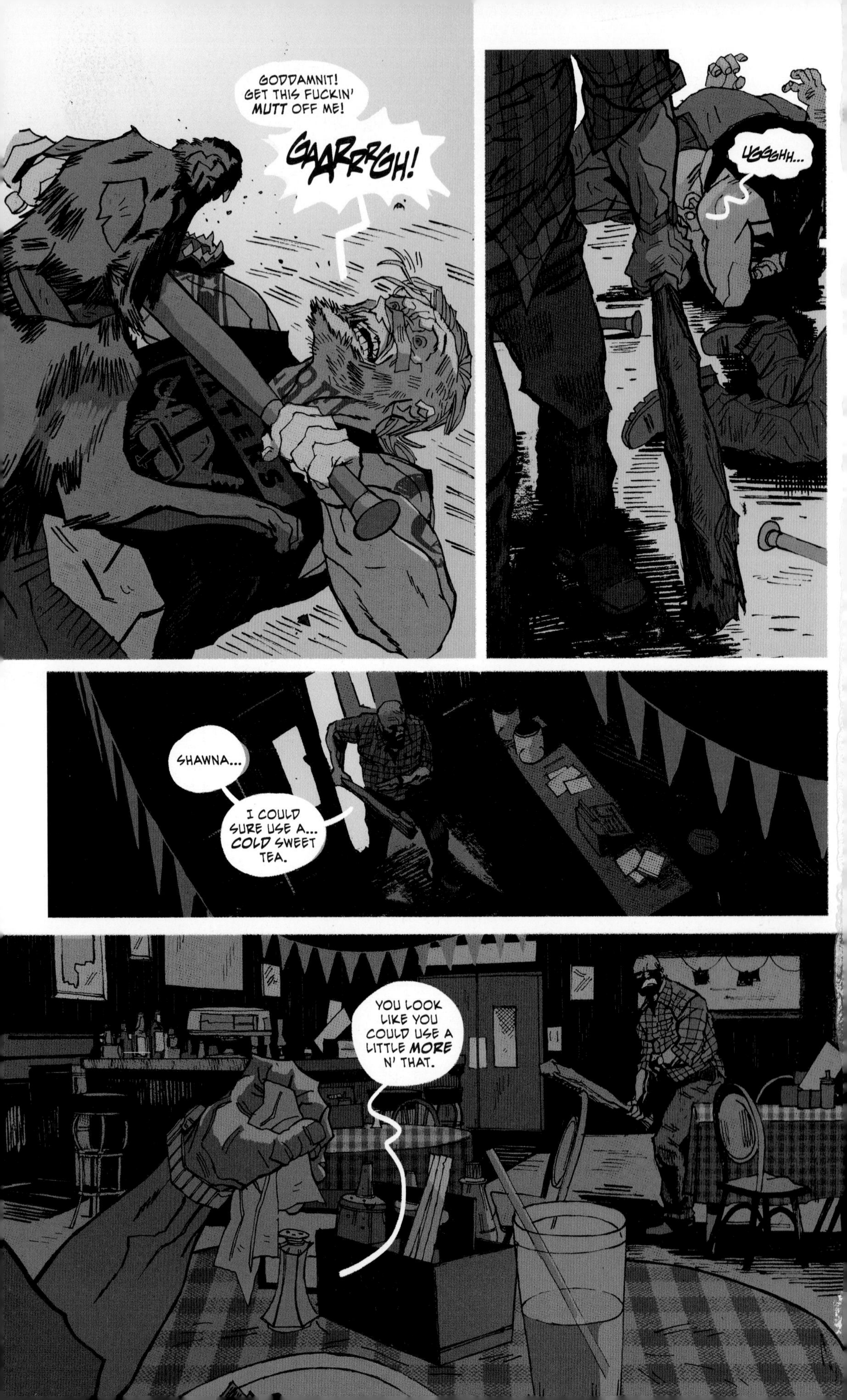

GODDAMNIT! GET THIS FUCKIN' **MUTT** OFF ME!
GAARRRGH!
UGGGHH...
SHAWNA...
I COULD SURE USE A... **COLD** SWEET TEA.
YOU LOOK LIKE YOU COULD USE A LITTLE **MORE** N' THAT.

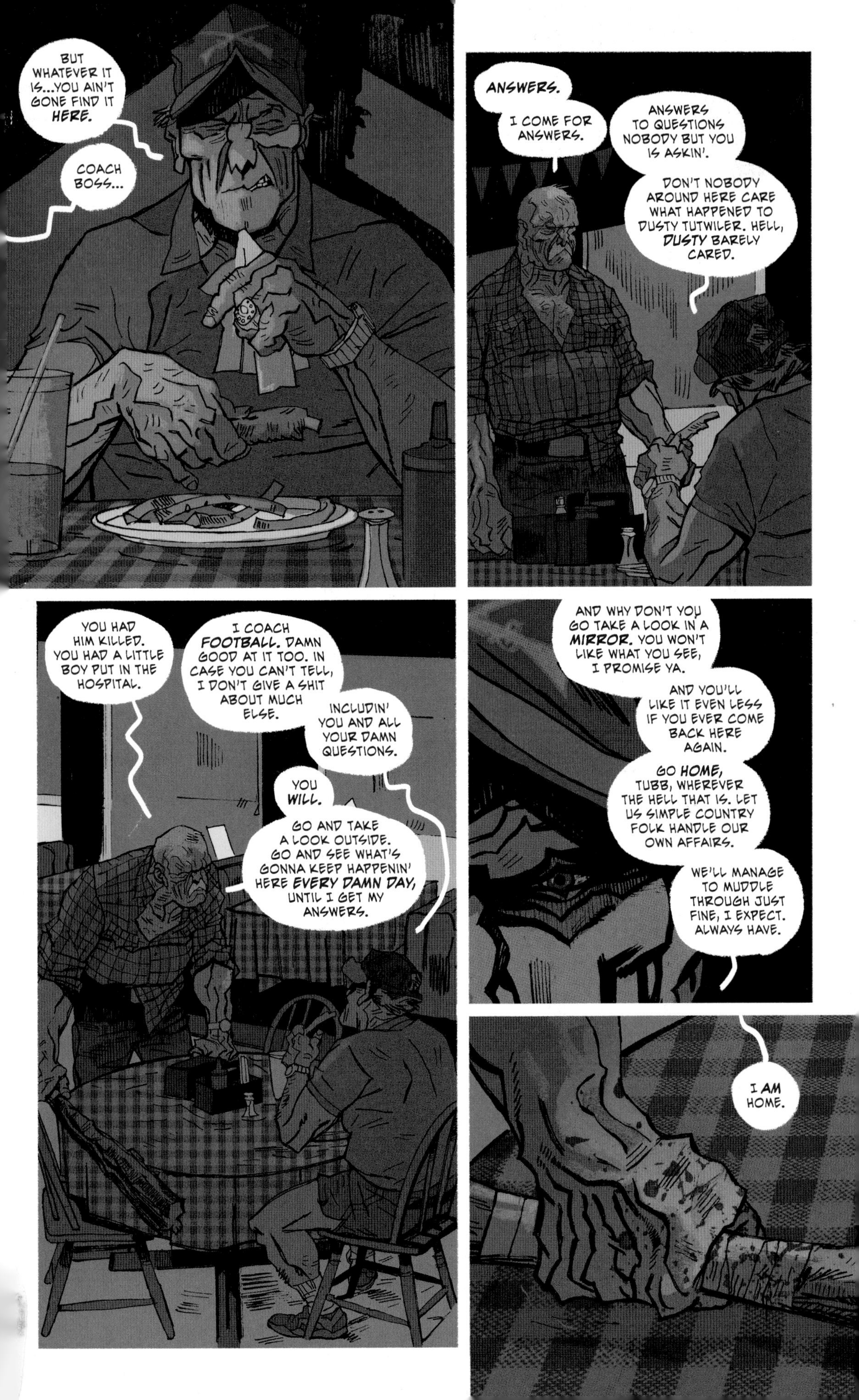
BUT WHATEVER IT IS...YOU AIN'T GONE FIND IT HERE.
COACH BOSS...
ANSWERS.
I COME FOR ANSWERS.
ANSWERS TO QUESTIONS NOBODY BUT YOU IS ASKIN'.
DON'T NOBODY AROUND HERE CARE WHAT HAPPENED TO DUSTY TUTWILER. HELL, DUSTY BARELY CARED.
YOU HAD HIM KILLED. YOU HAD A LITTLE BOY PUT IN THE HOSPITAL.
I COACH FOOTBALL. DAMN GOOD AT IT TOO. IN CASE YOU CAN'T TELL, I DON'T GIVE A SHIT ABOUT MUCH ELSE.
INCLUDIN' YOU AND ALL YOUR DAMN QUESTIONS.
YOU WILL.
GO AND TAKE A LOOK OUTSIDE. GO AND SEE WHAT'S GONNA KEEP HAPPENIN' HERE EVERY DAMN DAY, UNTIL I GET MY ANSWERS.
AND WHY DON'T YOU GO TAKE A LOOK IN A MIRROR. YOU WON'T LIKE WHAT YOU SEE, I PROMISE YA.
AND YOU'LL LIKE IT EVEN LESS IF YOU EVER COME BACK HERE AGAIN.
GO HOME, TUBB, WHEREVER THE HELL THAT IS. LET US SIMPLE COUNTRY FOLK HANDLE OUR OWN AFFAIRS.
WE'LL MANAGE TO MUDDLE THROUGH JUST FINE, I EXPECT. ALWAYS HAVE.
I AM HOME.

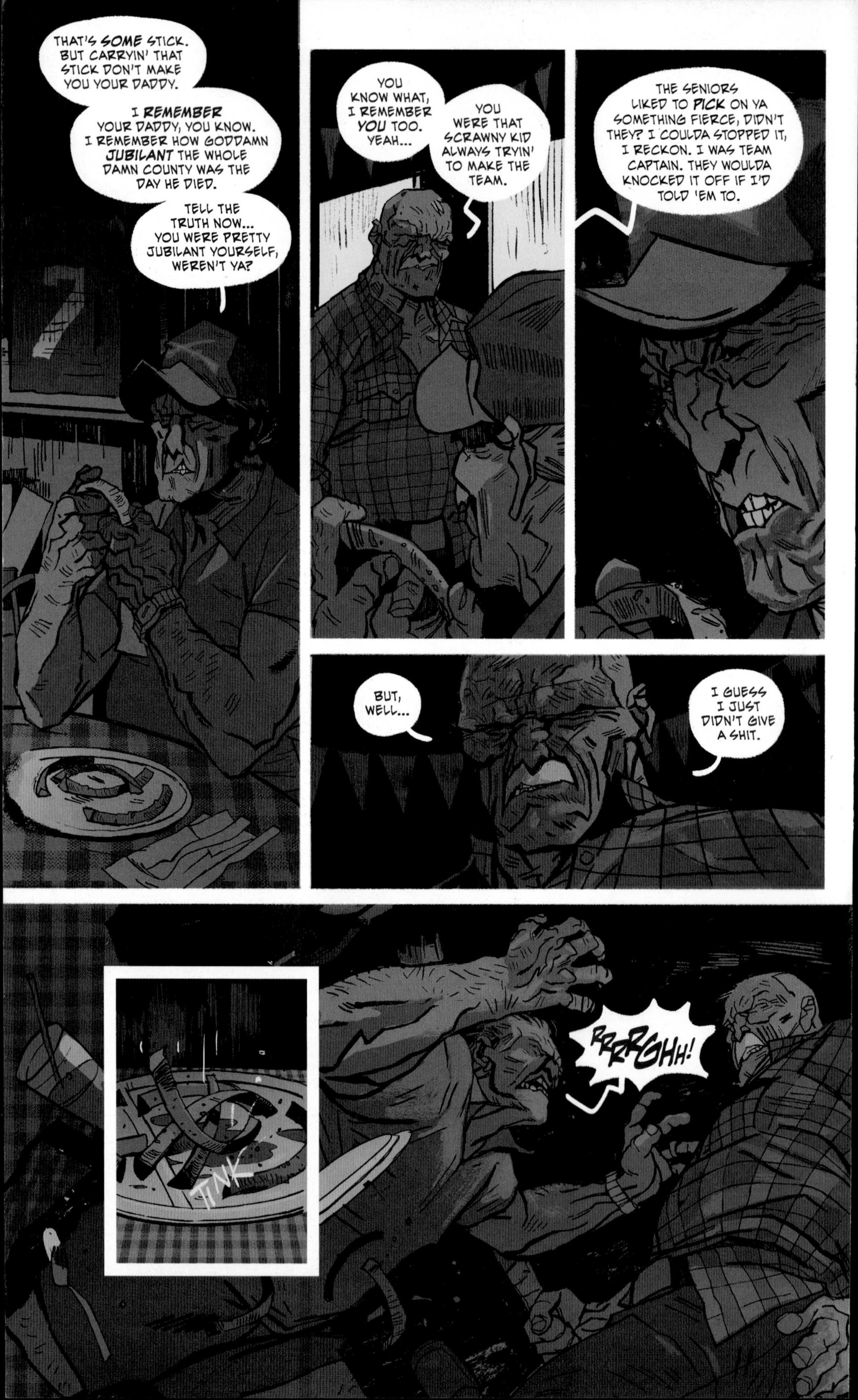
THAT'S SOME STICK. BUT CARRYIN' THAT STICK DON'T MAKE YOU YOUR DADDY.
I REMEMBER YOUR DADDY, YOU KNOW. I REMEMBER HOW GODDAMN JUBILANT THE WHOLE DAMN COUNTY WAS THE DAY HE DIED.
TELL THE TRUTH NOW... YOU WERE PRETTY JUBILANT YOURSELF, WEREN'T YA?
YOU KNOW WHAT, I REMEMBER YOU TOO. YEAH...
YOU WERE THAT SCRAWNY KID ALWAYS TRYIN' TO MAKE THE TEAM.
THE SENIORS LIKED TO PICK ON YA SOMETHING FIERCE, DIDN'T THEY? I COULDA STOPPED IT, I RECKON. I WAS TEAM CAPTAIN. THEY WOULDA KNOCKED IT OFF IF I'D TOLD 'EM TO.
BUT, WELL...
I GUESS I JUST DIDN'T GIVE A SHIT.
TINK
RRRRGHH!

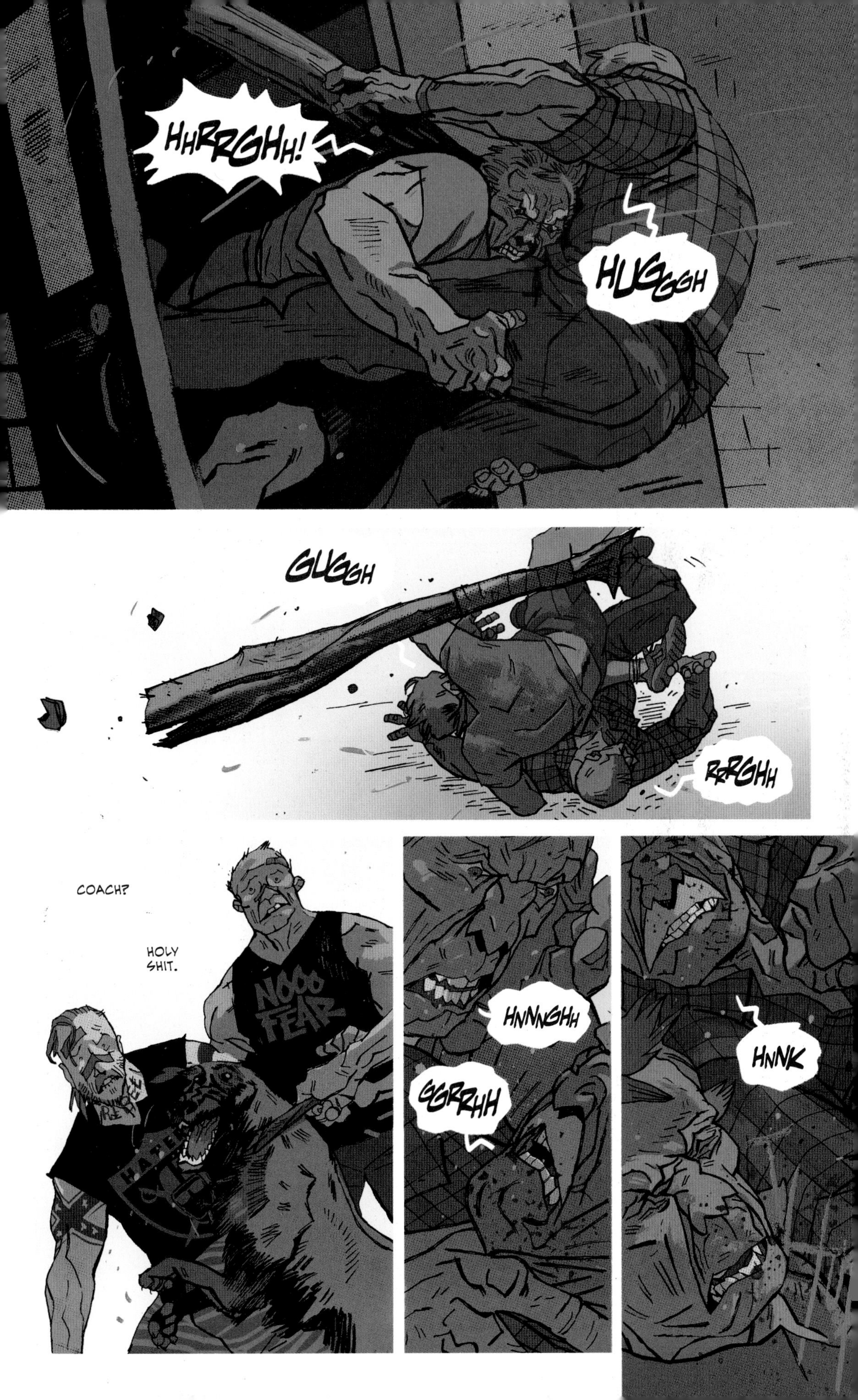
HHRRGHH!
HUGGGH
GUGGH
RRRGHH
COACH?
HOLY SHIT.
NOOO FEAR
HATER
HNNNGHH
GGRRHH
HNNK

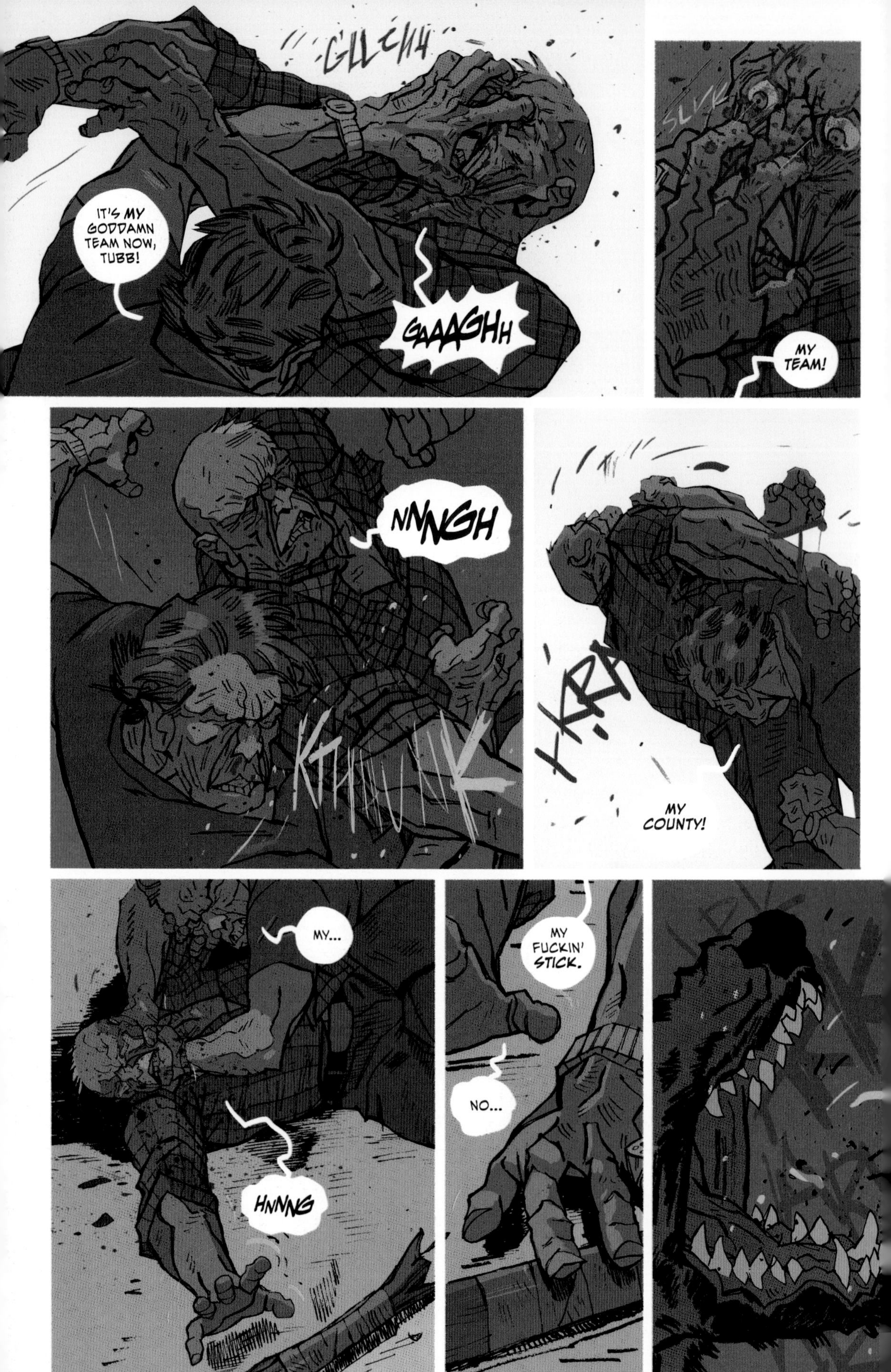
GLLCHH
IT'S MY GODDAMN TEAM NOW, TUBB!
GAAAGHH
SLUK
MY TEAM!
NNNGH
KTHUNK
KRA
MY COUNTY!
MY...
HNNNG
MY FUCKIN' STICK.
NO...

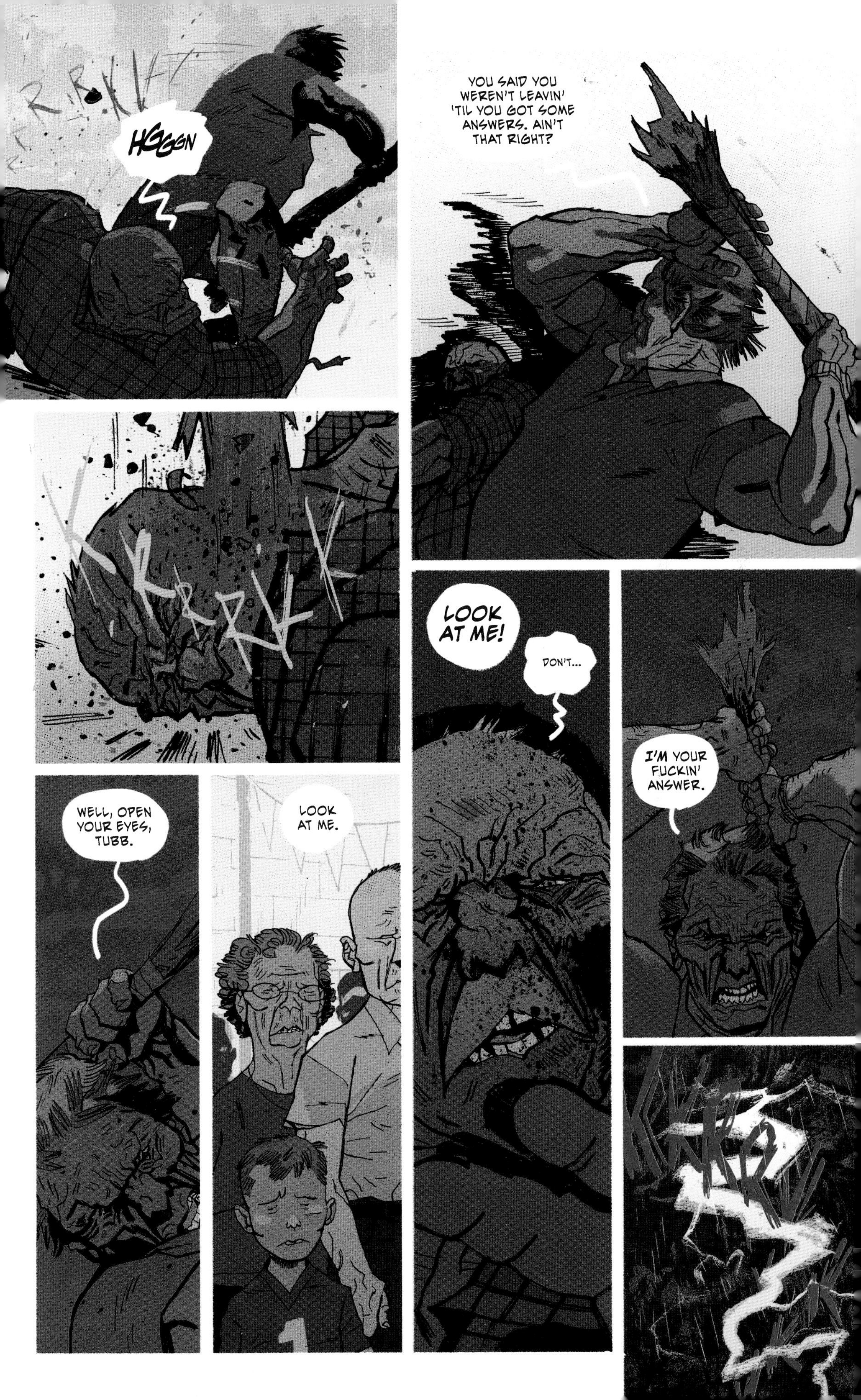
HGGGN
YOU SAID YOU WEREN'T LEAVIN' 'TIL YOU GOT SOME ANSWERS. AIN'T THAT RIGHT?
WELL, OPEN YOUR EYES, TUBB.
LOOK AT ME.
LOOK AT ME!
DON'T...
I'M YOUR FUCKIN' ANSWER.

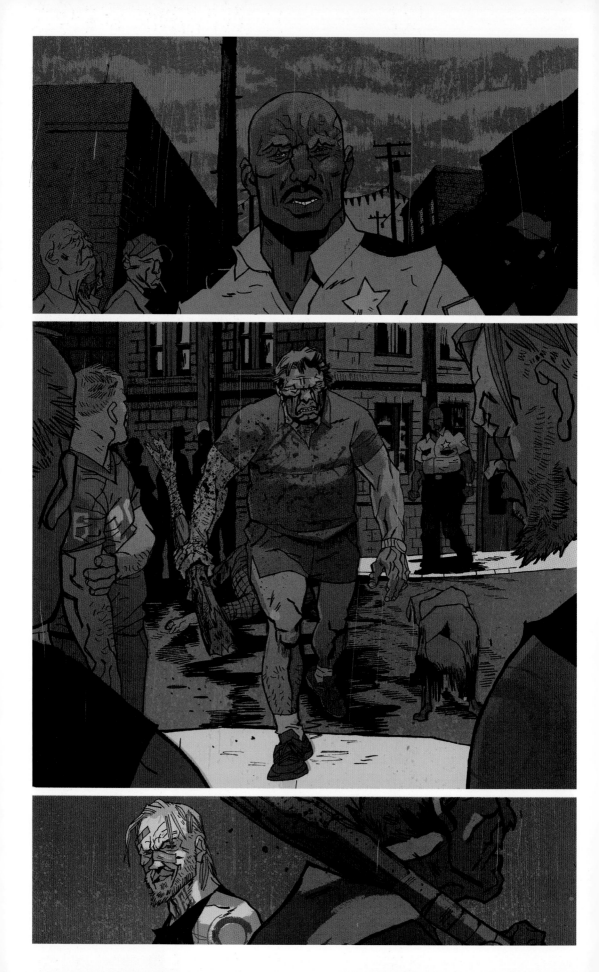

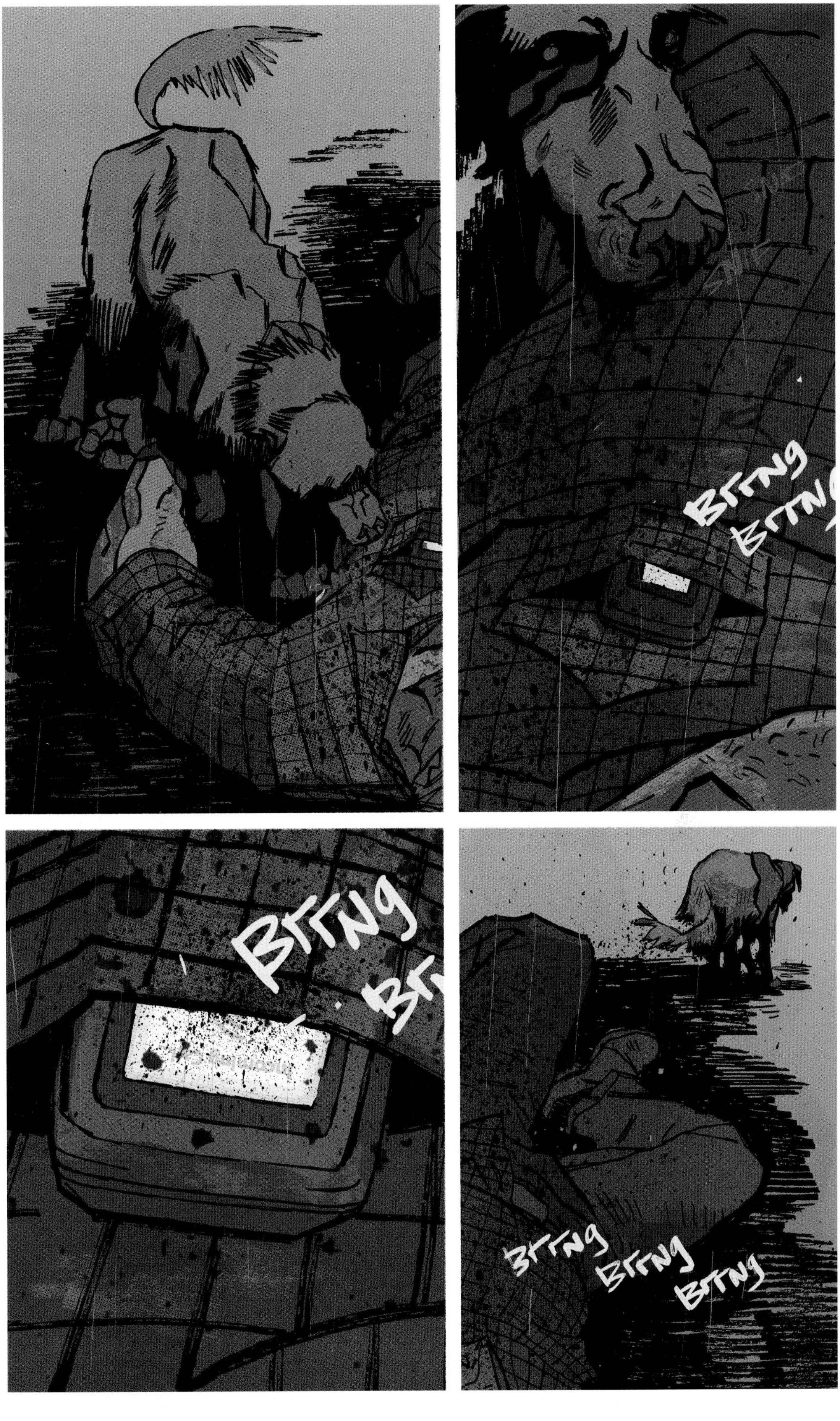

Brrng
Brrng
Brrng
Brrng
Brrng

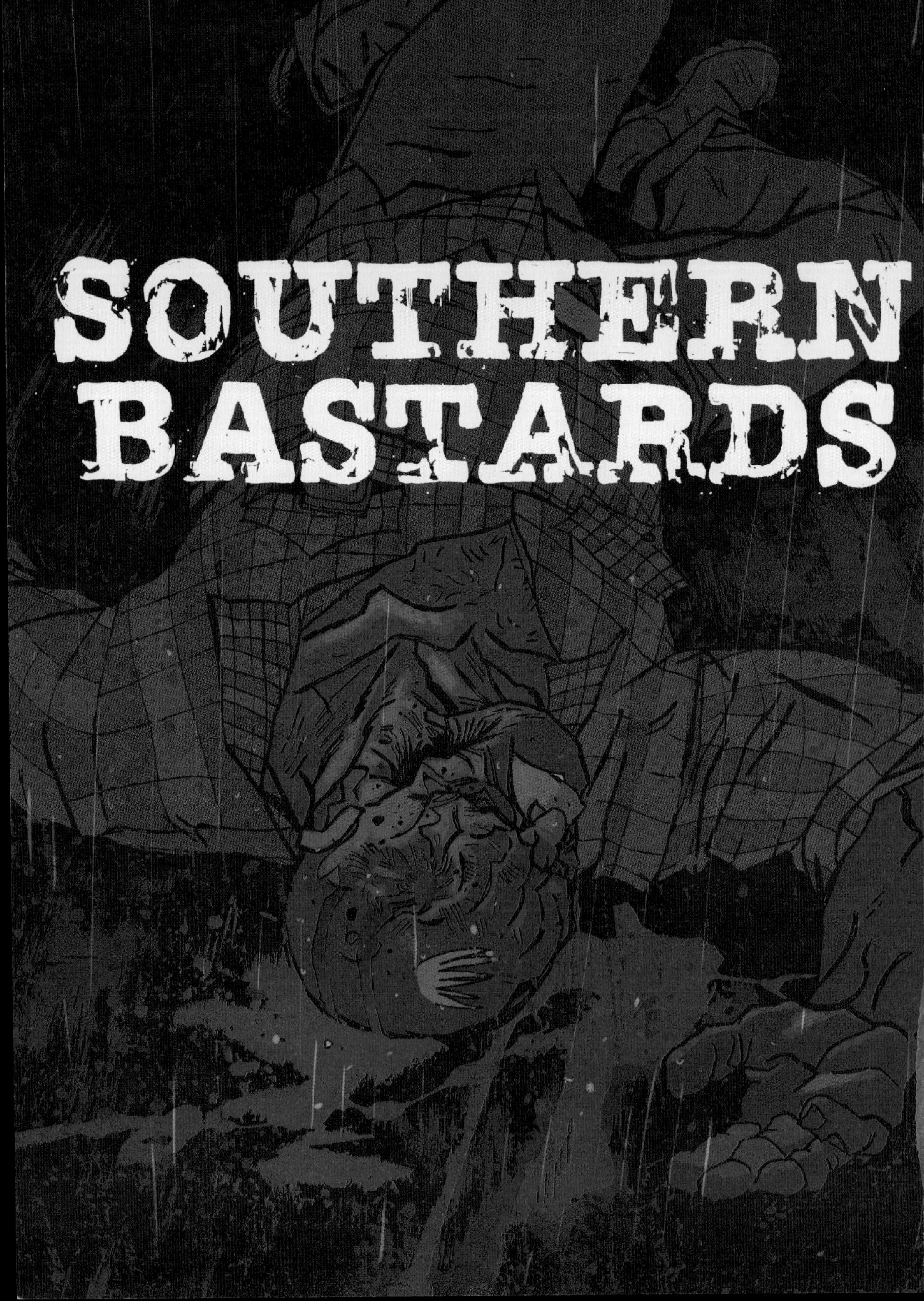
SOUTHERN
BASTARDS

"HERE WAS A MAN"

# epilogue

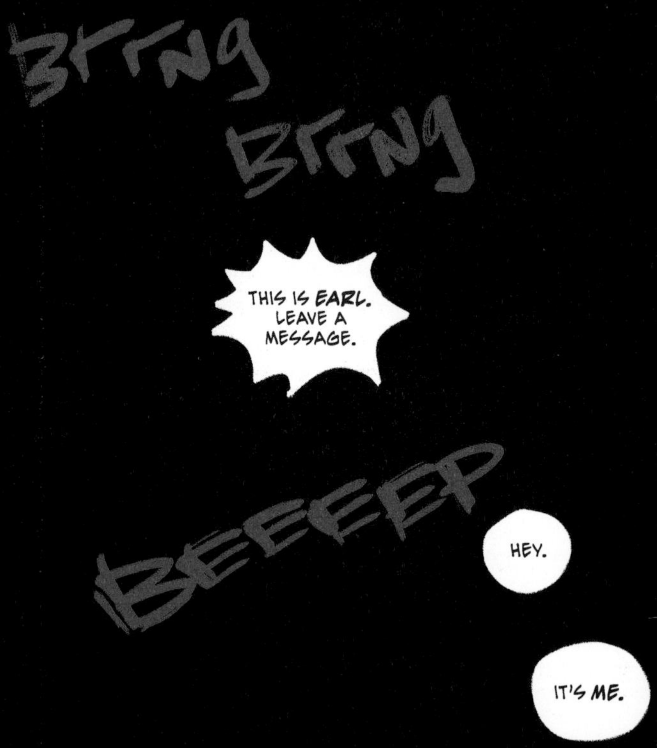
BRRNG
BRRNG
THIS IS EARL. LEAVE A MESSAGE.
BEEEEP
HEY.
IT'S ME.

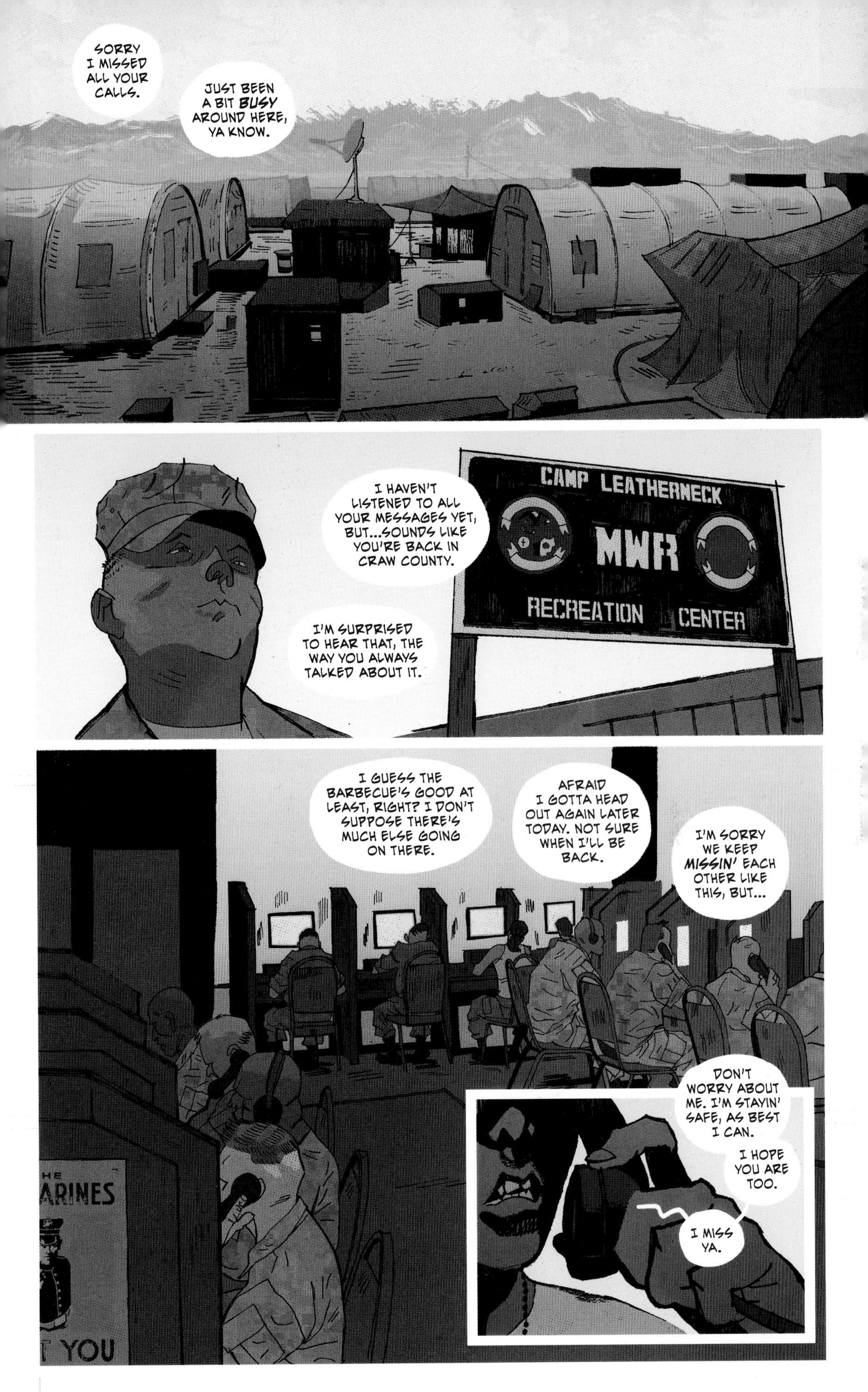
SORRY I MISSED ALL YOUR CALLS.
JUST BEEN A BIT BUSY AROUND HERE, YA KNOW.
CAMP LEATHERNECK
MWR
RECREATION CENTER
I HAVEN'T LISTENED TO ALL YOUR MESSAGES YET, BUT...SOUNDS LIKE YOU'RE BACK IN CRAW COUNTY.
I'M SURPRISED TO HEAR THAT, THE WAY YOU ALWAYS TALKED ABOUT IT.
I GUESS THE BARBECUE'S GOOD AT LEAST, RIGHT? I DON'T SUPPOSE THERE'S MUCH ELSE GOING ON THERE.
AFRAID I GOTTA HEAD OUT AGAIN LATER TODAY. NOT SURE WHEN I'LL BE BACK.
I'M SORRY WE KEEP MISSIN' EACH OTHER LIKE THIS, BUT...
DON'T WORRY ABOUT ME. I'M STAYIN' SAFE, AS BEST I CAN.
I HOPE YOU ARE TOO.
I MISS YA.

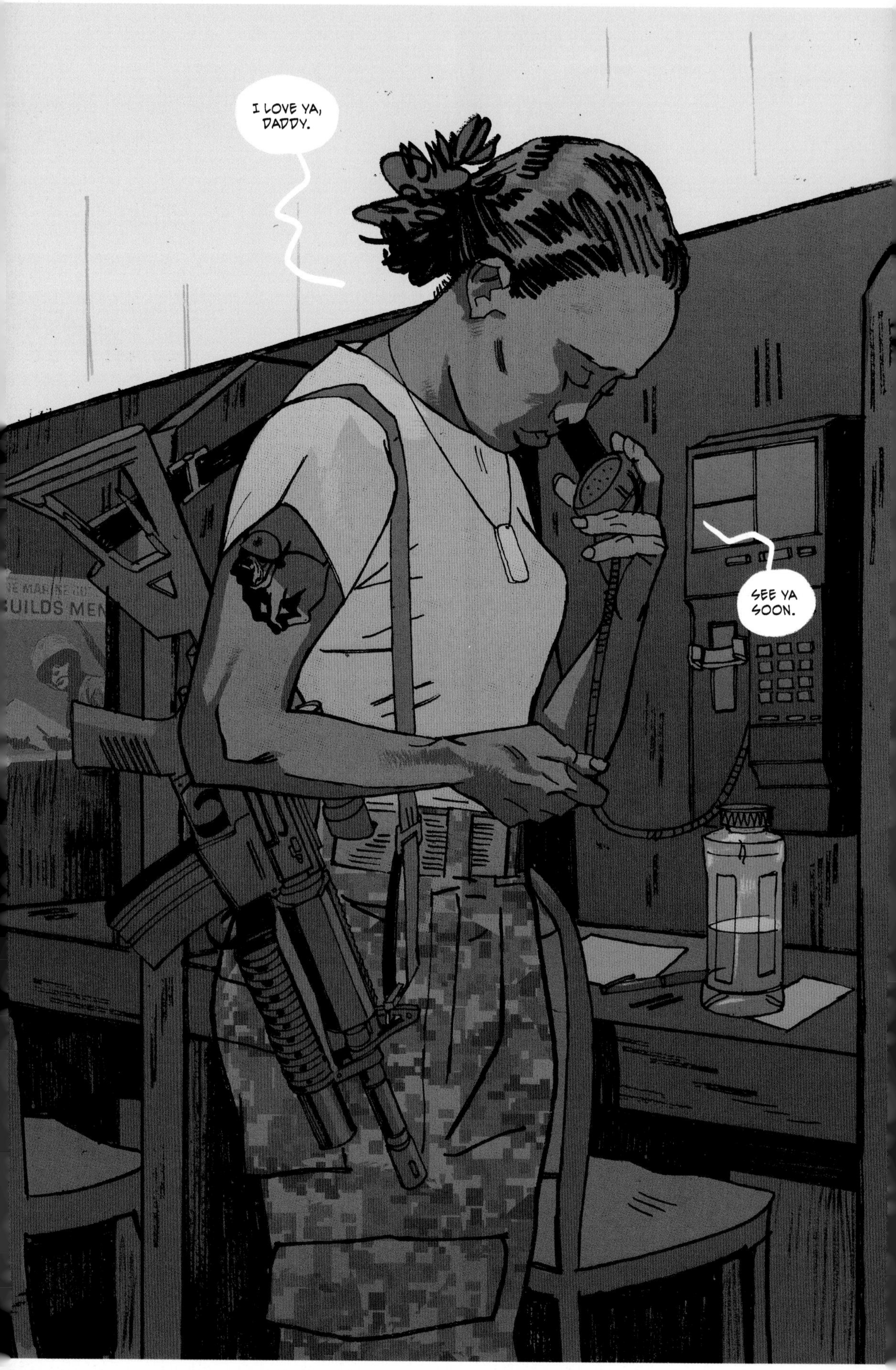
I LOVE YA, DADDY.
SEE YA SOON.
BUILDS MEN

**JASON AARON** writes comic books. Like the crime series SCALPED for DC/Vertigo and books like GHOST RIDER, WOLVERINE, INCREDIBLE HULK, PUNISHER MAX, and WOLVERINE AND THE X-MEN for Marvel.

His most recent projects include the Southern hitman series MEN OF WRATH at Icon, as well as STAR WARS and THOR at Marvel.

He was born in Alabama, but currently resides in Kansas City.

Jason enjoys many things, but shaving is not one of them.

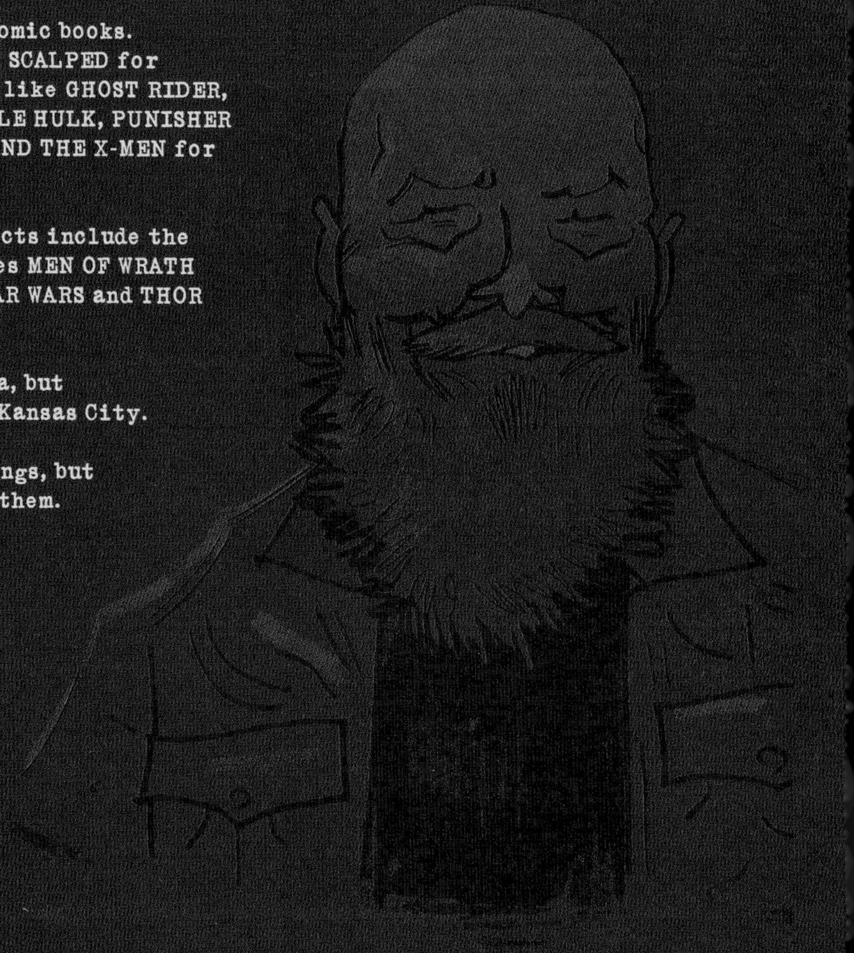

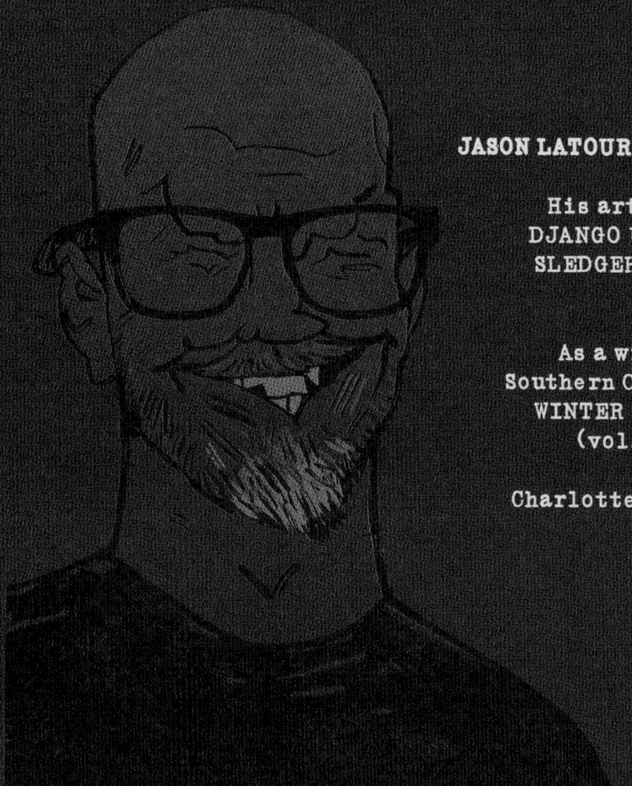

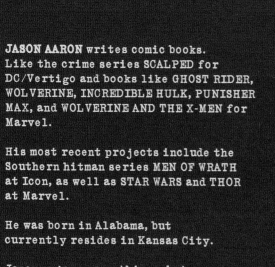

**JASON LATOUR** is a comic book artist and writer.

His art can be seen in Quentin Tarantino's DJANGO UNCHAINED, Mike Mignola's B.P.R.D., SLEDGEHAMMER 44, Marvel's WOLVERINE, and SCALPED for DC/Vertigo.

As a writer he's penned the creator-owned Southern Crime Romance: LOOSE ENDS, Marvel's WINTER SOLDIER, WOLVERINE AND THE X-MEN (vol. 2), and GWEN STACY: SPIDER-WOMAN.

Charlotte, NC is where he learned to draw(1).

## SOUTHERN BASTARDS

## COVER GALLERY
## & SKETCHBOOK

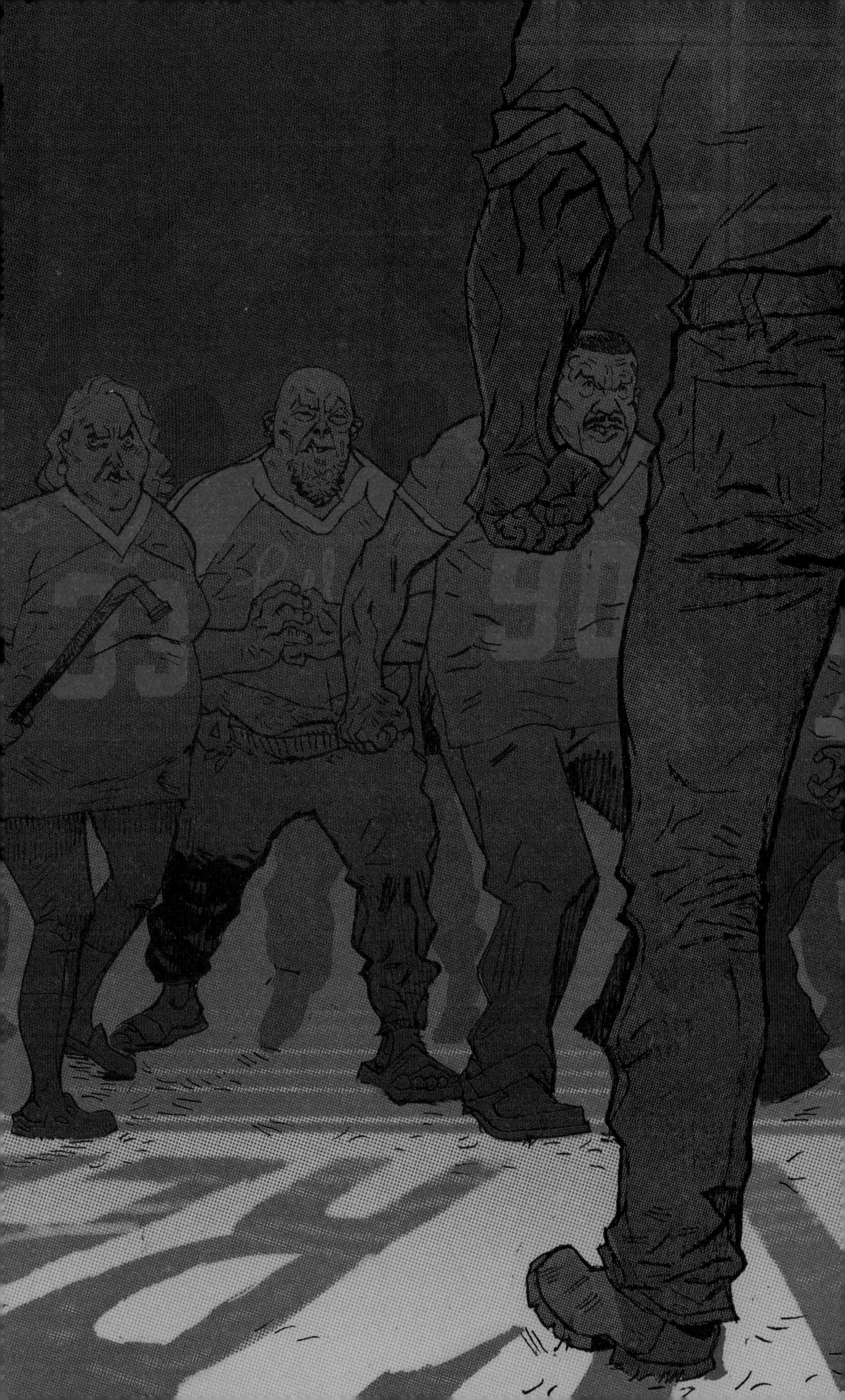

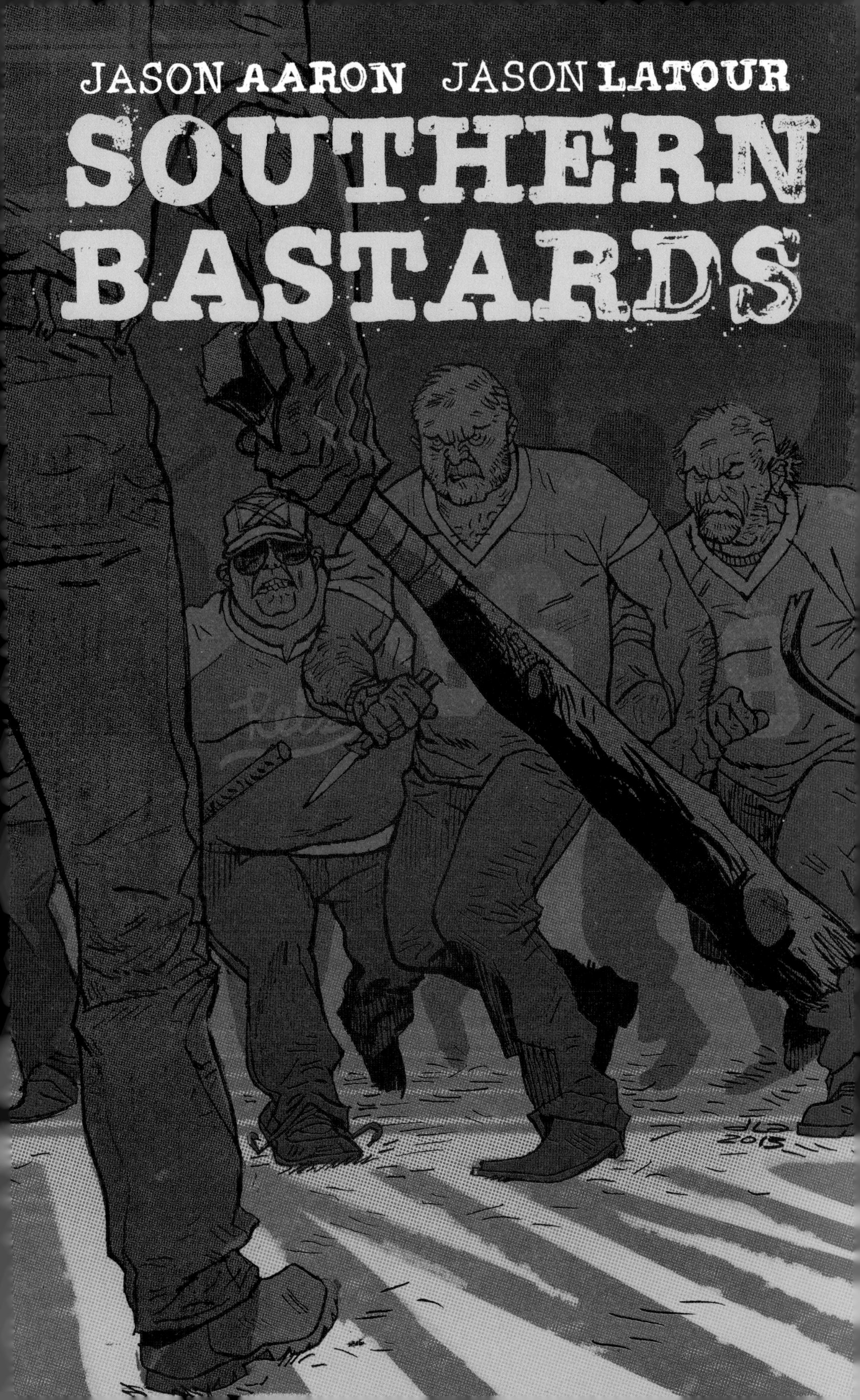
JASON AARON JASON LATOUR
SOUTHERN
BASTARDS
dla 2015

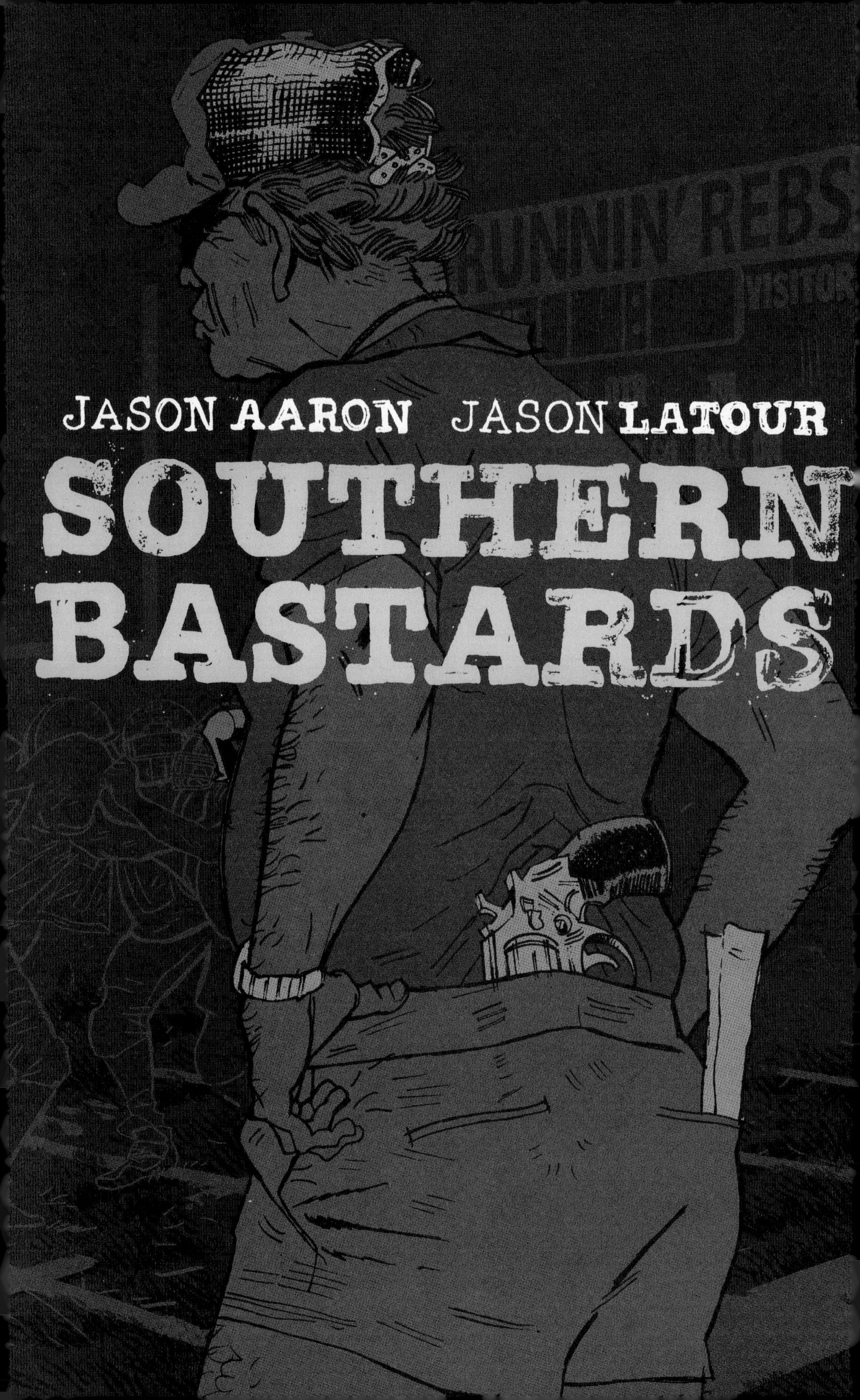

RUNNIN' REBS
VISITOR
JASON AARON
JASON LATOUR
SOUTHERN BASTARDS

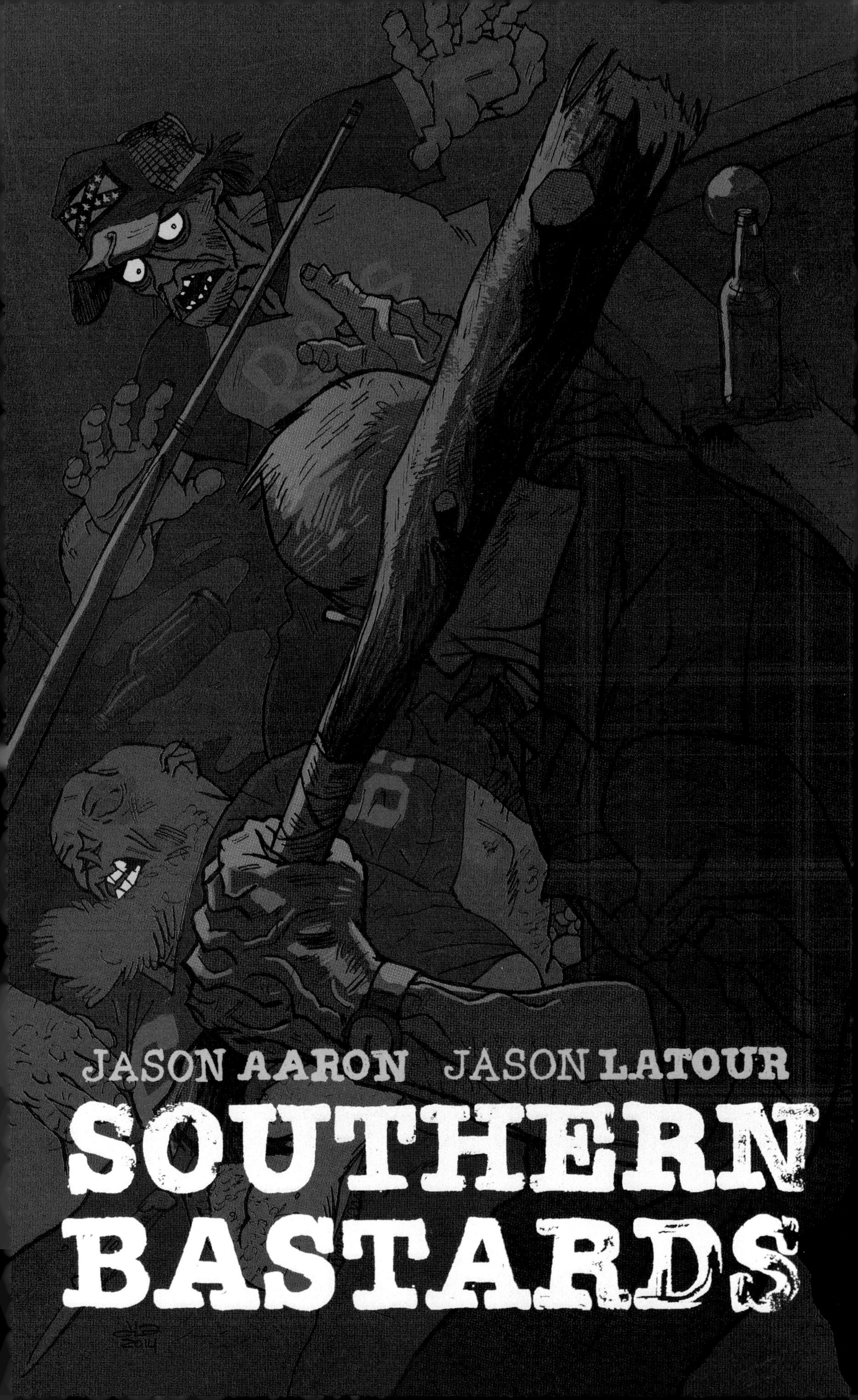
JASON AARON JASON LATOUR
SOUTHERN
BASTARDS

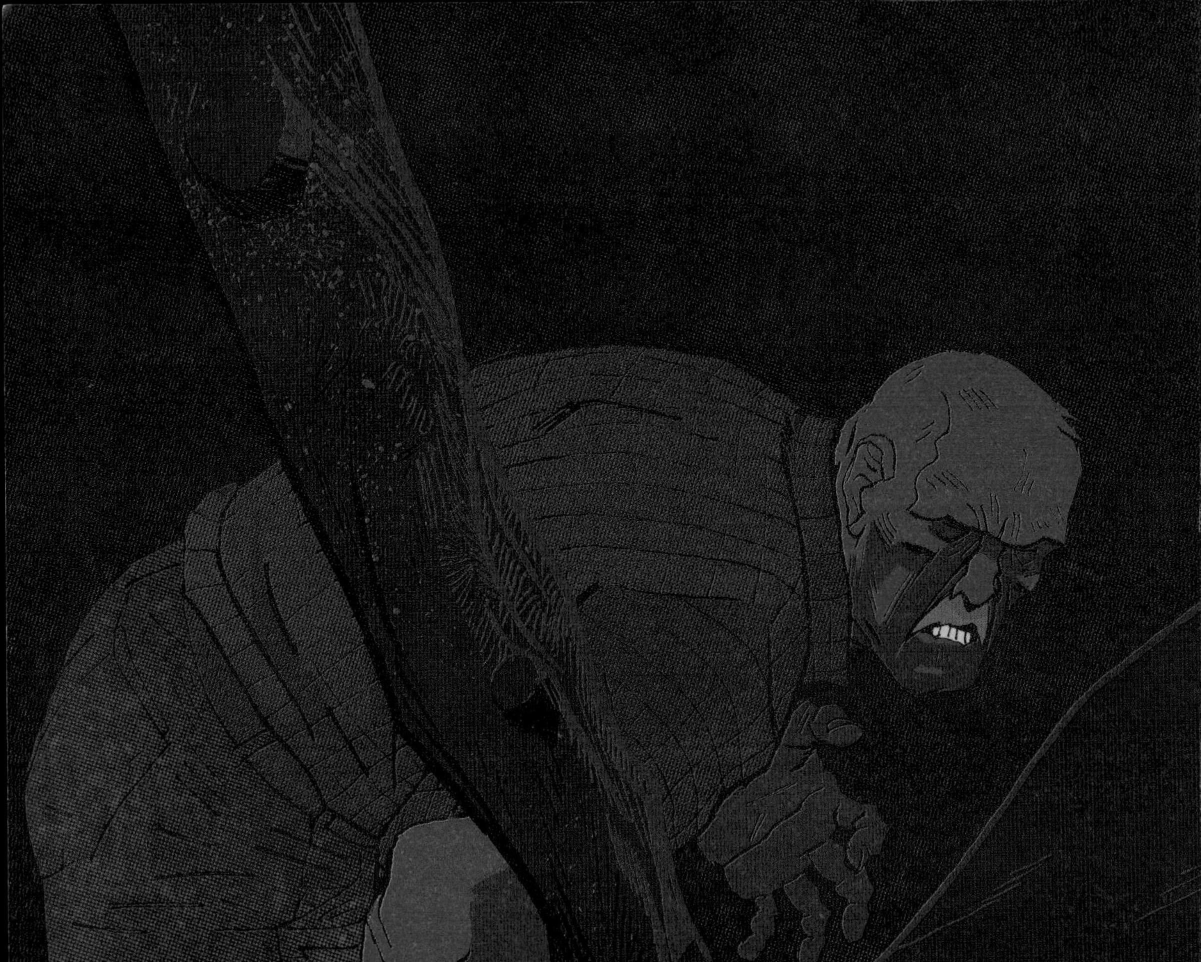

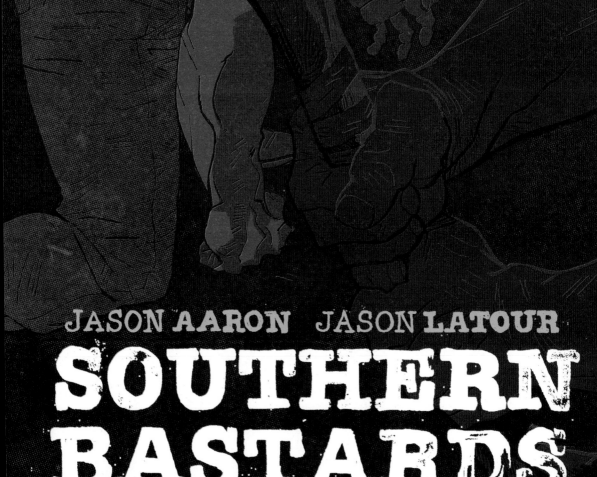

JASON AARON JASON LATOUR

# SOUTHERN BASTARDS

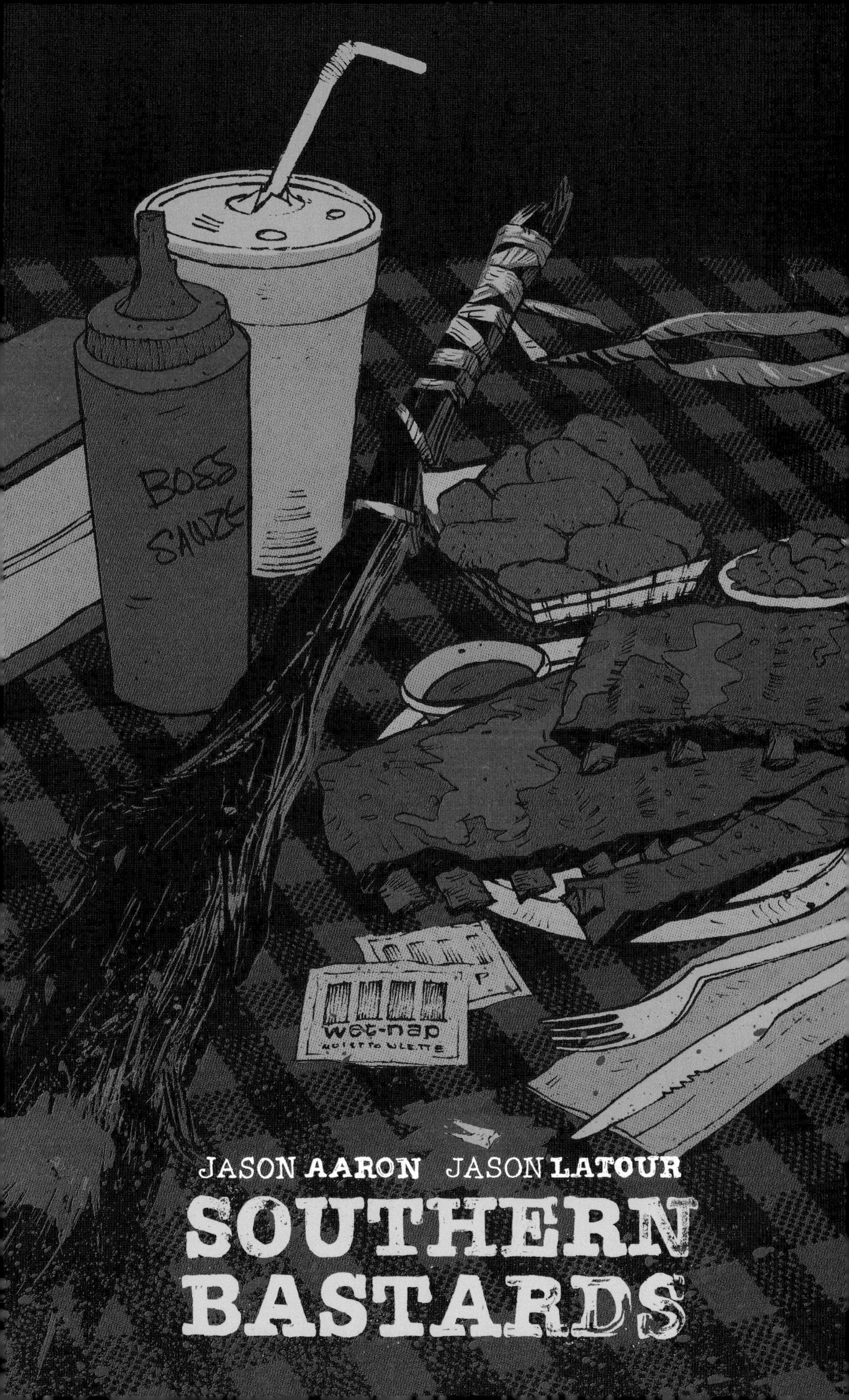
BOSS SAUCE
wet-nap
JASON AARON JASON LATOUR
SOUTHERN BASTARDS

JASON AARON JASON LATOUR
SOUTHERN BASTARDS
COMIC BOOK LEGAL DEFENSE FUND
CBLDF
APPROVED BY THE COMICS CODE AUTHORITY
1954 - 2011
ISSUE No. 1 VARIANT
IMAGE COMICS

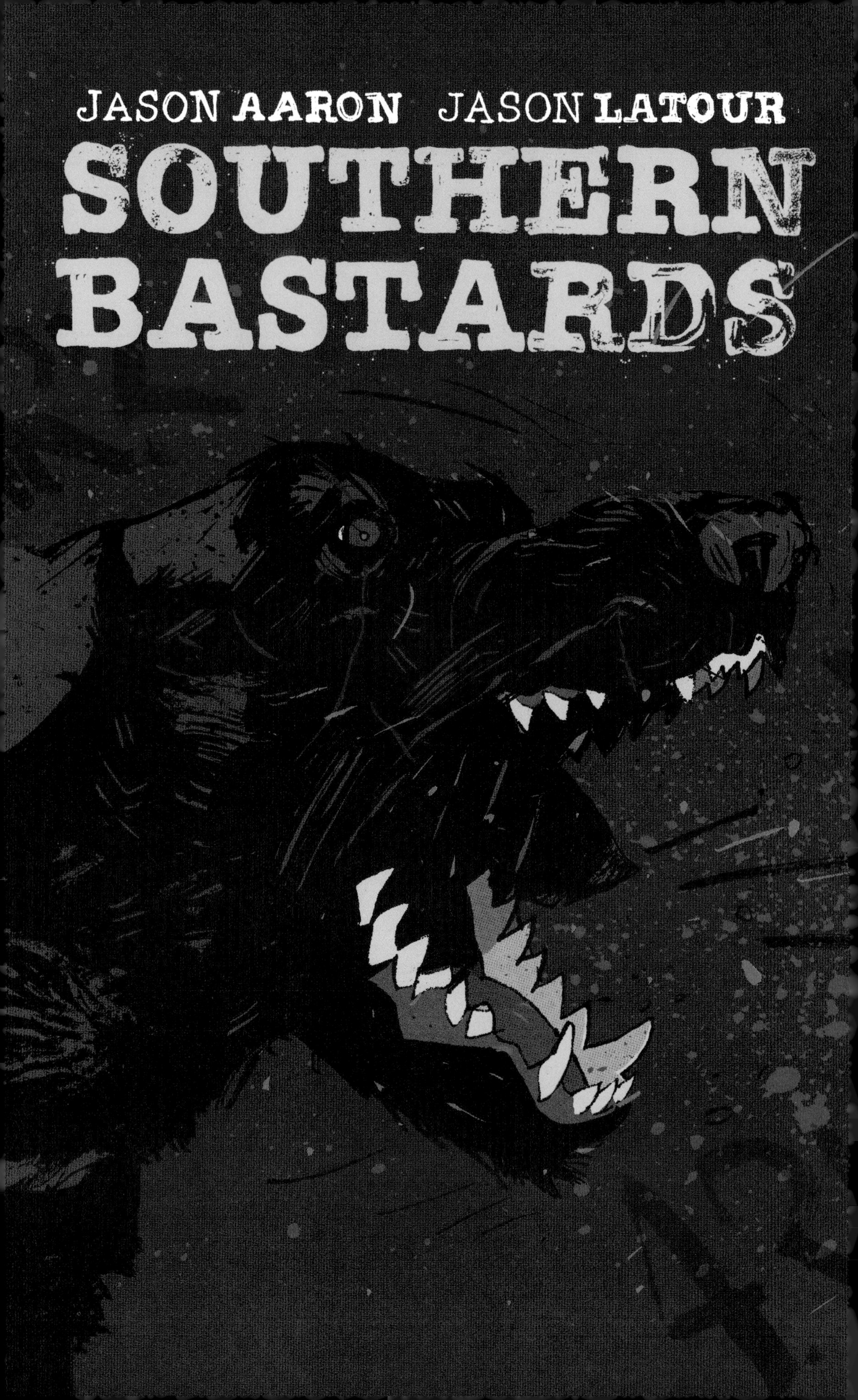
JASON AARON JASON LATOUR
SOUTHERN BASTARDS

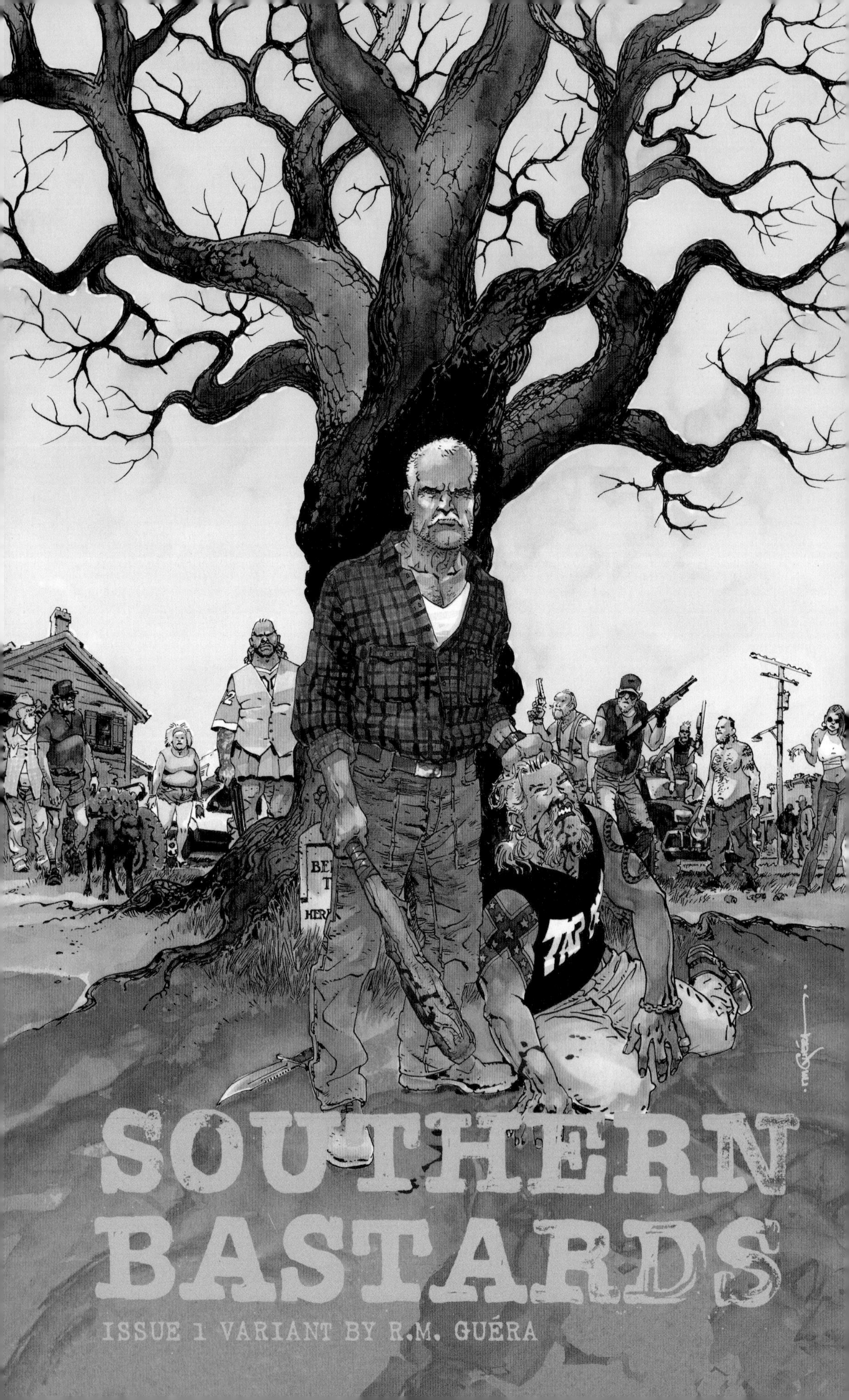
SOUTHERN
BASTARDS
ISSUE 1 VARIANT BY R.M. GUÉRA

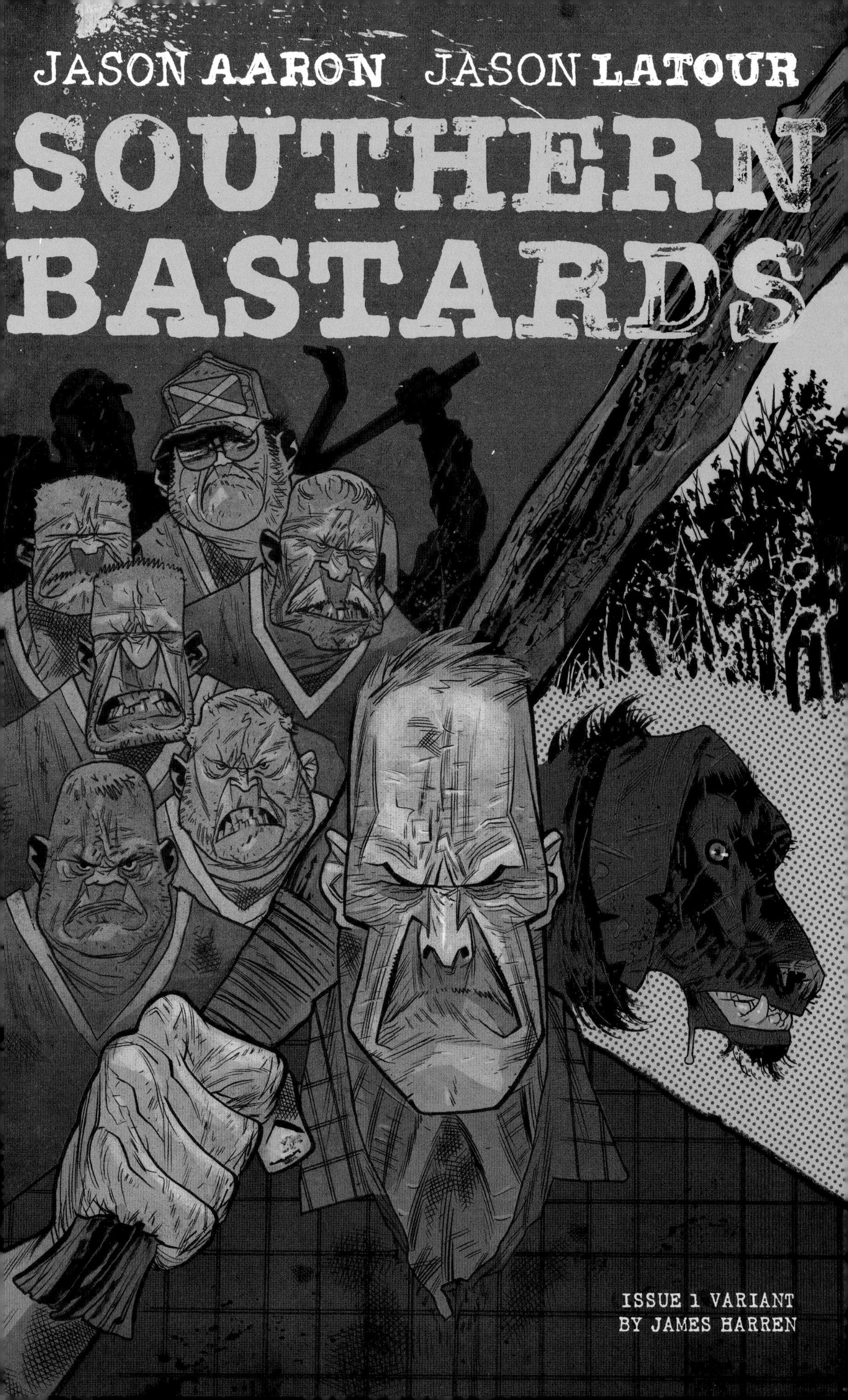
JASON AARON JASON LATOUR
SOUTHERN
BASTARDS
ISSUE 1 VARIANT
BY JAMES HARREN

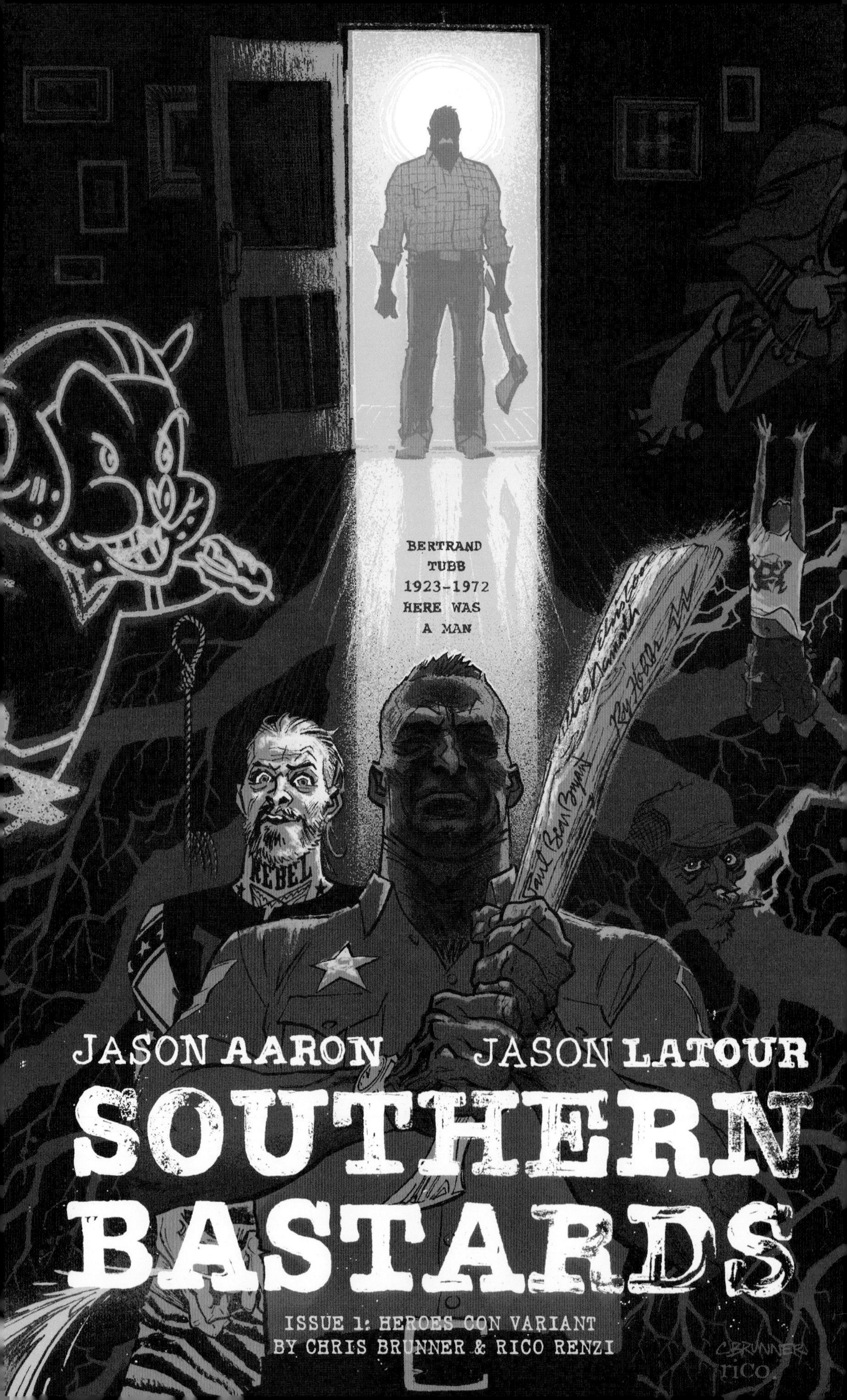
BERTRAND
TUBB
1923-1972
HERE WAS
A MAN
REBEL
JASON AARON
JASON LATOUR
SOUTHERN
BASTARDS
ISSUE 1: HEROES CON VARIANT
BY CHRIS BRUNNER & RICO RENZI
C.BRUNNER
rico.

# Recipe for FRIED APPLE PIES

*By Betty Aaron, Jason's mom*

## APPLE MIXTURE

4 medium sized apples, peeled and sliced (I like Granny Smith)
1/2 cup sugar
1/4 teaspoon ground allspice

Cook apples in small amount of water over medium heat until tender,
15 minutes or so. Stir occasionally. Drain well and mash lightly.
Add sugar and allspice. Let cool.

## PASTRY

1/3 cup shortening
2 cups self-rising flour
2/3 cup cold water

Mix shortening into flour until mixture resembles coarse meal. Add
water small amount at a time until all ingredients are moistened. On a
floured surface, roll pastry to about 1/8 inch thickness. Cut into 6 inch
or so circles (a small saucer works well for a pattern). Spoon about ¼
cup apple mixture onto half of a circle. Fold other half over and seal
edge with fork dipped in flour.

Heat at least 2 inches of oil in a heavy pan. Fry pies 2 or 3 at a time
until golden brown. Drain on paper towels.

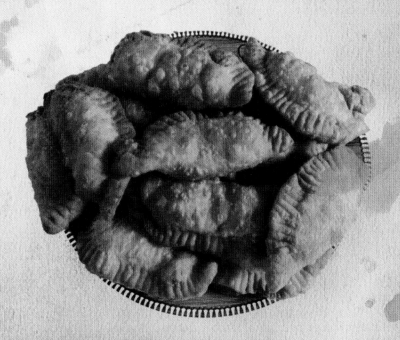

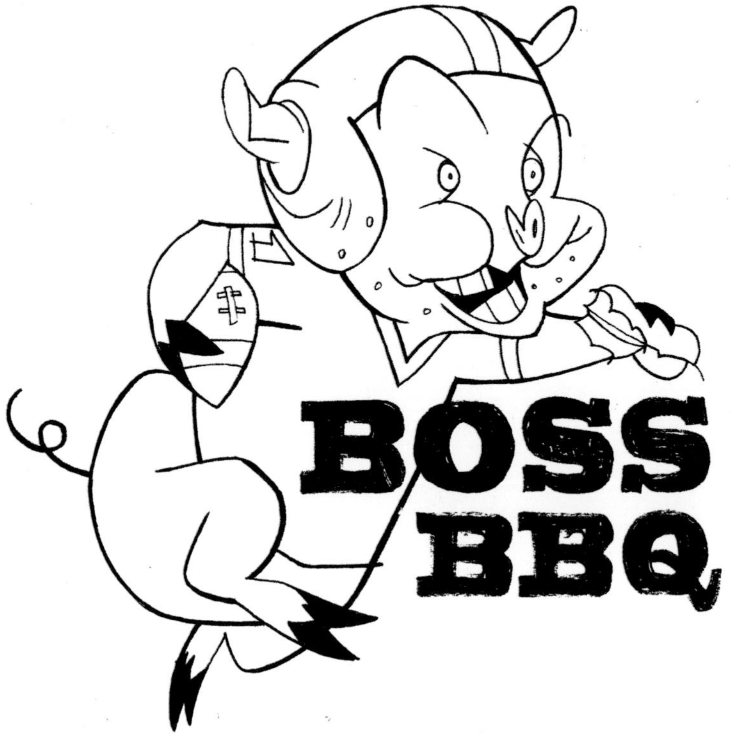
BOSS
BBQ

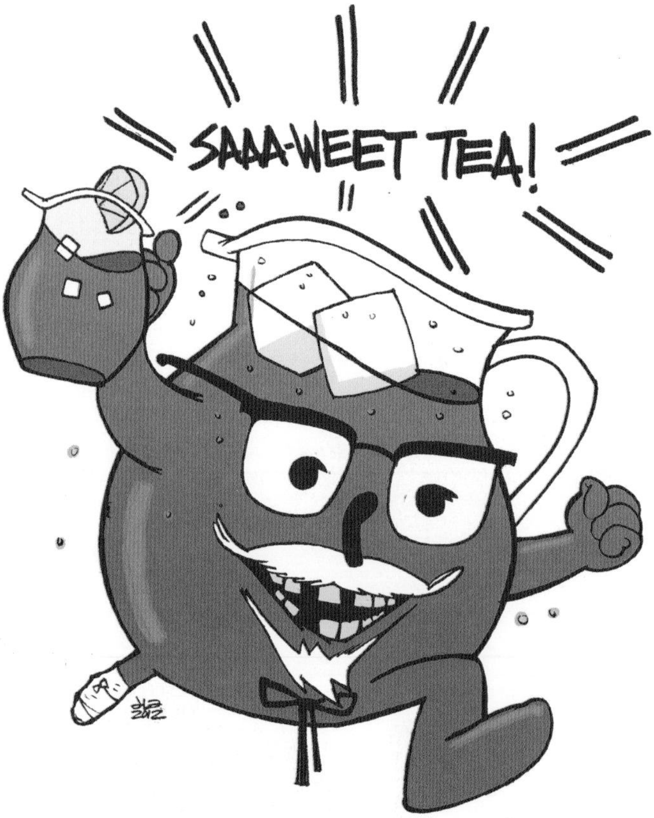
SAAA-WEET TEA!
NUTHIN' DIE-A-BEATS ME!

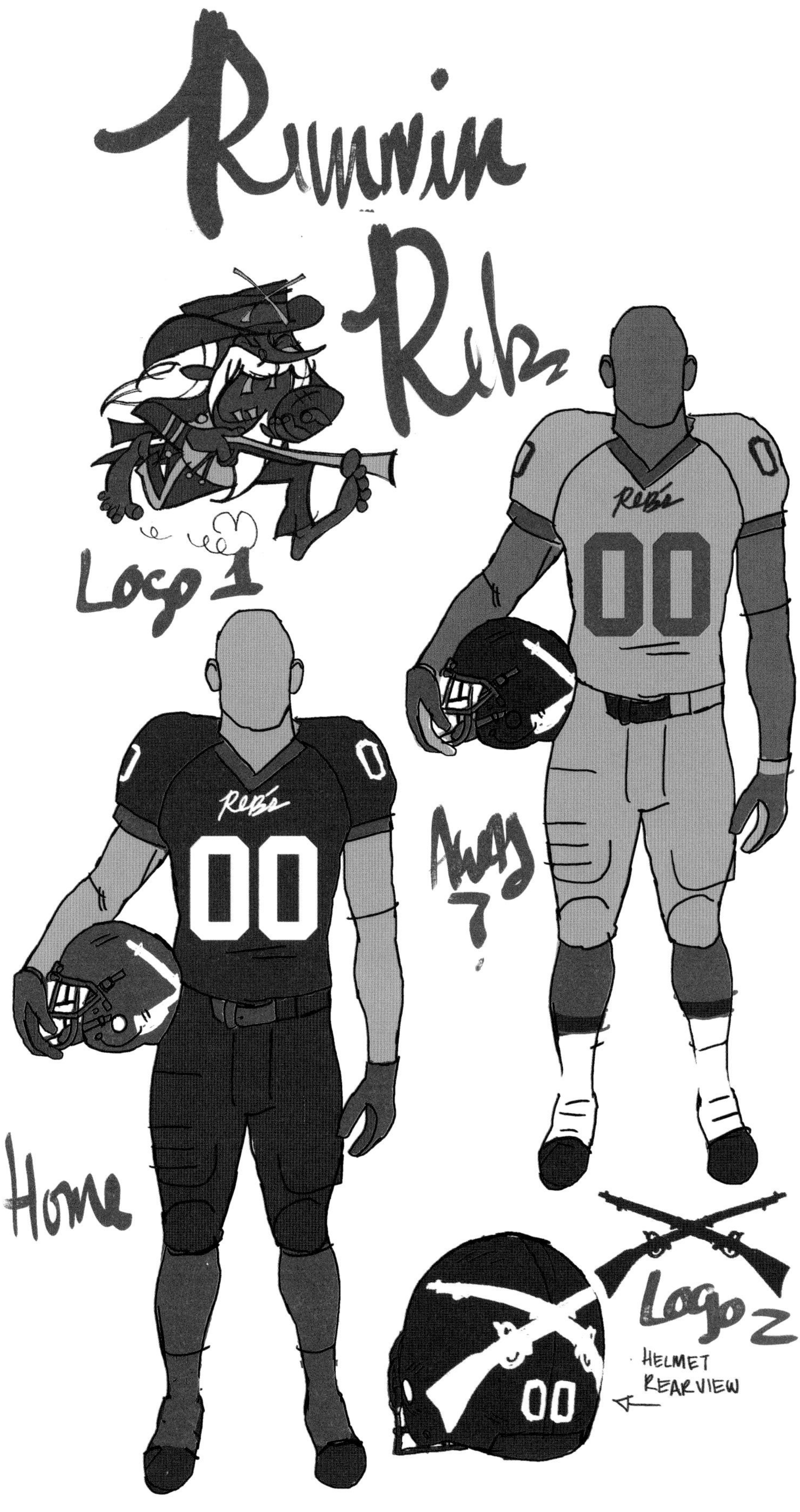
Runnin Rebs
Logo 1
Rebs
0
00
Away ?
Home
Logo 2
HELMET
REARVIEW
00

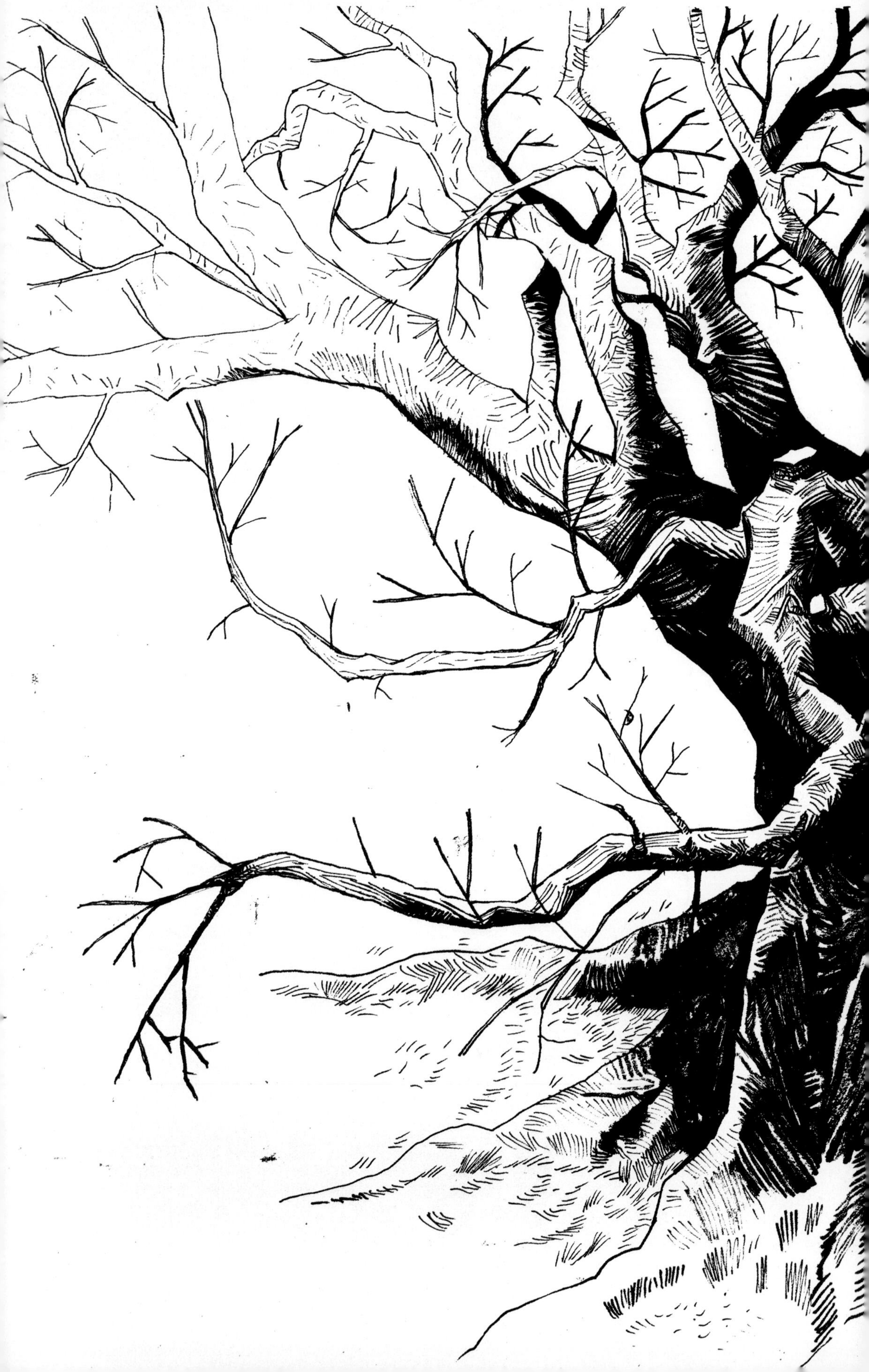

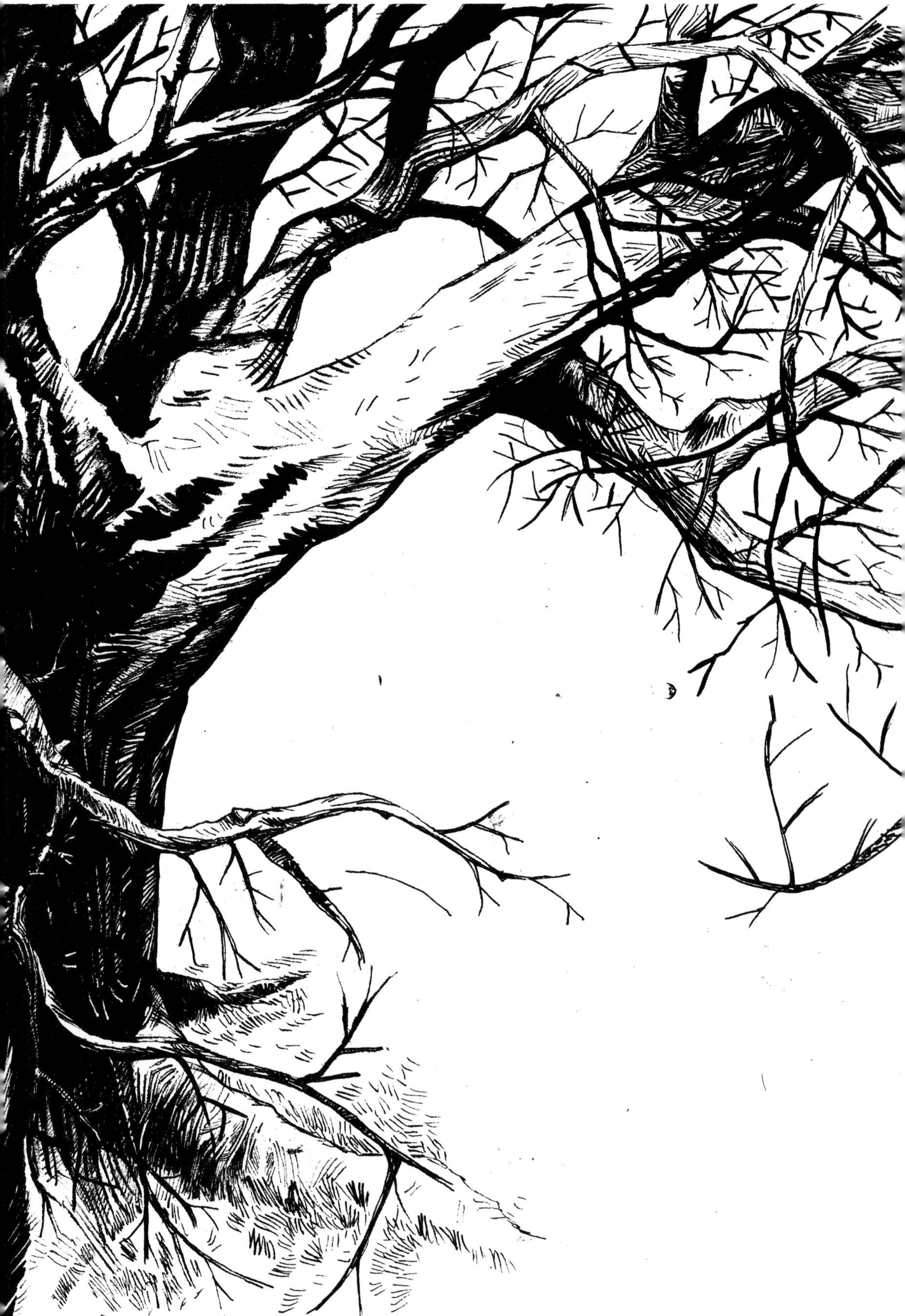

SOBAS#1-7

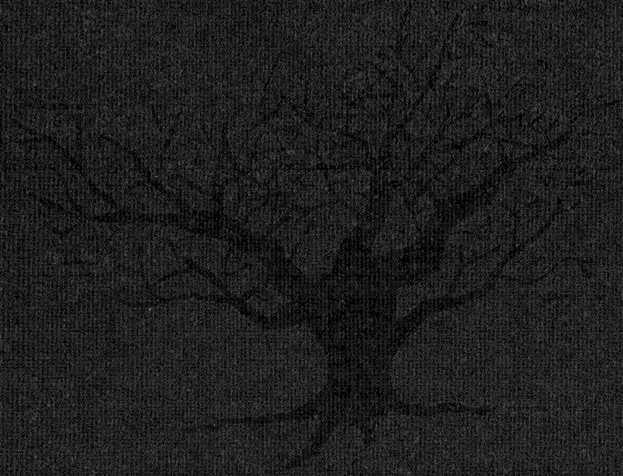

SOUTHERN BASTARDS

coming soon...
Volume 2: GRIDIRON